THE REVELS PLAYS

Founder Editor
1958–71: Clifford Leech

General Editors
F. David Hoeniger, E. A. J. Honigmann and J. R. Mulryne

THE NEW INN

FOR BEN,
BORN IN 1972

THE REVELS PLAYS

THE NEW INN

BEN JONSON

Edited by
Michael Hattaway

MANCHESTER
UNIVERSITY PRESS

Introduction, critical apparatus, etc.
© Michael Hattaway 1984

First published in 1984

Published by Manchester University Press
Oxford Road, Manchester M13 9PL
and 51 Washington Street, Dover,
New Hampshire 03820, USA

British Library cataloguing in publication data
Jonson, Ben
   The new inn.—(The Revels plays)
   I. Title   II. Hattaway, Michael
   III. Series
   822'.3   PR2616

Library of Congress cataloging in publication data
Jonson, Ben, 1573?–1637.
   The new inn.
   (The Revels plays)
   Includes bibliographical references and index.
   I. Hattaway, Michael.   II. Title.   III. Series.
PR2616.A2H37   1984   822'.3   84–5938

ISBN 0–7190–1530–8 *cased only*

This book has been published with the help of a grant from the Canadian
Federation for the Humanities, using funds provided by the Social
Sciences and Humanities Research Council of Canada.

Typeset by August Filmsetting, Haydock, St. Helens
Printed in Great Britain
by Bell & Bain Ltd., Glasgow

Contents

ILLUSTRATIONS   *between pages* 36 *and* 37

1 The title-page of the 1631 Octavo, taken from the British Library copy 643.b.31 (A).

2 The title-page of Burton's *Anatomy of Melancholy* which appeared the year before the play. See Introduction, p. 20. The melancholy lover on the left stands in a conventional pose with arms crossed.

3 A costume design by Inigo Jones for the Melancholic Despairing Lover in Jonson's masque celebrating Platonic love, *Love's Triumph through Callipolis* (1631). Reproduced by permission of the Trustees of the Chatsworth Settlement.

General Editors' Preface

The series known as the Revels Plays was conceived by Clifford Leech. The idea for the series emerged in his mind, as he explained in his preface to the first of the Revels Plays in 1958, from the success of the New Arden Shakespeare. The aim of the new group of texts was 'to apply to Shakespeare's predecessors, contemporaries and successors the methods that are now used in Shakespeare editing'. The plays chosen were to include well known works from the early Tudor period to about 1700, as well as others less familiar but of literary and theatrical merit: 'the plays included,' Leech wrote, 'should be such as to deserve and indeed demand performance.' We owe it to Clifford Leech that the idea became reality. He set the high standards of the series, ensuring that editors of individual volumes produced work of lasting merit, equally useful for teachers and students, theatre directors and actors. Clifford Leech remained General Editor until 1971, supervising the first seventeen volumes to be published.

The Revels Plays are now under the direction of three General Editors, F. David Hoeniger, E. A. J. Honigmann and J. R. Mulryne. The publishers, originally Methuen, are now Manchester University Press. Despite these changes, the format and essential character of the series will continue, and it is hoped that its editorial standards will be maintained. Except for some work in progress, the General Editors intend, in expanding the series, to concentrate for the immediate future on plays from the period 1558–1642, and may include a small number of non-dramatic works of interest to students of drama. Some slight changes have been forced by considerations of cost. For example, in editions from 1978, notes to the introduction are placed together at the end, not at the foot of the page. Collation and commentary notes will continue, however, to appear on the relevant pages.

The text of each Revels play, in accordance with established practice in the series, is edited afresh from the original text of best authority (in a few instances, texts), but spelling and punctuation are modernised and speech headings are silently made consistent. Elisions in the original are also silently regularised, except where metre would be affected by the change; since 1968 the '-ed' form is used for non-syllabic terminations in past tenses and past participles ('-'d' earlier), and '-èd' for syllabic ('-ed' earlier). The editor emends,

vi

as distinct from modernises, his original only in instances where error is patent, or at least very probable, and correction persuasive. Act divisions are given only if they appear in the original or if the structure of the play clearly points to them. Those act and scene divisions not found in the original are provided unobtrusively in small type and in square brackets. Square brackets are also used for any other additions to or changes in the stage directions of the original.

Revels Plays do not provide a variorum collation, but only those variants which require the critical attention of serious textual students. All departures of substance from 'copy-text' are listed, including any relineation and those changes in punctuation which involve to any degree a decision between alternative interpretations; but not such accidentals as turned letters, nor necessarily additions to stage directions whose editorial nature is already made clear by the use of brackets. Press corrections in the 'copy-text' are likewise included. Of later emendations of the text, only those are given which as alternative readings still deserve attention.

One of the hallmarks of the Revels Plays is the thoroughness of their annotations. Besides explaining the meaning of difficult words and passages, the editor provides comments on customs or usage, text or stage-business—indeed, on anything he judges pertinent and helpful. Each volume contains a Glossarial Index to the Commentary, in which particular attention is drawn to meanings for words not listed in *O.E.D.*

The Introduction to a Revels play assesses the authority of the 'copy-text' on which it is based, and discusses the editorial methods employed in dealing with it; the editor also considers his play's date and (where relevant) sources, together with its place in the work of the author and in the theatre of its time. Stage history is offered, and in the case of a play by an author not previously represented in the series a brief biography is given.

It is our hope that plays edited in this fashion will promote further scholarly and theatrical investigation of one of the richest periods in theatrical history.

F. DAVID HOENIGER
E. A. J. HONIGMANN
J. R. MULRYNE

Preface

My chief debt is to the general editor of this volume, Professor J. R. Mulryne, whose patience, knowledge and insight have saved me from more blunders than I should care to list. Professor David Hoeniger gave me some valuable advice in the early stages of the work. My colleagues at Kent, Professor R. A. Foakes, Dr K. E. McLuskie, and Dr P. W. K. Stone, have made very helpful comments on the portions of the introduction that I inflicted on them. Dr Shirley Barlow helped me with some classical references. The University of Kent at Canterbury provided me with some financial assistance towards the preparation of this edition, and my labours were eased by typists in Eliot College (U.K.C.) and by librarians at Kent, the British Library, the University of Massachusetts at Amherst, the University of Texas at Austin, Harvard, Yale, the Bodleian Library, Worcester College Oxford, the Victoria and Albert Museum and, particularly, the Folger Shakespeare Library. Anne Barton kindly sent me a copy of her article, '*The New Inn* and the Problem of Jonson's Late Style', *English Literary Renaissance*, IX (1979), 395–418, before it appeared in print.

MICHAEL HATTAWAY
Canterbury, 1984

Abbreviations

I. GENERAL

Abbott	E. A. Abbott, *A Shakespearian Grammar* (London, 1878 ed.).
B.L.	British Library.
Bacon, *Works*	Spedding, Ellis, and Heath edd., Francis Bacon's *Works* (London, 1857–74).
Bentley	G. E. Bentley, *The Jacobean and Caroline Stage*, 7 vols. (Oxford, 1941–68).
Brand	W. Carew Hazlitt ed., *Brand's Popular Antiquities of Great Britain* (London, 1905).
C.Q.	*Critical Quarterly.*
Chambers	E. K. Chambers, *The Elizabethan Stage*, 4 vols. (Oxford, 1923).
Cockeram	Henry Cockeram, *The English Dictionarie* (London, 1626).
Coleridge	*Essays and Lectures on Shakespeare*, Everyman ed. (London, n.d.).
Cotgrave	R. Cotgrave, *A Dictionarie of the French and English Tongues* (London, 1611).
D.N.B.	Leslie Stephen and Sidney Lee edd., *Dictionary of National Biography*, 21 vols. (London, 1908–9).
Dekker, *N.D.*	A. B. Grosart ed., *The Non-Dramatic Works of Thomas Dekker* (n.p., 1884–6).
E.C.	*Essays in Criticism.*
E.L.H.	*English Literary History.*
Florio	John Florio, *Queen Anna's New World of Words* (London, 1611).
J.E.G.P.	*Journal of English and Germanic Philology.*
J.W.C.I.	*Journal of the Warburg and Courtauld Institutes.*
Linthicum	M. C. Linthicum, *Costume in the Drama of Shakespeare and his Contemporaries* (Oxford, 1936).
M.L.N.	*Modern Language Notes.*
M.L.Q.	*Modern Language Quarterly.*
M.L.R.	*Modern Language Review.*
M.P.	*Modern Philology*
McPherson	David McPherson, 'Ben Jonson's Library and Marginalia', *S.P.*, LXXI (Texts and Studies, 1974), pp. 1–106.
Massinger, *P.& P.*	P. Edwards and C. Gibson edd., *The Plays and Poems of Philip Massinger*, 5 vols. (Oxford, 1976).
Montaigne	J. Florio tr., *The Essayes of Michael Lord of Montaigne*, Everyman ed., (London, 1910).
N.& Q.	*Notes and Queries.*
Nares	Halliwell and Wright edd., Robert Nares's *A*

	Glossary . . . of Words, Phrases, Names, and Allusions (London, 1905 ed.).
Nashe, *Works*	R. B. McKerrow ed., *The Works of Thomas Nashe*, rev. F. P. Wilson, 5 vols. (Oxford, 1958).
O.E.D.	*Oxford English Dictionary.*
Overbury	*The Overburyan Characters*, ed. W. J. Paylor (Oxford, 1936).
P.M.L.A.	*Publications of the Modern Language Association.*
P.Q.	*Philological Quarterly.*
Partridge, *Accidence*	A. C. Partridge, *The Accidence of Ben Jonson's Plays* (Cambridge, 1953).
Partridge, *Syntax*	A. C. Partridge, *Studies in the Syntax of Ben Jonson's Plays* (Cambridge, 1953).
R.E.S.	*Review of English Studies.*
Ren.D.	*Renaissance Drama.*
R.O.R.D.	*Research Opportunities in Renaissance Drama.*
S.B.	*Studies in Bibliography.*
S.E.L.	*Studies in English Literature.*
S.P.	*Studies in Philology.*
S.Q.	*Shakespeare Quarterly.*
Sh.Eng.	Sidney Lee and C. T. Onions edd., *Shakespeare's England*, 2 vols. (Oxford, 1916).
Shak.S.	*Shakespeare Studies.*
Simpson	C. M. Simpson, *The British Broadside Ballad and its Music* (Brunswick N.J., 1966).
Stone	L. Stone, *The Crisis of the Aristocracy, 1558–1641* (Oxford, 1965).
Sugden	E. H. Sugden, *A Topographical Dictionary to the Works of Shakespeare and his Fellow-Dramatists* (Manchester, 1925).
T.L.S.	*The Times Literary Supplement.*
T.N.	*Theatre Notebook.*
Tilley	M. P. Tilley, *A Dictionary of the Proverbs in England in the Sixteenth and Seventeenth Centuries* (Ann Arbor, 1950).

II. THE WORKS OF JONSON AND SHAKESPEARE

Quotations from other plays by Jonson are taken from Herford and Simpson's text and references are to their edition. Abbreviated titles that are unascribed are works by Jonson and the abbreviations are likewise those of Herford and Simpson:

Alc.	*The Alchemist.*
B.F.	*Bartholomew Fair.*
Beauty	*The Masque of Beauty.*
Blackness	*The Masque of Blackness.*
C.is A.	*The Case is Altered.*
C.R.	*Cynthia's Revels.*
Cat.	*Catiline.*

Christmas	Masque of Christmas.
Conv.Drum.	Conversations with Drummond.
D.is A.	The Devil is an Ass.
Disc.	Discoveries.
E.H.	Eastward Ho.
E.M.I.	Every Man in his Humour.
E.M.O.	Every Man Out of His Humour.
E.Althorp	The Entertainment at Althorp.
E.Blackfriars	The Entertainment at Blackfriars.
E.Bols.	Love's Welcome at Bolsover.
E.Highgate	The Entertainment at Highgate.
E.Welb.	The Entertainment at Welbeck.
Engl.Gr.	The English Grammar.
Ep.	Epigrams.
F.I.	The Fortunate Isles.
For.	The Forest.
G.M.	The Gypsies Metamorphosed.
H.W.	For the Honour of Wales.
Hadd.M.	The Haddington Masque.
Hym.	Hymenaei.
I.M.	The Irish Masque.
I.of D.	The Isle of Dogs.
K.Ent.	The King's Coronation Entertainment.
L.F.	Love Freed from Ignorance and Folly.
L.M.M.	Lovers made Men.
L.R.	Love Restored.
L.T.	Love's Triumph through Callipolis.
M.A.	The Masque of Augurs.
M.L.	The Magnetic Lady.
M.Owls	The Masque of Owls.
M.of Q.	The Masque of Queens.
M.V.	Mercury Vindicated from the Alchemists.
Mortimer	Mortimer his Fall.
N.I.	The New Inn.
N.T.	Neptune's Triumph.
N.W.	News from the New World in the Moon.
Oberon	The Masque of Oberon.
P.A.	Pan's Anniversary.
P.Hen.Barriers	Prince Henry's Barriers.
P.R.	Pleasure Reconciled to Virtue.
Poet.	The Poetaster.
S.N.	The Staple of News.
S.S.	The Sad Shepherd.
S.W.	Epicoene, or The Silent Woman.
Sej.	Sejanus.
T.of T.	The Tale of a Tub.
T.V.	Time Vindicated.
1 Theob.	The Entertainment of the Two Kings at Theobalds.
2 Theob.	An Entertainment of the King and Queen at Theobalds.

U.V.	*Ungathered Verse.*
Und.	*The Underwood.*
V.D.	*The Vision of Delight.*
Volp.	*Volpone.*

Quotations from Shakespeare are taken from the Tudor Edition of his works, ed. Peter Alexander. Abbreviated titles are those used by C. T. Onions, *A Shakespeare Glossary* (Oxford, 1911).

III. EDITIONS OF THE NEW INN

F3	Ben Jonson, *Works* (London, 1692) – the third folio.
G.	W. Gifford ed., *The Works of Ben Jonson* (London, 1816).
H. & S.	C. H. Herford and P. & E. Simpson edd., *The Works of Ben Jonson* (Oxford, 1925–52).
Oc.	Octavo copies of *The New Inn* containing corrected sheets (London, 1631).
Ou.	Octavo copies of *The New Inn* containing uncorrected sheets (London, 1631).
1716	*The Works of Ben Jonson* (London, 1716) – the Booksellers' Edition.
T.	G. B. Tennant ed., *The New Inn* (New York, 1908).
W.	P. Whalley ed., *The Works of Ben Jonson* (London, 1756).

Introduction

1. JONSON IN 1629

In 1625 King James, Jonson's patron and admirer, had died and the plague took his fellow dramatist John Fletcher the same year. Thomas Middleton died two years later. Jonson was to live until 1637,[1] the only major dramatist to produce major work in the reigns of Elizabeth, James and Charles. Yet there is no doubt that Jonson's greatest achievements fall within the reign of King James. Then he had joined vigorously in the battles of the theatre war and triumphed in public and private playhouses, at court and the universities with *Volpone* (1606), *The Silent Woman* (1609), *The Alchemist* (1610) and *Bartholomew Fair* (1614). The first collection of his *Works*, notoriously titled the *Opera* in imitation of ancient writers, had appeared in 1616, and throughout the reign he had provided the Jacobean court with a succession of brilliant masques that formed the centrepieces of their Christmas revels. After 1616, however, he had taken a vacation from the playhouses that was to last until 1625–6 when he produced *The Staple of News*.[2] During these years he continued to provide one or two masques annually but devoted the rest of his time to the other kinds of writing that were equally important to him, to divinity and to projects in *literae humaniores*: translations of Horace's *Ars Poetica* and of Barclay's *Argenis* (this last suggested by the king), an English grammar, a verse account of his journey to Scotland in 1618–19, a history of Henry V and work on the writings of the church fathers. There is no evidence, then, of a decline in Jonson's talent or energies – but he was beset by troubles. One of the most demoralising of these was the fire that destroyed his library in 1623: the poem he wrote after this catastrophe, 'An Execration upon Vulcan' (*Und.*, xliii), laments the loss of the projects just listed. Fortune afflicted him further with a paralytic stroke in 1628, and the very day, 19 January 1628–9, that *The New Inn* was licensed, he received a grant of £5 from the Dean and Chapter of Westminster that was recorded 'to M[r] Beniamin Ihonson in his sicknes & want'.[3] His income had been relieved the same year when he was made City Chronologer in succession to Middleton, but in 1631 the pension that accompanied the position was to be withheld because he had performed none of the requisite duties. So while *The Staple of News* had been moderately successful, there is no doubt that in the new reign Jonson's star had suffered an

eclipse. The stroke removed him from the taverns where he had held
a brilliant court among 'the tribe of Ben' (*Und.*, xlvii), although
friends and admirers did still visit him in his sick-chamber at
Westminster, described by Aubrey as 'the house under which you
passe as you goe out of the Churchyard into the old Palace'.[4]
Gentleman amateurs like Lodowick Carlell, Thomas Randolph and
Jasper Mayne had begun to produce plays for the stage but refused
payment for them, so threatening the very profession Jonson had
done so much to establish.[5] His style of masque was being supplanted
by more spectacular offerings as his erstwhile collaborator and now
his rival, the artist and architect Inigo Jones, rose in esteem at court.
Jonson held the traditional classical prejudice against spectacle: for
him, the 'show', however ingenious, formed only the 'bodily part'
which the poet's invention and verse had to animate.[6] So too he must
have experienced a very ambivalent pleasure in seeing plays by his
own protégé Richard Brome succeed in the same weeks that *The New
Inn* failed.[7] It was easy, therefore, for his old colleagues and his
audience to treat *The New Inn* as the product of a palsied brain and,
moreover, of a superannuated sensibility.

There is no doubt that the accession of Charles I precipitated
fundamental changes in the cultural life and artistic achievement of
the age. James had been a great patron of the drama; the number of
new plays performed slumped in the first years of his successor's
reign.[8] Besides losing their talented authors (Dekker too died,
probably in 1632) the dramatic companies seem to have been pausing
to absorb the spirit of the new court before they felt confident to start
commissioning new plays again. Meanwhile they played safe with
revivals of Beaumont and Fletcher. A list of the performances by the
King's Men at Hampton Court and then at the Cockpit in 1630
reveals that ten of the twenty evenings' entertainments were
provided by these dramatists, half of the plays being some fifteen
years old. Jonson was represented by a single performance of
Volpone.[9] Likewise in 1636 one performance of his *Silent Woman*
appears in a court season of twenty-two evenings.[10] As Herford and
Simpson remark, 'The young queen herself, with the fastidious
disdain of her French breeding, heightened by the delicacy of a
précieuse for all things English, was not likely to be captivated by this
"tun of a man", outwardly the most ruggedly English personage,
without doubt, in the entire Court circle'.[11] Although in this play
Lovel's speech on love might be, like the masques of *Chloridia* and
Love's Triumph through Persepolis (1631) a gesture of celebration to

Henrietta's Platonic courtesy, Jonson can scarcely have really expected his play to be a fashionable success, for the other great speech, Lovel's discourse on valour, is an implicit attack on everything Beaumont and Fletcher stood for.

Jonson refused to accommodate himself to new Caroline ideals of refinement and gentility. The subplot of *The New Inn*, a realist and neutrally presented slice of tavern life, belongs to a more robust time and is representative of the kind of drama that Beaumont and Fletcher, imitators of the conversation of gentlemen, excluded from the stage. Under their influence the subject matter of the plays presented at court and in the private playhouses narrowed: instead of depicting the whole range of society, dramatists devoted themselves to illustrating codes of manners for the court coterie. Low-life characters are pastoralised into worthy rustics or comic servants. The deference of Fletcher and his collaborators to the newly-rich burghers forced them to suppress that deep-rooted anti-commercial prejudice that had given point and energy to the satiric citizen comedies of Dekker, Middleton and Jonson himself. The epicentre of many plays moved from 'action' to 'plot' in that these dramatists were concerned more with telling a story than with any criticism of life. Instead of analysing the deep rifts that were appearing in the structures of English society, Caroline dramatists tended to ignore them. Monarchical claims for absolutism that were the Stuarts' answer to the rising power of the city were implicitly endorsed by private playhouse dramatists like Ford and Shirley (as they had been by Fletcher): there was none of the dramatic probing of the origins of regal power, the exploring of the relationship between a man and his office that Shakespeare had undertaken in his history plays. In their place were written countless plays built around amorous intrigues where sexual passion is named love and where chastity or subservience to the will of a king are the bases of honour.

In his own way Jonson too was an uncompromising royalist. For his patron James he had written masques and entertainments that allegorised the virtues that were supposed to cluster round the throne. Two years after the performance of *The New Inn* his Platonic masques incarnated the particular ideals of the Caroline court. As Roy Strong says of them, they 'propound the same principles of absolutist rule: power, they say, is love; opposition and rebellion are unleashed passions, both human and cosmological, the King is order, gentle, civilised, nature and peace'.[12] Jonson's two tragedies, *Sejanus* (1603) and *Catiline* (1611), depict the justice meted out to rebels who misguidedly challenge the legitimate ruler, and in two characters from *The Alchemist* and *Bartholomew Fair*, Tribulation Wholesome and Zeal-of-the-Land Busy, he satirises the excesses of the opposing puritan zealots, their elevation of inspiration and enthusiasm over reason and reasonableness, and their consequent hypocrisy and rapaciousness. Other aspects of puritanism, however, its emphasis on decency and comeliness, its almost Platonic advocacy of unmediated spiritual apprehension, are part of Jonson's make-up. Jonson deplored the elevation of the flesh over the spirit, the pursuit of fashions rather than ideals. Lovel's meditation on beauty in this play can accordingly be placed in the tradition of Spenser's *Four Hymnes*.

Yet unlike his younger contemporaries, Ford and Davenant for example, Jonson did not welcome the changes in the state of the body politic. He realised that the old humanist dream of one nation and one culture that is enshrined in Sidney's *Arcadia* and Spenser's *Faerie Queene* had been shattered. *The New Inn*, like many of the late masques and *A Tale of a Tub* (which may in fact be his last play and not the revision of an earlier work[13]), is infused with nostalgia for a vision of Elizabethan England. Not only do we find in the masques, between the great harmonies of Jonson's classical learning, a surprising affection for the stuff of country life – clowns called Cockerel, Clod, Townshead and Puppy, wenches named Prudence, Frances, Meg and Christian (*The Gipsies Metamorphosed*) – but, like those earlier poets, he postulates a government based on right reason, consensus and moral earnestness. To a contemporary who visited him in 1632 he appeared in fact as a simplifying idealist:

> Behind the Abbey lives a man of fame;
> With awe and reverence wee repeat his name,
> *Ben Johnson*: him we saw, and thought to heare
> From him some flashes and fantastique Guere;
> But hee spake nothing lesse. His whole Discourse
> Was how Mankinde grew daily worse and worse,
> How God was disregarded, how Men went
> Downe even to Hell, and neuer did repent,
> With many such sadd Tales; as hee would teach
> Vs Scholars, how herafter Wee should preach.
> Great wearer of the baies, looke to thy lines,
> Lest they chance to bee challeng'd by Divines:
> Some future Times will, by a grosse Mistake,
> Johnson a Bishop, not a Poët make.[14]

Indeed we look in vain in Jonson's last plays for glimpses of the realities of political life. Nowhere here does Jonson hold up a mirror for magistrates to reveal the power a favourite might gain by manipulating the personality of the monarch. Money features only as a moral symbol, one root of evil, and not as the necessary and inevitable nexus between governor and governed: Jonson does not, unlike Shakespeare for example in *Richard II*, even glance at the problems of taxation.

Jonson was, however, aware of other realities, in particular of changes in the social structure. In the case of our play he is lamenting the destruction of the household. In the sixteenth century it is true to say that the household was the centre not only of family but of economic and even political life. This is obviously true in rural areas, and even in the City masters gave not only professional but moral training to their apprentices, who lodged as well as worked under their roofs.[15] This world had been lost. The transfer of power and wealth from country estate to urban institution had hastened the separation of families as the provincial aristocracy found it necessary to establish residences in London to be near the court or the Royal Exchange. There they might measure their power by their proximity to the royal person or consolidate their fortunes by marriages to city women. Further separations were the result of better transport: the development of the coach (alluded to in the play several times) enabled women to travel about the land more comfortably and decorously than when they had to ride on horseback. Complicated changes in attitudes towards personal relationships had led to a vast number of marital separations among the aristocracy.[16] This is some of the background to this play. For some unknown reason the Lord Frampul has deserted his obligations, ended up as Host of a public inn whither he is unwittingly followed by his flighty daughter Frances. Although there is some sense of 'conversation' or community at the Inn of the Light Heart, it is a household held together only by convenience, vulnerable to the follies and vices represented by Tipto and the Stuffs, and enlivened only by the passing whim of a great lady pursued there by her 'servants' to play an amorous game. No wealth, hospitality or lasting love can be generated there and the play ends, unusually for Jonson, with the characters converted from their wandering humours and ready to commit themselves to life together once more. Jonson in other words is recording not the division of England between economic or political factions but the decay of the one living English culture, epitomised by a country seat like Penshurst, home of the Sidneys,[17] a disintegration of a way of life where wisdom derived from well-doing and not just well-knowing (see Lovel's sterile devotion to entomological knowledge) and where love encompassed not just the pursuit of sexual gratification but the care of children and the bonds between master and servant.

Jonson, Shakespeare and the Blackfriars

In *The New Inn* Jonson was celebrating another debt to the past, to Shakespeare. Both dramatists had spent the greater part of their playwrighting and acting lives with the same troupe, the King's Men, the company which had, by the time Charles attained the throne, surpassed all its rivals. *The New Inn* was written for performance in their private playhouse, the Blackfriars, referred to in the Prologue as 'the old house' (l. 2) which, with the Globe, had seen the first performances of Shakespeare's last plays twenty years before. In 1629 when *The New Inn* was performed, the disposition of the stage and staging techniques remained unchanged – perspective or changeable scenery was not yet in use.[18] (The building had been used as a fencing school before it became a playhouse and it may be that Jonson is recalling that era in II.v.) As the critical introduction will argue, in this play Jonson seems to have realised that the dominant dramatic genre of a generation before, the romance, may have its own kind of truth. However, the audiences that had enjoyed the extravagances and mysteries of *Pericles*, *The Winter's Tale* and *The Tempest* now wanted a different kind of escapism, what Jonson parodied as 'Phancies, Figures, Humors, Characters, Idaeas, Definitions of Lords, and Ladies'.[19] Despite the great act of homage that the King's Men had paid Shakespeare in 1623 by printing in folio his *Comedies, Histories, and Tragedies* (not, be it noted, his '*Works*'), his memory was not honoured by frequent performances. Bentley records sixteen performances of his plays between 1616 and 1642 compared with fifty of Beaumont and Fletcher.[20] In this awkward piece of nostalgia, therefore, Jonson was out of key with the times, almost inviting criticism from his audience.

Situated close to the Inns of Court and the important commercial and social quarter centred around St Paul's, the Blackfriars playhouse attracted an extremely privileged audience of courtiers, wits, dandies, men about town, wealthy students of law, soldiers thrown into idleness by the peace – and their fashionable women.[21] Its audience must have been drawn there too by their knowledge that this was the house of the players who were most frequently called upon to perform at court – Jonson hoped that this play would be seen there.[22] The King's Men were celebrated for their modulated natural playing: Carew hails them in 1630 as 'the true brood of Actors, that alone/Keepe naturall vnstray'nd Action in her throne' and compares the styles of the suburban Red Bull and Cockpit playhouses 'where not a tong / Of th'untun'd Kennel, can a line repeat / Of serious sense'.[23] Boxes at the Blackfriars were the scene of several *affaires d'honneur*,[24] and if the audience was there as Jonson alleged in the dedication to this play to see and to be seen, the company seems to have been willing to allow the spectators to play their part in the spectacle. Music was performed between the acts,[25] an invitation to the audiences to rise and woo their mistresses or pursue court intrigues, and those who wanted to be most conspicuous could pay two shillings for a stool on the stage itself. (A seat in a box cost half a crown and it was a habit for a wealthy man to entertain his retinue by taking up a whole box.) Jonson was quite unwilling to compromise his values by writing to please such a throng. In his next play, *The Magnetic Lady*, he satirised the stage-sitting gallant in the figure of Damplay, but as Alexander Gill rather reasonably pointed out in some verses on the play, such adherence to unfashionable values courted failure:

Is this your loadstone, Ben, that must attract
Applause and laughter at each scene and act?
Is this the child of your bed-ridden wit,
And none but the Blackfriars to foster it?
If to the Fortune you had sent your Lady
'Mongst prentices and apple-wives, it may be
Your rosy fool might have some sport begot
With his strange habit and indefinite knot.
But whenas silks and plush and all the wits
Are called to see and censure as befits,
And if your folly take not, they perchance
Must hear themselves styled 'Gentle Ignorance',
Foh, how it stinks! What general offence
Gives thy profaneness and gross impudence.[26]

Jonson should scarcely have been surprised therefore, that with its resurrection of a Shakespearean mode and its damnation of Fletcherian morals, *The New Inn* failed to please the benches of wit at the Blackfriars.

II. DATE AND STAGE HISTORY

According to Malone, 'Ford's play [*The Lover's Melancholy*] was exhibited at the Blackfriars on the 24th November, 1628, when it was

licensed for the stage, as appears from the office-book of Sir Henry
Herbert, Master of the Revels to King Charles the First, a
manuscript now before me . . . and Jonson's New Inn on the 19th of
January in the following year, 1628–9'.[27] Although the office-book
has disappeared there is no reason to doubt the accuracy of the
transcript, but presumably Malone (who was followed by Tennant[28]
and Herford and Simpson[29]) was in error in assuming that the date of
licensing was also the date of first performance: no company would
want to take the risk of preparing a play that might be suppressed.
The date of performance on Jonson's title-page is 1629, and if we
assume that the play was produced a few weeks after the date of
licensing, in fact shortly after the new year began on Lady Day (25
March), Malone's evidence is in accord with this.

There is ample testimony that the play was not well received at its
first performance. This derives chiefly from the 'Ode to Himself'
which circulated widely before it was appended to the first printing of
the play and which drew many comments and replies (see Appendix
I). The sentiments we find in that poem, however, are to be found in
many of Jonson's invectives against the manners and lack of
judgment of his audiences right from the time of *Every Man in his
Humour*, and indeed it is difficult to find any specific reasons for the
play's failure or to discover whether, as it is commonly alleged, there
was only one performance, and if only one, whether the players gave
up their task part-way through the play. In his dedication Jonson
speaks of 'a hundred fastidious impertinents, who . . . by their
confidence of rising between the acts . . . make affidavit to the whole
house of their not understanding one scene'.[30] Yet there are
references to a similar habit in works as early as Dekker's *The Gull's
Hornbook* (1609) and Day's *The Isle of Gulls* (1606): ''Tis growne into
a custome at playes if anyone rise (especially of any fashionable sort)
about what serious busines soeuer, the rest thinking it in dislike of the
play, tho he neuer thinks it, cry "Mew! by Jesus, vilde!" and leaue the
poore hartlesse children to speake their Epilogue to emptie seates.'[31]
Moreover Jonson was not present at the Blackfriars to witness the
performance – the Epilogue speaks of how 'he sent things fit' from his
sick-bed. His invectives are therefore based on memory and com-
monplace rather than his own testimony to the events.

Nor can one argue that the appearance in the preliminary matter of
the Octavo of a 'character' of the personages and an 'argument' is a
tacit admission that the play had been or might be incomprehensible
on the stage; such guides for the reader occur elsewhere in Jonson's

work.[32] Certainly there is no evidence to support the nineteenth-
century editor Gifford's claim, the substance of which has percolated
into so many critical commentaries, that the play was not 'heard to
the conclusion' or to validate his portrait of Ben as 'the sick lion'. He
goes on: 'his enemies had too little respect for his enfeebled condition
to forego so good an opportunity of insulting him with impunity'.[33]
But as Tennant pertinently remarks, the heading to the second
Epilogue which Jonson had written in expectation of a court
performance gives no hint that he was under attack from a cabal of
enemies: 'Another Epilogue there was, Made for the Play in the
Poet's Defence, but the Play Lived not, in Opinion, to have it
Spoken.' Indeed the mere existence of this second Epilogue, written
after the play had been performed, is evidence that the play's
reception had been successful enough for a court performance to be
considered. Jonson's reference in the Dedication to the 'impertinents' who were present on 'the first day' does not imply even that
there was only the one performance. A Broadside of 1679 is probably
based on this phrase and has little status as historical testimony:

> Poets, who others can Immortal make,
> When they grow *Gray*, their Lawrels them forsake;
> And seek young Temples where they may grow Green;
> No Palsie-hands may wash in *Hippocrene*;
> 'Twas not terse Clarret, Eggs and Muskadine,
> Nor Goblets Crown'd with *Greek* or *Spanish* Wine
> Could make new Flames in Old Ben Johnsons Veins,
> For his Attempts prov'd lank and languid strains:
> His *New Inn* (so he nam'd his youngest Play)
> Prov'd a blind Ale-house, cry'd down the first Day:
> His own dull Epitaph – *Here lies Ben Johnson*,
> (Half drunken too) He Hickcupt – *Who was once one*.[34]

In the same second Epilogue Jonson gives us a possible clue for the
play's unhappy reception when he refers to

> such as will not hiss

Because the chambermaid was named Cis.   (ll. 7–8).
(The Chambermaid's name was later changed to Pru.) Although Cis
was a generic name for a maid – the name is given to one of the
wenches in *The Gipsies Metamorphosed* and to a character in Nabbe's
Tottenham Court (1638) – a ready hypothesis would be that here is
evidence of a specific topical allusion that inflamed an unsympathetic
but not necessarily hostile audience. Yet it is unlikely that we have in
this name a key to the play's failure, for the habit of looking for veiled
personal allusions was common. 'Application, is now, growne a trade

with many' complained Jonson in his Dedication to *Volpone* (l. 65), and John Aubrey and Margaret Duchess of Westminster both provided keys to the characters in *The Alchemist*. Webster, Fletcher and Nabbes too complained, perhaps disingenuously, of the habit.[35] In 1632, Jonson again inveighed against the particular application of his general satire in the Chorus at the end of Act II of *The Magnetic Lady*. A more recent commentator, Fleay, made much of the reference to 'secretary Cis' in one of the 'Charis' poems (*Und.*, II.viii.25): he had identified Charis with Elizabeth, Lady Hatton.[36] But the simplest explanation is that the sound of the name suggested hissing[37] to a restive and philistine audience upon whom, on one occasion at least, a desultory performance was inflicted – Jonson refers on the play's title-page to the negligent playing of the actors. The play does not feel like a *pièce à clef* and there is no reason to doubt the truth of Jonson's expostulation in the second Epilogue:

> We think it would have served our scene as true,
>   If, as it is, at first we'd called her Pru;
> For any mystery we there have found,
>   Or magic in the letters or the sound.
> She only meant was for a girl of wit
>   To whom her lady did a province fit;
> Which she would have discharged and done as well,
>   Had she been christened Joyce, Grace, Doll, or Nell. (ll. 9–16)

Finally the press variants reveal that Jonson had not completed the task of correcting the name when he sent his manuscript to the printer: had the reference to 'Cis' been the sole cause of the play's failure he would presumably have scoured the text more thoroughly.

It is possible that the judgment offered in the play on their manners, in particular their pursuit of fashion, offended the 'better and braver'[38] members of the audience. Indeed there is some evidence that they found the corrosive tone of the Prologue offensive and that this prejudiced their reception of what ensued. We may infer this from the Boy's remark in the Induction to *The Magnetic Lady* that Jonson would not be entreated to give that play a prologue: 'He has lost too much that way already, hee sayes' (ll. 120–1). All such conjectures, however, must remain hypothetical.

No other performances of the play are recorded until a modern revival at the Chelsea Arts Club in 1903 by members of the Old Vic Company under the direction of C. R. Ashbee.[39] Like Herford and Simpson, I have failed to obtain any account of it.

III. THE TEXT

Two years after its performance, on 17 April 1631, *The New Inn* was entered to the bookseller Thomas Alchorne in the Stationers' Register:

17mo die Aprilis 1631

Thomas
Alchorne

Entred for his Copye vnder the handes of Sir HENRY HERBERT and Master Kingston warden a Comedy Called *New Inne* written by Ben: Johnson . . . vjd.[40]

Alchorne may have taken on the play after Robert Allot, who had published *Bartholomew Fair*, *The Devil is an Ass* and *The Staple of News*, had turned it down. Fleay conjectured that Jonson's cryptic epigram 'To My Bookseller' (*Und.* lviii) is addressed to Alchorne.[41]

The New Inn was the only one of Jonson's plays to appear in Octavo. Twenty-two plays had been printed in Quarto, and the author's first collection of 'Works' was published in 1616 in Folio. After his stroke in 1628, Jonson began to publish individual plays in Folio in preparation for a second volume to accompany this first collection.[42] John Beale printed *Bartholomew Fair*, *The Devil is an Ass* and *The Staple of News* in 1631 in this format. But Jonson must have been disappointed: work in Beale's shop was slovenly and these texts are full of uncorrected blunders. Anger at their fate as well as disappointment at the reception of the play may therefore have encouraged him to seek a new publisher as well as a new printer. It was a good move: the new printer, Thomas Harper, who had printed the third edition of the *Annals* (1629) and was to print the fifth edition of the *Remains* (1636) of Jonson's old schoolmaster Camden, provided the author and posterity with a text that presents remarkably few problems.

The copy for the printer
The title-page reads:

THE / NEVV / INNE. / OR, / *The light Heart.* / A COMOEDY. / As it was neuer acted, but most / negligently play'd, by some, / the Kings Seruants. / And more squeamishly beheld, and censu-/red by others, the Kings Subiects. / 1629. / Now, at last, set at liberty to the Readers, his Maties / Seruants, and Subiects, to be iudg'd. / 1631. / By the Author, *B. Ionson.* / Hor . . . *me lectori credere mallem:* / *Quàm spectatoris fastidia ferre superbi.* // *LONDON,* /¶ Printed by *Thomas Harper,* for *Thomas Alchorne,* and / are to be sold at his shop in Pauls Church-yeard, / at the signe of the green Dragon. / *MDCXXXI.*

If the wording of this, in particular the motto which means 'I prefer to entrust myself to a reader rather than to bear the disdain of a scornful spectator', suggests that Jonson himself prepared a careful copy for the printer to compensate for the misfortunes of the play's performance, examination of Harper's text readily confirms this hypothesis. It bears all the signs of having been set up from holograph copy or at least a scribal transcript that had been scrupulously read by the author. As well as that elaborate title-page the Octavo provides us with a full collection of prefatory matter (Dedication, Argument, a detailed *Dramatis Personae*), as well as two Epilogues and the Ode written after the play's failure. The play was set up by page rather than by forme and, unusually, the sequence of signaturing of the gatherings begins on pages carrying the prefatory matter – which indicates that this was supplied to the printer along with the text of the play itself and was printed first.[43] The text is carefully divided into acts and scenes and, according to the convention for learned drama, the names of the characters are massed at the head of each scene irrespective of whether they enter at its beginning or midway through its action. The absence of a large number of entrances and exits helps confirm the hypothesis that the copy for the printer came from Jonson's study rather than from any manuscript associated with a playhouse.

Printing the text

Once copy reached the printer it was subject to alteration or corruption at two stages, the type-setting and proof-reading. It is convenient to examine the second process first.

The evidence suggests that, as was customary, the proofs were read during the printing or 'machining' of the play, and that in this case the reader was Jonson himself. The text is remarkably clean although the extant copies display a large number of variant readings on the inner formes of Sheets B and C. The variants reveal a meticulous correction of spelling, capitalisation, punctuation and italicisation, and this may conceivably have been done by a zealous reader in Harper's shop. The corrections to the metre at I.iii.155, I.vi.166, II.ii.8–9, II.ii.13–5, II.ii.20, II.iv.25, II.v.7 and II.v.85, however, involving, as they do, changes to substantive readings suggest that these were authorial. So almost certainly are the corrections of the name of Lady Frampul's chambermaid: in I.vi 'Cis' and 'Cicelie' are changed to 'Pru' and 'Prudence' in the scene-heading, the stage directions at ll. 22.1 and 25.1, the speech prefixes

at ll. 29 and 32, and within the text at ll. 25 and 46. In the Selden copy
in Bodley (a presentation copy?) there is a cancel slip pasted over the
uncorrected version of the chambermaid's name at I.vi.0.1. There is
no correction to her name at I.v.11. This evidence suggests that the
possibly bedridden Jonson was sent proofs as the play was set up but
failed to get Sheets B and C returned before printing of them had
started.[44] The other five press corrections (at I.i.12, III.i.183,
III.ii.166, IV.i.15 and IV.ii.74) were probably done by Harper's
reader. I have recorded only substantive corrections in the collation;
the complete list can be found in *H.& S.*, VI, 385–94.

An alternative hypothesis for the large number of press corrections
on B and C would be that these sheets were assigned to a less skilled
compositor. Variations in spelling and between conventions of
indentation for the first lines of scenes throughout the play, however,
reveal no consistent pattern. In Sheet C the compositor ran short of
roman 'I's, but the italic substitutes are found on *all* subsequent
sheets and increase in frequency merely towards the bottoms of the
pages. So too '*J*' is sometimes substituted for '*I*' in the running title
but in no discernible pattern. The convention of marking entrances
with a very long dash, a brace bracket and the words '*to them*'
increases in frequency on the last sheets of the play, but the nature of
the play's catastrophe makes such entrances more frequent, and '*to
them*' is a Jonsonian idiosyncrasy and not necessarily a compositorial
one.[45] The evidence therefore suggests that the Octavo text derives
from authorial fair copy, was set up by no more than one compositor,
and was proof-read by the author.

Later editions
Because of its different format, this play could not be bound up with
its predecessors and was therefore not included in the second Folio
volume of *The Workes of Benjamin Jonson* which appeared in 1640,
three years after the author's death.[46] Its title appears as the last of a
sequence of fourteen plays by Jonson that were allotted to Killigrew
about 12 January 1668/9. The list is headed 'Plays Acted at the
Theatre Royall. A Catalogue of part of his Ma^tes Servants Playes as
they were formerly acted at the Blackfryers & now allowed of to his
Ma^tes Servants at ye New Theatre'.[47] The play was, however,
included in the third Folio, *The Works of Ben Jonson*, in 1692 (Sigs.
[4Z1]–5B4v.). This volume carries the statement on its title-page:
'To which is added A COMEDY CALLED THE NEW INN'. The text was set
up from a copy of the Octavo which included an uncorrected inner

forme of Sheet C (I.vi.113–II.vi.9); it corrects a few minor misprints in *O*, modernises some spelling and elision conventions, and alters the lineation at IV.ii.35–7. The uncorrected readings descended to the texts reprinted in Volume 6 of the Booksellers' edition (6 vols., 1716–7) which was reprinted from the 1692 Folio, and in Volume 4 of Whalley's edition (7 vols., 1756) which was reprinted from the Booksellers'. Whalley made some changes to accidentals and one change of substance: 'He that did loue in Oxford' to 'He that did liue in Oxford' (I.v.59). The greatest of the early editors of Jonson was William Gifford who printed *The New Inn* in Volume 5 of his nine-volume edition of 1816. Although he set up his text from Whalley's edition, he did undertake a collation, an imperfect one, of seventeenth-century editions of Jonson. There is no evidence, however, that he consulted the Octavo of *The New Inn*. He was concerned to increase the number of readers of Jonson and accordingly modernised the text, expanded elisions, eliminated archaic word-forms, redivided the acts according to more familiar conventions and added scene locations, entrances and exits. He had a keenly intelligent sense of stage action and it is rarely that a modern editor has to emend his stage directions. The Everyman edition of E. Rhys (2 vols., 1910) is what Herford and Simpson tactfully describe as 'a lax reprint of Gifford'.[48] The play was last edited on its own by G. B. Tennant (Yale Studies in English, XXXIV, (1908)) who was fortunate to use the British Library volume that includes corrected states of Sheets B and C as his copy. Tennant's glossary is useful, his annotations full although seldom concise, but his labours must have given him little joy for his critical introduction damns the play with the faintest of praise. The usefulness of Herford and Simpson's edition of the complete works (11 vols., 1925–52) needs no comment here. The perspicuity, thoroughness and knowledge contained in their apparatus and annotation is apparent to every reader of their text: all a later editor can do is report on the preternatural accuracy of this text and its collation. The two or three misprints, errors of transcription or mistakes in collation that I discovered were trivial and were true exceptions to the rules of excellence that govern their work.[49]

This edition

This edition is based on the Octavo of 1631. The copy I have worked from is the British Library copy 643.b.31 (A). With this I have collated the following:

The Selden copy in the Bodleian Library (B1)
The Malone copy in the Bodleian Library (B2)
The Dyce copy in the Victoria and Albert Museum (C)
The Forster copy in the Victoria and Albert Museum (D)
The Wise copy in the British Library (E)
The Holgate–Toller copy in the Folger Library (Fo)
A copy in the Sterling Library of the University of London (G)
The Bridgewater copy in the Houghton Library at Harvard (H1)
Another copy at Harvard (H2)
A copy at the University of Texas at Austin (T)
A copy at Worcester College, Oxford (W)
A copy at Yale (Y)

Herford and Simpson print a full table of press corrections.[50] I have indicated in Appendix III how the copies I have collated which were unknown to them would appear in their table.

In accordance with the conventions of the Revels series I have, without further annotation, regularised speech prefixes, corrected literal misprints, expanded contractions (L. for Lord, M^r. for Master etc.), modernised spelling, capitalisation, italicisation and most archaic forms ('hanches', 'loose' for 'lose', etc.). Jonson's latinate spellings can be traced in the collation. I have, however, retained 'phant'sie' as this indicates a more precise meaning than the modern 'fancy' and because it is a key word for the meaning of the play. I have also retained Jonson's scene divisions to harmonise with Herford and Simpson and the other Jonson plays in this series, but have distributed the massed names of characters that appear at the head of each scene according to their actual entrances and exits. These and any added stage directions appear within square brackets. I have not thought fit to suggest locations for any scenes or report the suggestions of former editors. I have regularised all elided forms of 'them' to ''em', and have printed 'yo'are' as 'you're', but have noted other changes in elision in the collation as readers or actors may disagree with my sense of Jonson's metre. Greek words have been transliterated. My punctuation, like that of all editors of modernised versions of Jonson, is considerably lighter than the original. Jonson punctuated logically and grammatically rather than rhetorically:[51] my sole concern has been to clarify meaning and aid an actor's emphasis. Any changes of punctuation that affect the sense I have recorded in the collation. Occasionally, where only a slight pause is called for, I have omitted a comma from the end of a line at a place where, were the passage in prose, it might nowadays be used. I have done this as it seems to me that line division is itself a natural and subtle form of punctuation. Any reader who needs to check minutiae of this kind will in any case consult Herford and Simpson's edition of the play rather than my own.

The collation lists the substantive press corrections, substantive differences between the seventeenth-century editions, added stage directions (principally Gifford's) and any of my own modernisations that are debatable or which cannot be decided according to the editorial principles of this series.

Many commentary notes necessarily derive from Herford and Simpson, although I have provided a much larger glossarial apparatus than they did,[52] expanded the cross-references to other passages in Jonson, added somewhat to their historical allusions and tried to provide more material and references that would be helpful to critics and actors.

I have modernised the texts in Appendix I, the poems associated with the play. Unmodernised texts are accessible in Herford and Simpson but their sense for modern readers is often obscure.

IV. THE PLAY

Unity and verisimilitude

In the words of the Induction to Jonson's next play, *The Magnetic Lady*, the inn of *The New Inn*, the Light Heart at Barnet, is a 'Center attractive, to draw thither a diversity of Guests, all persons of different humours'.[53] As Shakespeare had done in his middle comedies, Jonson in *The New Inn* thus defines a comic world within the play. At the Light Heart, as in the Forest of Arden in *As You Like It*, the characters congregate to revel for the duration of the action and from there, at the end, are about to depart again to the city. 'Centers attractive' – the fair in *Bartholomew Fair* is another example – allowed Jonson and Shakespeare to depict a wide spectrum of human types and classes. Unlike Shakespeare, however, Jonson carefully observed the neo-classic unities of time and place. The action takes place within a single day (II.vi.257–8) and is confined to the Inn itself – the play does not begin, say, in the Frampul household as *As You Like It* begins on the de Boys estate. We are merely told of and not shown the events which sent the characters to Barnet. Whether or not Jonson maintained the third unity, unity of action, is a critical problem to which much of this introduction will address itself.

Jonson also departed from Elizabethan precedent in making his comic world 'real' and not romantic. It is quite unlike Illyria, the Forest near Athens or even the city of Ephesus. Manners are contemporary, there is no magic, nor are there exotic trees and beasts, for the scene, a coaching inn a few miles from London resembles many such resorts of the times (IV.iii.71–2). Again Jonson was obeying classical precept, in using comedy as an 'imitation of life', or in the words of his translation of a famous tag, to hold up 'the glass of custome (which is Comedy)';[54] a modern revival of this Caroline play might benefit from the use of representational scenery.[55] There were, of course, no painted flats on the Blackfriars stage, although the tiring-house façade may have borne some resemblance to an inn. A visual contrast between the reality of the set and the self-deceptions of some of the characters would point up many moments in the dialogue.

It is crucial to an understanding of the play to realise the implications of this particular combination of framework plot and realistic mode. Without the establishment of the comic world the play would lose its delicacy of touch and be either an unsuccessful comedy of sentiment or a satire of contemporary manners. What the device does is remind us that this play, like so many Renaissance plays, is also a game. We know that actors imitate real people, but setting the action in a place of resort or revelry reminds us that imitation or acting is characteristic of life as well as of art, that men and women as well as actors perform and play games, maintain illusions, ape and reflect one another's roles. As always Jonson is explicit about his intentions. Although Lord Frampul is himself involved in the complications of the plot, he can, like Prospero, be seen as a figure of the author (V.v.91–100n.), a manipulator of the story, and a chorus to discern the nice distinction between action and acting. It is not surprising that a version of the familiar *topos* of the *theatrum mundi* appears early in the play.[56] The disguised Lord Frampul – who is himself playing a part, Goodstock, host of the inn – reflects:

> I imagine all the world's a play:
> The state and men's affairs, all passages
> Of life, to spring new scenes, come in, go out,
> And shift and vanish.

(I.iii.128–31)

Our reactions to the characters will be very much determined both by our notions about whether or not they admit they are playing a part and by our feelings about the amount of playing that is tolerable in our own lives. Tipto, the very type of Hispanified braggart captain, can win little sympathy. Lovel, by contrast, who first appears merely as a melancholy stereotype, deserves our compassion even though he chooses to profess theatrically his love in public, where his self-righteousness colours his protestations, and where the growing intimacy between him and Lady Frampul is governed by the rules of the Court or 'Parliament' of Love before which they have chosen to appear. Jonson who knew so well how a play could take over an author –

> I had thought to ha' sacrificed
> To merriment tonight i' my Light Heart, Fly,
> And like a noble poet to have had
> My last act best; but all fails i' the plot.

(V.i.24–7)

– had some sympathy with those whose parts took over their natures.

The New Inn has not had a happy critical history. Dryden dismissed the last plays of Jonson's career as 'dotages'[57] and his judgment together with the circumstances of the play's first production have combined to discourage readers from spending much time with it. The first critical task is probably to see whether the play does in fact possess unity of action. A common judgment is that it does not, although it can be argued that this verdict was reached in the nineteenth century when it was very common to confuse 'plot' with 'action'. An age of which the dramatic achievement pointed towards melodrama was unlikely to be able to discern the informing principles of poetic drama. So *The New Inn* was then and is still commonly thought to be a confused and unpalatable mixture of romantic comedy and humorous satire.[58] The fine sentiments of the noble lovers, it has been supposed, could not be integrated into the play along with the fustian of the Inn's servants and swaggerers. Although it would be precipitate to give here a full description of the play's action (readers may wish at this stage, however, to consult Jonson's own 'Argument') it should be pointed out that action is inseparable from tone and irony, from the perceived life of the play on the stage. Even the definitions of action we can select from Jonson's own work, and from the vein of self-monitoring that runs through this play, do not in fact do justice to its distinctive quality, a fine control of satirical awareness and genial tolerance. First, it is certainly an error to assume that Jonson intended a romantic play, a simple idealisation of love. In the Induction to *The Magnetic Lady* he

noted that he considered *The New Inn* to be of the same kind as his
early satiric plays:

> The *Author*, beginning his studies . . . with *every man in his Humour*; and
> after, *every man out of his Humour*: and since, continuing in all his *playes*,
> especially those of the *Comick* thred, whereof the *New-Inne* was the last,
> some recent humours still, or manners of men, that went along with the
> times.
>
> (*M.L.*, Ind. 100–4)

The implications are that Jonson considered that the play's action
was informed by its characterisation. The basis for this characterisation was humour psychology, that elaborate late classical and
medieval science which held that an individual's disposition was
determined by the combination and balance of four fluids or
'humours': black and yellow bile, phlegm, and blood. Jonson argued
that this physiology provided a set of analogical descriptions of
psychological conditions or mental states: as he pointed out in the
explanatory Induction to *Everyman Out of his Humour*, when some
'one peculiar quality' took possession of a man he could be said 'by
metaphor' to exemplify that humour and be held up as an example to
be corrected of folly or vice. Accordingly in the first scene of the play
he establishes Lovel and the Host as melancholic and sanguine.
Their humours of black bile and blood were associated with the
planets Saturn and Jupiter, and Jonson uses the adjectives 'saturnine' and 'jovial' designedly in that scene. Similarly among the minor
characters, Tipto is obviously martial and Lady Frampul and
Pinnacia Stuff in their various ways are venerean. Jonson does not,
however, castigate the principal characters as he had in the earlier
plays castigated those who had affected a humour, like Master
Stephen, the country gull in *Every Man in his Humour*, who calls for a
stool 'to be melancholy upon' (1616 version, III.i.100). Lovel has a
particular cause for his melancholy, his unrequited love for Lady
Frampul. In fact his nature is suggested as much by his name as by
his humour, and his name is ambiguous: 'is your name Love-ill, sir,
or Love-well?' (I.vi.95). Similarly the name of his beloved and in fact
of the Host, 'Frampul', means both 'peevish' and 'high-spirited'.

It is also crucial to realise that in this play the characters are no
longer static types but are subject to change and able to reform.
Lovel's melancholy is purged by his love for Lady Frampul. It may
be that Jonson knew the schematic treatment of melancholy devised
by Henry Cornelius Agrippa, the inspiration of Dürer's famous
engraving 'Melancholia I', and set out in Book I of his *De Occulta*

Philosophia (1531). Agrippa argues that the melancholic is not incapacitated by his grief but on the contrary is the type of genius. He might progress through 'a threefold apprehension of the soul, *viz.* imaginative, rationall, and mentall'.[59] Lovel's devotion to ento-mology is characteristic of the imaginative man whose powers are confined to measuring and the manual arts. On the engraved title-page to Burton's *Anatomy of Melancholy*, this type appears like Lovel in seclusion and is explained by this verse:

> Old *Democritus* under a tree,
> Sits on a stone with book on knee;
> About him hang there many features,
> Of Cats, Dogs, and such like creatures,
> Of which he makes Anatomy,
> The seat of Black Choler to see.
> Over his head appears the sky,
> And Saturn, Lord of Melancholy.

In IV.iii it is reported that Lovel has purged the body politic of its 'Centaurs' – Tipto and his crew – an action representative of rational control in the sphere of moral and political action. The play might be read alongside Chapman's allegorical poem *The Shadow of Night* (1594) which Dame Frances Yates has suggested in a recent lecture is based on the threefold melancholic scheme of Agrippa:

> Therefore Promethean Poets with the coles
> Of their most geniale, more-then-humane soules
> In liuing verse, created men like these,
> With shapes of Centaurs, Harpies, Lapithes,
> That they in prime of erudition,
> When almost sauage vulgar men were growne,
> Seeing them selues in those Pierean founts,
> Might mend their mindes, asham'd of such accounts.
> So when ye heare, the sweetest Muses sonne,
> With heauenly rapture of his Musicke, wonne
> Rockes, forrests, floods, and winds to leaue their course
> In his attendance: it bewrayes the force
> His wisedome had, to draw men growne so rude
> To ciuill loue of Art, and Fortitude.   ('Hymnus in Noctem', ll. 131–44)

Lovel's progress culminates in his poem (IV.iv.4ff.) when he adds the Orphean harmony mentioned by Chapman to his Herculean vigour, and accomplishes a supreme act of intuitive 'mind', a 'vision' (IV.iv.2) such as Agrippa prescribed, of the realm divine.

Jonson's meticulous and unifying control of his satirical tone can be shown by an analysis of the so-called 'sub-plot'. There are qualities as well as follies to be found among the below-stairs characters, so that this group also serves a critical function for the play, and reinforces its particular satiric structure. In an important passage Jonson points out that the two groups in the play, what he calls 'fine' company and 'wild' company, are analogues of one another:

> Why do you bring me in wild company?
> You'd ha' me tame and civil in wild company?
> I hope I know wild company are fine company,
> And in fine company, where I am fine myself,
> A lady may do anything, deny nothing
> To a fine party . . . (IV.ii.92–7)

The unity of the action, therefore, as always in Jonson, is poetic. It derives not simply from a satisfying story, from analogies between situations, from the interplay of characters, but from a method of characterisation. It also derives from linguistic decorum, the establishment of an appropriate spectrum of verbal styles, from the enactment of themes, from the indication of appropriate techniques of acting, and from the stance of the author, his particular and constantly-renewed balance of sympathy and judgment. I shall, for clarity, separate my discussion of the play's satire from my discussion of its romantic elements, but these are only aspects of what is indivisible at any one moment of a theatrical realisation.

The tone of the satire

Although the play looks backwards towards romance, Jonson has displaced the romantic assertions of Elizabethan comedy and looks forward to Restoration comedy of manners. We can begin to define the theme of the play by looking at the nature of the comic world within the play, the character of the Inn itself. A festive and merry place, like Rabelais' Abbey of Thélème, Lovel desecrates it by entering with his melancholic humour: his heavy heart cannot be accommodated in the Inn of the Light Heart. But the Inn has a motto: 'a heavy purse makes a light heart'. The phrase is proverbial, but Jonson again extends its ordinary meaning. 'Light' here means not only happy but fickle and self-indulgent. Jonson hints that the humours and vapours of his company are the luxuries of the rich. He gently satirises the introversion and brooding of 'fine company', the indolent Caroline nobility, as preoccupied with love and masquerade as the merchants of *Volpone* and *The Alchemist* had been obsessed with gold.[60]. As Lovel himself recognises, the pursuit of love is as consuming a passion as the pursuit of wealth:

B

Host. But yet the lady, th' heir, enjoys the land.
Lovel. And takes all lordly ways how to consume it
      As nobly as she can: if clothes and feasting
      And the authorised means of riot will do it.
Host. She shows her extract, and I honour her for it.   (I.v.77–81)

It is also significant that the play is set in an inn and not a house. The Inn serves as the anti-type of Penshurst, the home of the Sidneys and celebrated in Jonson's famous poem, a place were all men may lodge but no man dwells, a thoroughfare for all, and a figure therefore for the social mobility, fashion following and rootlessness of the times. In his 'whirls and bouts of fortune', Burst was once 'a citizen, since a courtier, / And now a gamester' (III.i.171–2), and it is the servants' humour to call one another by inflated titles, a reflection of the inflation of honours, the creation and promotion of baronets and peers by the Stuarts.[61] To emphasise this Jonson inserts a panegyric of the world that had been lost, of the chivalric education that had been acquired by men of good stock in the houses of the old aristocracy.[62] The ancient 'Academies of Honour' had been invaded by the ways of the tavern: the habit now is to

            carry messages to Madam Cressid;
      Instead of backing the brave steed o' mornings,
      To mount the chambermaid; and for a leap
      O' the vaulting-horse, to ply the vaulting-house;
      For exercise of arms, a bale of dice
      Or two or three packs of cards to show the cheat
      And nimbleness of hand; mistake a cloak
      From my lord's back, and pawn it; ease his pockets
      Of a superfluous watch, or geld a jewel
      Of an odd stone or so; twinge three or four buttons
      From off my lady's gown: these are the arts
      Or seven liberal deadly sciences
      Of pagery, or rather paganism,
      As the tides run.   (I.iii.71–84)

Invectives and passages of social criticism like this can be paralleled by passages in Jonson's poems – some may indeed derive from the poems as the notes to this edition indicate – but we are dealing with a play and not a poem, and what a responsible production could reveal of the play need not be in total accord with these passages of explicit moralising. The Inn is indeed a metaphor, a figure for the life of the times. Like the Fair of St Bartholomew, the Light Heart draws to itself a wild company of rogues and swaggerers from the London underworld. The Host describes how his premises have become a thieves' academy, a working-class counterpart of the nobility's Academy of Lust:

> The school, then, are my stables or the cellar
> Where he doth study deeply at his hours
> Cases of cups, I do not know how spiced
> With conscience, for the tapster and the ostler: as
> Whose horses may be cosened, or what jugs
> Filled up with froth. (II.v.34–9)

The use of generic names for the minor characters, Tipto, Fly, Burst, etc., might also lead us to expect a 'comicall satyre', a concourse of humours.[63] But the play is not merely a social parable: a ferocious assault upon the audience's conscience, mounted by turning all the characters into moral grotesques, would be inappropriate for a modern revival. For the Inn is a jovial place where people go about their jobs cheerfully and honestly enough – their villainies can be construed as mere 'pranks of ale and hostelry' (III.i.125) – and so it sets off the vapourings of the idle rich and the morose toils the Saturnine Lovel has imposed upon himself. (His profession of studying insects aims a glancing satirical blow at the *virtuosi* of the time.[64]) The Light Heart is not decorous – although it is the outsider Ferret who is offensive with his joke about the 'scotch warming-pan' (I.iii.8ff.) – but the talk there, even if the speakers like any pub bores insist on exhausting their subjects, is often good and racy, good enough to make Tipto forget his suit to Lady Frampul. There is no snobbery or false gentility there: Goodstock's confident humour accompanies his fair-trading, and servants and lords can join together in convivial banter on the fashions and topics of the day. A modern director should not succumb to the temptation to cut as merely topical or irrelevant, say, the discussion of fashions in fencing (II.v) and of Spaniards (IV.ii). The subject-matter of these conversations is unimportant, but Jonson has captured masterfully the atmosphere of pub talk, its languor and nostalgia, the insistence of bar-room pundits on displaying their factual knowledge, the inability of the wits to refrain from *double entendres*.

The bar is presided over by Fly who is literally the *donné* of the place – he was inherited by Goodstock when he acquired the Inn.[65] Fly has a smattering of learning and his humour is to run the house as a militia, a harmless if quaint and strained practice. (One could compare the drinking school with tankards named as beasts in *The Silent Woman*.) Tipto happily joins in, and extends, this language game in III.i, where Jonson defines artfully the characters of the

Braggart Captain and the Inn's parasite, as Fly's natty speech deftly exposes Tipto's fustian humour. Perhaps Jonson intended in this passage some satire on the decline of enthusiasm among the nobility for serving in the real militia and on their preoccupations with skirmishes in the fields of love – but that might be difficult to realise in a production now. The moral status of the Inn is rather like that of the tavern in *2 Henry IV*. In one sense, Shakespeare's tavern is a place of resort for the ageing Doll and Falstaff and for the theatrical huffing of Pistol, and so serves as a figure for the declining fortunes of Bolingbroke's reign. But in another, like the Light Heart, it is a place where, as Nashe had written, 'Familiarity and conference' are 'the sinews of societies',[66] a place of talk, wit and toleration.

The real iniquities of the Inn have been imported from the nobility. We see this most notably in the episode of the tailor Nick Stuff and his wife Pinnacia. Her humour is to be richly dressed, to ape the conspicuous display of fine company,[67] his to 'preoccupy' her in the borrowed robes which serve to rouse his jaded sexual appetites. They are the centre of the play's satire on modishness: it is set in a 'New Inn' where there is 'news brought of a new lady, a newer coach, and a new coachman' (Arg. 82) – Jonson's previous comedy, *The Staple of News*, had dealt with the theme in a different mode.[68] As 'Pinnace', the wife is a whore, and together they are part of the general satire on role-playing, seeming what one is not. The Hispanified Tipto is infected with this new-fangledness and remonstrates with the Host for appearing plainly dressed – 'in *cuerpo*' as he insists on saying (II.iv.48ff.). (Ironically, in fact, the Host is the disguised Frampul.). In particular, Stuff and his wife live for their mechanical sex, measured by its variety, valued in the terms of a tavern-reckoning as they 'score up sums of pleasure' (*Volpone*, III.ii.433). Jonson's savagery emerges in the fantasies of Lady Frampul and Pru as they devise sadistic punishments for the tailor, and yet their reason for displeasure, his late delivery of a robe, is a mark of the trivial torments of those that live the 'good' life. The poetic justice that is meted out to the Stuffs, blanketing for him, stripping of finery for her, is a punishment for folly rather than vice, even if Stuff does beg Pru for mercy. On the stage the main effect would be of a couple of splendid grotesques: Pinnacia is enormous, a gross dame in 'yellow, glittering, golden satin' (III.ii.274), and Stuff, her 'protection', is a 'toy', 'a slight mannet' (IV.i.27–8).

When Jonson turns his attention to the cozening tricks played by Pierce and Peck (III.i) we feel that the nobility are merely receiving condign punishment by being robbed themselves. The vanity of the 'pampered breed' (III.i.165) emerges in Tipto's disdain for Burst, the vile snobbery of a reduced gentleman aping the *hauteur* of the nobleman:

> A broke-winged shopkeeper? I nose 'em straight.
> He had no father, I warrant him, that durst own him;
> Some foundling in a stall or the church-porch;
> Brought up i' the Hospital; and so bound prentice;
> Then master of a shop; then one o' the Inquest;
> Then breaks out bankrupt or starts alderman:
> The original of both is a church-porch.   (IV.ii.6–12)

The servants of the Inn have a fashion that becomes them far better than the plush robes and posturings of the nobility: a fashion of speech that is quite their own. The vigour, wit and discrete signs of individuality and characteristic action in a passage like the following indicate that the 'wild company' have a naturalness and a knowingness which elude those of 'finer' disposition:

> *Fly.*   . . . you must pray
>   It may be revealed to you at some times
>   Whose horse you ought to cozen; with what conscience;
>   The how, and when. A parson's horse may suffer –
> *Pierce.*   Whose master's double beneficed; put in that.
> *Fly.*   A little greasing i' the teeth; 'tis wholesome,
>   And keeps him in a sober shuffle.
> *Pierce.*   His saddle too
>   May want a stirrup.
> *Fly.*   And, it may be sworn,
>   His learning lay o' one side, and so broke it.
> *Peck.*   They have ever oats i' their cloak-bags to affront us.
> *Fly.*   And therefore 'tis an office meritorious
>   To tithe such soundly . . .   (III.i.139–50)

A scene like this gives the lie to the old charge that Jonson created merely 'flat' characters. It was first made in the seventeenth century when Felltham alleged that the 'jests so nominal' in this play 'throw a stain through all the unlikely plot';[69] was given aphoristic force when Moulton argued that Jonson 'alleged' his characters rather than presented them;[70] and has been repeated relentlessly in this century under the influence of Forster's *Aspects of the Novel* and Eliot's essay on Jonson. In this scene we see Fly inflaming the smouldering wit of Pierce and Peck who know that the nobility rob them as much as they rob the nobility. Fly in fact does not possess their first-hand social awareness, but is amused to be drawn into the game in invective fantasy. His wit runs before that of the others, but he returns to egg them on or to display his superiority with a pedantic correction:

> *Peck.* ... I wish he may be founder'd.
> *Fly.*   Foun-der-ed:
>   Prolate it right.   (III.i.166–7)

Jonson is scrutinising a narrow milieu, the ambivalent morality of the working class and the niceties of social distinctions there. But the 'personality' that Jonson's unsympathetic critics demand *is* there, as much determined by the characters' relationships with their fellows as by the inward workings of their minds. Only a master playwright could have portrayed the structure and dynamics of that group with such economy, and a company of actors with a developed social sense could turn this scene from, to use the terms of the play, 'phant'sie' to 'vision'.

Yet the play is not an earnest elevation of working class morality above that of the upper classes. This society below stairs is unsupported by any ideals or aspirations. It has no visions, deceptive though these may be, and its valour consists only of brave words. Jonson banishes this crew from the play in the middle of Act IV after Burst and Huffle have provoked Tipto over Pinnacia. Their exit in fighting confusion is an emblem of their nature, and of the disorder that will befall a group that cannot look beyond their preoccupations. Unlike the noble lovers, their minds are untransfigured, unordered by Love, and their images of fantasy lead only to inconstancy.

The romance elements

In Jonson's next play, *The Magnetic Lady*, a speech from a boy actor leaves us in no doubt as to the author's attitude towards popular romantic drama:

> if a child could be borne, in a *Play* and grow up to a man i'th first Scene, before hee went off the Stage: and then after to come forth a Squire, and bee made a Knight: and that Knight to travell between the Acts, and doe wonders i' the holy land, or else where; kill paynims, wild boores, dun Cowes, and other Monsters; beget him a reputation, and marry an Emperour's Daughter for his Mistris; convert her Fathers Countrey; and at last come home, lame, and all to be laden with miracles.
>
>   (Chorus I.16–24)

The direction of the satire here is that taken by Beaumont in *The Knight of the Burning Pestle*, and there are some side glances at the Iberian originals for these popular narratives scattered throughout *The New Inn*. Yet it is too simple to assume, as Larry S. Champion[71] and Douglas Duncan[72] have done, that *The New Inn* is essentially a

parody of romance conventions and a satire on the Caroline cult of
Platonic love. Jonson, it is true, in his Ode written after the play's
failure, growls at the taste for 'mouldy tales' like *Pericles*, and *The
New Inn* has a plot that subsumes episodes deriving ultimately from
Greek romance: a long-separated husband and wife, a mother in
disguise caring for her child and revealing herself only when family
divisions are to be healed by marriage, lovers overcoming obstacles to
their love, and fine sentiments about love and valour. Jonson, it could
be argued, has brought the tale within the bounds of his particular
decorum by setting the airy nothing of his story in a local habitation,
observing the unities of time and place, and concentrating his action
on its final unfolding. Nature and Fortune have been domesticated
and internalised: instead of tempests and providential rescues, we
have gusts of passion and accidental encounters; and by keeping
some of the episodes of this kind of romance off stage, reducing
others to absurdity – the lost mother disguised as a one-eyed Irish
nurse, for example – Jonson, according to this interpretation, is
rescuing what little he could from a genre he disdained. There is
evidence outside the play: he had called the first poem of *The Forest*
'Why I Write not of Love' and one could argue that the corpus of his
writings as a whole indicates that his creative impulses run towards
satire based on right reason, sanity and the Roman virtues of
mediocritas and *pietas* – those central and human values of Christian
humanism – and towards the making of artefacts of which the
excellence depends on their firmness and the strenuous and sinewy
labours of their verse. An early commentator, Edmond Gayton,
described *The New Inn* as a play of this kind, designed to appeal to an
audience who would expect romance to be banished from their
presence: 'though the Comoedy wanted not its *prodesse, & delectare*,
Had it been exhibited to a scholastick confluence; yet men come not
to study at a Play-house'.[73]

The play, however, does not feel like that. For one thing there is no
hint of *parodic* intention in the Argument (although it suggests, as I
have argued, some satire on fashion), and for another the opposition
between the classical and the romantic is unhistoric: romance
episodes are as intrinsic to classical comedy as satiric episodes. Early
in his career Jonson had written *The Case is Altered* (1597) and based
its double plot on two plays of Plautus, the major one on the *Captivi*
and the minor one on the *Aulularia*. As Madeleine Doran points out,
'the romantic elements of the main plot are similar to those in *The
Comedy of Errors*, but they actually play a larger part in the plot – loss

of children, far wandering over many years, fortunate recognition at a moment of imminent peril, and final happy reunion of parents and children'.[74] The parallel with Shakespeare is interesting, for both men at the end of their careers returned to this kind of romance. *The New Inn* is I would submit Jonson's recension of Shakespeare's last plays.[75] He is as intrigued as his predecessor with the 'truth' that could be extracted from what was strange or improbable, as aware as Shakespeare had been of the possibilities of amplifying the conclusion of his play with a recognition scene that tends towards revelation. Both men had known the patterns of pastoral and masque; but where Shakespeare celebrates the miraculous and hints at the coming of a new order, Jonson anatomises the unions that may be possible and invokes old traditions that may just hold together in a whirling world.

The burgeoning love of Lovel and the Lady Frampul serves as a positive in the play. At first we might think Lovel merely one of Love's fools, a middle-aged scholar, squeamish about being exposed to the hurly-burly of the revels in the Inn, but playing the conventional love games, sending his lady 'toys, verses, and anagrams, / Trials o' wit, mere trifles she has commended, / But knew not whence they came' (I.vi.104–6). Later, we realise that he had not told his love because he had promised to take care of Lord Beaufort's son, the debonair Beaufort who had ventured his own suit to the lady. On the occasion of the Parliament of Love called by Lady Frampul, Lovel decides to press his case obliquely and not only wins the lady but converts her from her flippant and careless pursuit of pleasure. The mode of the story is that of the sequence of 'Charis' poems in *The Underwood* where the poet recognises not only the imperfections of his beloved and his own folly, but the transfiguring nature of the love that might bind them. The Lady may be Frampul, descended from the house of Silly, but she is not a totally unworthy subject for the immaculate meditation on beauty that Lovel delivers in IV.iv. There it is called a 'vision' and the word marks a progression in Lovel's self-confidence: he had feared that his obsession was mere 'phant'sie' (I.iv.17). There is no more need to think that he is totally self-deluded than there is doubt whether her conversion is in fact more profound than her new profession of love suggests. Neither has yet found a fit style for new emotion, and so resorts to what is familiar and conventional. Their union may be uncertain – Jonson does not prognosticate. What he concentrates on are those delicate moments when Lovel is stirred from his throttling diffidence and Lady

Frampul steered from her unhappy sportiveness.

In his use of the terms 'phant'sie' and 'vision' Jonson is following the distinction drawn by Macrobius between the deceptions of fantasy and the truth that may be revealed in vision.[76] The distinction is usefully developed by Puttenham in *The Arte of English Poesie*, a copy of which Jonson owned:

> For as the euill and vicious disposition of the braine hinders the sounde judgement and discourse of man with busie & disordered phantasie . . . so is that part being well affected, not onely nothing disorderly or confused with any monstrous imaginations or conceits, but very formall, and in his much multi-formitie *vniforme*, that is well proportioned, and so passing cleare, that by it as by a glasse or mirrour, are represented vnto the soul all maner of bewtifull visions, whereby the inuentiue parte of the mynde is so much holpen, as without it no man could deuise any new or rare thing . . . the phantasticall part of man (if it be not disordered) [is] a representer of the best, most comely and bewtifull images of things to the soule and according to their very truth.[77]

At the end of the play Lovel comes to a fine point of recognition when he asks that his vision, his 'dream of beauty', might be sung (V.iv.149): the conflation of the two species of apprehension, 'vision' and 'phant'sie', is analogous to the awakening of the lovers in *A Midsummer Night's Dream*, when the lovers look with parted eyes, when everything seems double, when each has a love who is his own and not his own. Lovel's poem is a still point amid the chaos of the Inn. It is because of Lovel's self-knowledge that his moments of excessive declamation reduce him no more in our eyes than do those of Orsino in *Twelfth Night*. And it is this self-knowledge that draws him and the Host together in the opening scenes. Both know the ways of the world, its follies and deceptions, although Lovel does not know whether his name means Love-ill or Love-well (I.v.95). But whereas Lovel chooses to pursue his ideal, the Host waits for events to overtake him as his wife and children are returned to his family. His ironic cheerfulness is as self-indulgent as Lovel's sentimental melancholy.[78] At the end of the play, however, the Host realises that the true natures of Lovel and Lady Frampul have been touched and that their love is more than a casual alliance formed in the spirit of revelry:

> I had thought to ha' sacrificed
> To merriment tonight i' my Light Heart, Fly,
> And like a noble poet to have had
> My last act best: but all fails i' the plot.   (V.i.24–6)

Parliaments of love

It remains to define the nature of the play's central scenes, the love games of the noble characters. Jonson drew on three traditions for the wooing scenes: medieval Courts or Parliaments of Love,[79] Renaissance 'banquets' or *symposia*[80] and, in so far as the parliament is presided over by a servant, the tradition of Feasts of Misrule which were common occasions in Elizabethan revelry.[81] This last tradition establishes an ironic perspective on this important part of the action. Like all games, ceremonies of misrule combined both jest and earnest, and were times (like masked balls) when the roles of 'art' and 'life' coincided. They therefore are related to Jonson's explicit description of the *theatrum mundi* (I.iii.128–31) and reinforce our impression that the truest moments of the lovers' dialogues are, as Touchstone remarked, the 'most feigning'.

The Court of Love has a long history: as a parliament it was an assembly in which noble men and women assembled to hear 'questions' of love, definitions or praises of love, or to discuss matters of etiquette; as a court it served to resolve differences. Various decisions in love cases are described in the early thirteenth-century *Tractatus de Amore* of Andreas Capellanus (II.vii), Chaucer alluded to the tradition in *The Parliament of Fowls*, and a Court of Cupid tries the proud Mirabell in VI.vii of *The Faerie Queene*. Her companion, the squire Disdain, 'did stryde / At euery step vppon the tiptoes hie' (VI.vii.42) and, like Tipto in the present play, is vanquished by a hero, Arthur himself.[82] The proceedings of a Court of Love are fully set out in the *locus classicus*, the *Aresta Amorum, sive Processus inter Amantes cum Decisionibus Parlamenti* of Martial d'Auvergne (*c.* 1430–1508). This work, generally known by its French title, *Les Arrets d'Amour*, was written about 1455 and went through more than thirty-five editions between 1500 and 1734.[83] Jonson may have known a derivative work that had recently appeared over the name of 'Cupidon', *Plaidoyers et Arrests d'Amours Donnez en la Cour & Parquet de Cupidon* (Rouen, 1627). Actual assemblies of this type had been held in European courts, but there is no evidence that any such was ever held in England[84] although certain entertainments offered to Queen Elizabeth bore some resemblance to the form.[85] (Perhaps Jonson was thus striking another faint note of nostalgia.) From an early stage playwrights had seen the dramatic potential of the occasion: John Heywood's *Play of Love* (1533) has characters called The Lover Loved, The Lover not Beloved, Neither Lover nor Loved and The Woman Beloved not Loving.[86] Marston constructed the fifth act of *The Fawn* (1604) around a Parliament of Love to which the humorous characters are summoned to hear edicts of love and receive condign punishment for their follies and crimes against social form. Massinger's *The Parliament of Love* (1624) which survives only in a mutilated form and may never have been acted, is a play of amorous intrigue in the manner of Beaumont and Fletcher. The parliament which is called in its fifth act is a Court of Love, presided over by the monarch before a statue of Cupid carried in by a priest. There the protagonists are summoned to listen to a discourse on the decline of love and to answer for the crimes they had committed in the pursuit of their passions.

The second tradition is that of the academic debate or symposium. The classical archetype is Plato's dialogue on love (*The Symposium*). Courtship scenes in prose romances like Sidney's *Arcadia* are also often cast in the form of debates. Some features of the love debate in *The New Inn* recall the structure of the Renaissance archetype, Book IV of Castiglione's *The Courtier*. Like Cardinal Bembo, Lovel propounds a doctrine of love that is conventionally neo-Platonic (although it is apparent that Jonson went directly to Ficino for his formulations). As with Bembo, Lovel's oration is interrupted and cynically undercut by an Ovidian sensualist, Lord Beaufort, whose practice exposes the sophistries of assuming that the beautiful is the good and that love can last without a descent to the flesh:

Lovel.	. . . Love is a spiritual coupling of two souls,
	So much more excellent as it least relates
	Unto the body; circular, eternal,
	Not feigned or made, but born; and then, so precious
	As nought can value it but itself; so free
	As nothing can command it but itself;
	And in itself so round and liberal
	As where it favours, it bestows itself.
Beaufort.	And that do I: here my whole self I tender,
	According to the practice o' the court. (III.ii.104–13)

Jonson's assembly is both a court of justice to which Lovel brings a Bill of Complaint for the disrespect he has 'conceived if not received' (II.vi.143) from Lady Frampul, and a parliament in which he propounds *quaestiones* of love and valour. The problem is whether the scene is intended as a comic exposure of Lovel's pretensions in particular and perhaps as a general satire on fashionable Platonism. Jonson does refer (III.ii.205) to the work that had inspired the craze, Honoré d'Urfé's pastoral novel, *Astrée*. This had appeared in France in 1607–10, and had been first translated into English in 1620. But in

1629, the year of *The New Inn*, it is unlikely that Platonism at court was as fashionable as it was six or so years later.[87] In a letter of 2 June 1634, James Howell writing to a friend in Paris suggests that the craze was just then catching on:

> The Court affords little News at present, but that there is a Love call'd Platonick Love, which much sways there of late; it is a Love abstracted from all corporeal gross Impressions and sensual Appetite, but consists in Contemplations and Ideas of the Mind, not in any carnal Fruition. This Love sets the Wits of the Town on Work; and they say there will be a Mask shortly of it, whereof Her Majesty and her Maids of Honour will be part.[88]

(The masque was Davenant's *The Temple of Love* presented on Shrove Tuesday, 1635.) If Jonson was not therefore satirising that particular cult it is still possible that, as E. B. Partridge argues, he was exploiting the inherent comic possibilities of Platonic love:

> Usually, these scenes are interpreted as romantic expositions of Platonic love and Aristotelian valour, static and dull, though interesting as rhetorical pieces. But such an interpretation misses the delicate comedy in a chambermaid's pretending to be Queen for a day and tyrannizing over her mistress, or in Lovel's discriminating, with Aristotelian precision, the causes of love while looking at the beautiful Lady Frampul. His exquisite definition is comically counterpointed by Beaufort's more earthy love and by the Nurse's drunken misunderstanding of both Lovel and Beaufort (III.ii.91–118). The comic – and earthy – touch is also kept by Pru, especially in her remark after Lady Frampul had said that she would give Lovel twenty kisses: 'Beware, you doe not coniure vp a spirit / You cannot lay'   (III.ii.250–51).[89]

Yet this, it seems to me, is but a partial reading of a scene which gains its effect by both celebrating and mocking Lovel's earnestness. Like Henrietta Maria, Jonson took his Platonism seriously, and considered it as a way of reforming sexual morals. Separation, adultery and divorce were becoming more prevalent among the nobility in Charles's reign[90], but it was only in the 1630's that 'Platonic Love' provided a cover for more zealous love-making. 'Platonic wooing became an exaggerated prudery combined with coquetry, a love relation not always pure, a series of intricate manoeuvres according to false standards, one which proclaimed marriage a mere slavery.'[91] If Jonson had intended a satire on triviality and hypocrisy in *The New Inn*, is it not likely that his play would have pilloried those who enacted the empty rituals of the *Plaidoyers et Arrests d'Amour*? '*Vne Dame demande raison de son amy pour luy auoir mis la main sur le tetin, & mouillé le deuant de sa cotte (xii) . . . Vne ieune Dame se complaint de son mary, pour cause qu'il ne veut qu'elle port robbe ne chapperon à la nouvelle façon* (xxxi).' None of those who wrote poems on the play suggest that it failed because of its satire (see Appendix I), and the tone of *The New Inn* is quite different from Davenant's professed satire on the theme, *The Platonic Lovers* (1635):

Castraganio.	My sister, signior, is inquisitive,
	Guilty of my offence, she ask'd me ere
	You came, why you endeavour'd thus to have
	The lady married to another, whom you meant to love?
Fredeline.	That's the platonic way; for so
	The balls, the banquets, chariot, canopy,
	And quilted couch, which are the places where
	This new wise sect do meditate, are kept,
	Not at the lover's but the husband's charge.
	And it is fit; for marriage makes him none,
	Though she be still of the society.
Amadine.	And may, besides her husband, have
	A sad platonical servant to help her meditate.
Fredeline.	All modern best court authors do allow't.
Amadine.	You give good light into the business, sir.
Fredeline.	Were Eurithea married, I would teach
	Her the true art: she is unskilful yet.
Amadine.	Hymen may burn his taper to a snuff
	Before we see her wedding day; there's nothing comes
	So seldom in Theander's thought.
Fredeline.	But are you serious?
Amadine.	I've newly dress'd her like a shepherdess;
	And he, i'th' old Arcadian habit, meets
	Her straight, to whine and kiss. That's all they do.
Fredeline.	How? 'Tis two full hours since the prefix'd time
	Our artist did prescribe his charm should operate;
	I hope he hath not us'd us thus. Castraganio!
	Captain, I'd forgot. Dear sir, hasten, and see
	How it doth work with Gridonell.[92]

Jonson elsewhere seems to have been happy to celebrate the myths of Plato. In his masque *Love's Triumph Through Callipolis* (1631) Euphemus, with lines that quote from Lovel's discourse, opposes Platonic constancy to the giddy whirls of sensual lovers.[93] So it is reasonable to take the pleas of Lovel seriously: he appears after all not simply in a court to judge folly but in a parliament for debate. The tone is festive and the tradition of revelry where servants monarchise over their superiors is as much associated with celebration as with satire.[94] There is comedy in the scene, but all lovers are easily made fools in the world's eyes. On stage, Lovel's discourses might seem pedantic and long-winded – but they are perfectly in character. The dramatic interest comes not only from an ironic contrast between

Lovel's idealism and Beaufort's sardonic reminders of the reality of contemporary manners, but from the embarrassment Lovel and Lady Frampul display after their love has thus been exhibited in public. Lovel cannot decide whether to be cynical or ecstatic after the first kiss Pru awards him before the court (II.vi.114ff.) and Lady Frampul resorts to a string of conventional conceits to cover the real feeling she feels growing within her and then suddenly stops to take a reasonable view of the match.

> Now I adore Love, and would kiss the rushes
> That bear this reverend gentleman, his priest,
> If that would expiate – but I fear it will not.
> For though he be somewhat struck in years and old
> Enough to be my father, he is wise,
> And only wise men love, the other covet.
> I could begin to be in love with him,
> But will not tell him yet because I hope
> T'enjoy the other hour with more delight,
> And prove him farther.   (III.ii.226–35)

Lovel covers up his shock at Lady Frampul's conversion to his cause by gruffly voicing a suspicion that his love is merely playing her part:

> Tut, she dissembles; all is personated,
> And counterfeit comes from her! If it were not,
> The Spanish monarchy with both the Indies
> Could not buy off the treasure of this kiss
> Or half give balance for my happiness.   (III.ii.258–62)

Lady Frampul and Lovel are Jonson's versions of Beatrice and Benedick: both couples have erected protective shells about selves that are more vulnerable than other revellers who surround them realise. In his prefatory verses to the Beaumont and Fletcher Folio (1647) William Cartwright, possibly thinking of this play, wrote:

> *Johnson* hath writ things lasting, and divine,
> Yet his Love-Scenes, *Fletcher*, compar'd to thine,
> Are cold and frosty, and express love so,
> As heat with Ice, or warme fires mix't with Snow.[95]

Yet the pieties and embarrassments of these two lovers bring more realities to mind than do the galleries of idealising but sexually obsessed characters who pass through the plays of the two younger dramatists. Richard Lovelace in what purports to be a compliment in a poem in the same volume exactly captures the limitations of their simplifying talent when he describes how

> Virgins as *Sufferers* have wept to see
> So white a Soule, so red a Crueltie.[96]

Jonson steadfastly refused to portray such melodramatic simplic-
ities, and if a modern spectator finds Lovel's long speeches undramatic he must bear in mind that Jonson's contemporaries had been
brought up on the declamations in the *Arcadia*, and that Beaumont
and Fletcher themselves had catered to the liking for what Dryden
was to call later 'argumentation and discourse'.

   In the second sitting of Love's Parliament, Jonson not only
presents Lovel as a man of action to add perspective to our knowledge
of his contemplative parts, but delivers a firm verdict on contemporary notions of valour. The shift in power from the great country
house to the metropolitan court over the forty years or so preceding
Jonson's play and the relatively peaceful reign of James had
dislocated the moral codes of the aristocracy. Valour which had been
a duty for the country knight had become a cult for the urbane
courtier, and the chastity that Jonson celebrated as one of the moral
foundations of Penshurst had been reduced to the good reputation of
the court lady. Middleton and Rowley satirised 'vaporous' duelling
in *A Fair Quarrel* (1614) but Beaumont and Fletcher accepted the old
codes without registering the new realities. Their characters are
swayed by absolute claims of love and honour, and after dishonour
resort only to vengeance. These dramatists, progenitors of the heroic
vacuities of Restoration tragedy, pandered to the tastes of an affluent
but rootless audience whose moral sense was based on a pious
nostalgia for a chivalric age long since passed. The gentlemen of the
Blackfriars audience affected the valour of warriors – the plague of
duels is one manifestation of this – and their wives or mistresses
played the role of Venus' nuns. Fletcher and his collaborators
dramatised these projected roles and not the true identities of their
audiences; Jonson was not prepared to accept this simplification,
although his refusal may have cost his play its success. Backed by an
arsenal of Senecan *sententiae*, he reminded the court and his fellow
dramatists that valour is honour, that it is based on moral wisdom and
not the adherence to the code of a narrow social caste. Lovel's speech
is an amplification of the proverb 'Discretion is the better part of
valour' (Tilley, D354) which is the distillation of several Renaissance
discussions of the relationship between *fortitudo* and *sapientia* and
which Falstaff so wittily perverts:[97]

> It is the greatest virtue, and the safety
> Of all mankind; the object of it is danger.
> A certain mean 'twixt fear and confidence:
> No inconsiderate rashness, or vain appetite

> Of false encount'ring formidable things;
> But a true science of distinguishing
> What's good or evil. It springs out of reason
> And tends to perfect honesty; the scope
> Is always honour and the public good:
> It is no valour for a private cause.

Beaufort.   No, not for reputation?
Lovel.   That's man's idol
> Set up 'gainst God, the maker of all laws,
> Who hath commanded us we should not kill;
> And yet we say we must for reputation.   (IV.iv.39–52)

These lines have the authority of a repentant convert: Jonson himself had killed the actor Gabriel Spencer in a duel.[98] If Beaufort had been a voice of sense in the earlier scene, here he is *advocatus diaboli*, and Lovel's true valour has been proved by his efficient dispatching before the scene of the epitome of false valour, the blustering and mischief-making Tipto.[99]

Resolution and recognition

It is Jonson's skill in the characterisation of Lovel and Lady Frampul that gives the final act of the play its interest, and prevents it being merely the completion of an intrigue written to a burlesque formula. Tennant cited some challenging remarks of Coleridge comparing the resolutions of Shakespeare's plays with those of Jonson: 'As the feeling with which we startle at a shooting star, compared with that of watching the sunrise at the pre-established moment, such and so low is [the] surprize [of Jonson] compared with expectation [aroused by Shakespeare's plays]'.[100] It would be easy to argue that the catastrophe depends for its effect on surprise, that it is imposed by the demands of the kind of plot Jonson had employed, that the three marriages and the reuniting of the Frampul family are at odds with the elements of satiric humour in the play or are a parody of romance conventions. Yet the surprise of the *dénouement* can be historically as well as critically justified. One can go most conveniently to the theory of Guarini whom Jonson knew and admired and to the practice of Beaumont and Fletcher as well as of Jonson himself in his earlier plays. Guarini, combining Aristotle's praise of Sophocles' *Oedipus* and Donatus' commentary on Terence, had advocated a plot based on complication or 'knotting' and a *dénouement* involving a change to good fortune through revelation.[101] According to Giraldi, the audience should be prepared for the revelation by certain hints but unable to foretell its exact outcome.[102] Jonson therefore, accepting

THE
NEVV INNE.
OR,
The light Heart.
A COMOEDY.
As it was neuer acted , but moſt
negligently play'd,by ſome,
the Kings Seruants.

And more ſqueamiſhly beheld,and cenſu-
red by others, the Kings Subiects.
1629.

Now,at laſt,ſet at liberty to the Readers,his Maties
Seruants,and Subiects,to be iudg'd.
1631.

By the Author, *B. Ienſon.*

Hor. . . . . *me lectori credere mallem :*
Quàm ſpectatoris faſtidia ferre ſuperbi.

LONDON,
¶ Printed by *Thomas Harper,* for *Thomas Alchorne,*and
are to be ſold at his ſhop in Pauls Church-yeard,
at the ſigne of the greene Dragon.
MDCXXXI.

---

1 The title-page of the 1631 Octavo, taken from the British
Library copy 643.b.31 (A).

B*

2 The title-page of Burton's *Anatomy of Melancholy* which appeared the year before the play. See Introduction, p. 20. The melancholy lover on the left stands in a conventional pose with arms crossed.

3 A costume design by Inigo Jones for the Melancholic Despairing Lover in Jonson's masque celebrating Platonic love, *Love's Triumph through Callipolis* (1631). Reproduced by permission of the Trustees of the Chatsworth Settlement.

these principles, gives the disguised Laetitia the name Frank to associate her with her sister, Frances, Lady Frampul; hints that Frank may be playing a part ('he prates Latin / And 'twere a parrot or a play-boy' (I.iii.4–5)); has the Host reveal that his name is Goodstock (I.iii.98); and gives the Nurse one eye to symbolise her knowledge of her daughter and ignorance of her husband – a laborious jest, it is true. Contemporary audiences seem to have relished surprise endings: Bellario does not reveal that she is the disguised Euphrasia until the end of *Philaster*; Arbaces' true parenthood is revealed to save him from incest at the end of *A King and No King*; and Jonson himself concealed the sex of Epicoene until the end of *The Silent Woman*. What distinguishes the *dénouement* of *The New Inn* from those of Beaumont and Fletcher, however, is that discovery and recognition involve two generations, a whole family, and not just pairs of lovers rescued from sensational and titillating predicaments. This gives the scene – and Shakespeare did the same thing in his last plays – a moral resonance that the other dramatists failed to achieve.[103]

If Jonson's preparation for the final act does seem laboured, and the sudden recognition of Lord Frampul, his wife and daughter so improbable as to be ridiculous, the betrothal of Lovel and Lady Frampul continues the psychological realism Jonson had established in the first parliament scene.[104] At the end of his discourse on valour, Lovel complains that Lady Frampul's reward was but 'half a kiss' (IV.iv.246). True to her name, Prudence ignores his plea and dissolves the court; Lovel retires to bed to nurse his disappointed ardour while proclaiming that what was probably an accident was an emblem of 'Love's ungrateful tyranny' (IV.iv.265). Lady Frampul remonstrates with Pru for not having stopped him, and defends her own confusion at the accident as well as the strength of her feelings by claiming that her earlier 'frowardness' (IV.iv.293) had been just an act. Once more they cover their feelings with poeticisms,[105] but Latimer, the interpreter, is again there to tell us they are serious (III.ii.253–5, IV.iv.147 and 273). A permanent separation is averted only by the complications that arise from Beaufort's precipitate marriage with Laetitia. The news saves Lady Frampul from her descent into Petrarchan misery, the Host's jest turns to earnest as it is revealed that the boy he dressed as a girl was in fact a girl, and Lovel and Lady Frampul can be brought together in the midst of general laughter before their self-defences rise again. Beaufort is rescued from his uncomfortable snobbery, and Latimer who had been so perceptive of the way Lady Frampul had revealed herself in her acting, is matched with the spirited Pru who had likewise made herself a lady by acting out that part.

Every critic of Jonson is left with the disconcerting feeling that he has uncovered no more and no less in a poem or play than Jonson put into it, that explication is the basis of both the interpretation and evaluation of his works.[106] For this reason source and analogue study are less illuminating than in the case of Shakespeare: Jonson thoroughly digests his materials; his intentions are usually clear, and everything in the play is aligned with them. Shakespeare remains closer to his sources, and his intentions can be only inferred from comparisons with them. When it comes to the production of Jonson's plays, the best productions will confine themselves within the hard outlines of Jonson's vision, whereas a good Shakespearean production may realise meanings that are merely latent in the text or which may be applied to it in the light of a modern director's own experience. No one could accuse Jonson of botching his job in this play: its craftsmanship as always is impeccable. Although there is the possibility that his moral insistence on appropriate social order would be as unpleasing to a fashionable modern audience as it was to a contemporary one, the realities of the below-stairs scenes and of the central love-match deserve the attention of the 'understander' and will repay with enjoyment. The play has probably suffered because even modern critics adopt a neo-classic approach: they have been so concerned to prove that it is wholly a romance or wholly a parodic satire that they have missed the fine mixture of genres and expectations the author has created, his hatred of public showiness and viciousness and his commensurate sympathy for the acting that all are called upon to resort to in the course of their lives. In particular they have missed his respect for lovers who do not have youth on their side to prevent their uncertainties from appearing as insincerities. It is important to remember that Jonson did not consider that generic purity was the prime criterion of excellence in his plays: the dominant position of the title-page of his first Folio is occupied by Tragi-comedy, standing above the figures of Comedy and Tragedy. The mixed genre, therefore, combines with accurate class dialect and Jonson's definition of social stereotypes to give the play its unique kind of realism. *The New Inn* deserves new examination and indeed a new production.

NOTES

1 Volume I of *H.& S.* is devoted to Jonson's life and there is a good short biographical sketch in the introduction to F. H. Mares's Revels edition of *The Alchemist* (London, 1967). For a general guide to the period, see Rachel Fordyce, *Caroline Drama: A Bibliographic History of Criticism* (Boston, Mass., 1978).

2 This long fallow-time was commented on by contemporaries: see Carew's 'To Ben Jonson upon Occasion of his Ode to Himself' (Appendix I), ll. 29ff.

3 *H.& S.*, I, 244.

4 Cited by *H.& S.*, I, 103.

5 See W. J. Lawrence, 'Playwriting for Love', ch.xii of his *Speeding up Shakespeare* (London, 1937), pp. 179–201.

6 *Blackness*, ll. 90–1; *H.& S.*, VII, 172.

7 The plays were *The Lovesick Maid* which, according to Malone, 'was so popular, that the managers of the King's Company, on the 10th of March, presented the Master of the Revels with the sum of two pounds, "on the good success of [the play];" the only instance I have met with of such a compliment being paid him' and *The Northern Lass* (Bentley, I, 105). Jonson revised the 'Ode to Himself' to expunge the jealousy of Brome that he first exposed there.

8 Alfred Harbage, *Annals of English Drama*, rev. S. Schoenbaum (London, 1964) reveals that in 1623 there were forty plays, masques or academic dramas performed for the first time, in 1624 thirty-six, in 1625 only eighteen, a figure curtailed by the court's mourning and by an exceptionally disastrous outbreak of plague (see Bentley, I, 19). 1626 saw twenty-three new plays, but the number declines to a low in 1630, (fifteen in 1627, thirteen in 1628, eighteen in 1629, nine in 1630).

9 Bentley, I, 27–8.

10 Bentley, I, 51–2.

11 *H.& S.*, I, 90–1.

12 *Splendour at Court* (London, 1973), p. 232.

13 See *H.& S.*, I, 279ff.

14 Written by Michael Oldisworth of Wotton-under-Edge, cited *H.& S.*, I, 113n.

15 See Peter Laslett, *The World we have Lost* (London, 1965); a good essay on Caroline culture is P. W. Thomas's 'Two Cultures? Court and Country under Charles I' in C. Russell ed., *The Origins of the English Civil War* (London, 1973), pp. 168–96; contemporary views and legislation concerning the proliferation of inns in the period may be pursued in Robert Ashton, 'Popular Entertainment and Social Control in Later Elizabethan and Early Stuart London', *The London Journal*, IX (1983), 3–19.

16 See Stone, ch.xi., 'Marriage and the Family', and his later work, *The Family Sex and Marriage in England 1500–1800* (London, 1977).

17 For Jonson's continuing relationships with members of the Sidney family see *H.& S.*, I, 53ff.

18 See Kenneth R. Richards, 'Changeable Scenery for Plays on the Caroline Stage', *T.N.*, XXIII (1968), 6–20, and John Freehafer,

'Perspective Scenery and the Caroline Playhouses', *T.N.*, XXVII (1972), 98–113.

19 *M.L.*, Ind. 2–3, *H.& S.*, VI, 508.

20 Bentley, I, 109–15 and 127–30.

21 See William A. Armstrong, 'The Audience of the Elizabethan Private Theatres', *R.E.S.*, n.s. X (1959), 234–49. A subtle defence of the taste of these audiences is provided by Michael Neill, '"Wit's most accomplished Senate": the audience of the Caroline private theatres', *S.E.L.*, XVIII (1978), 341–60.

22 See *The New Inn*'s second Epilogue.

23 Verse epistle to Davenant's *The Just Italian* (1630), A4r.

24 See Herbert Berry, 'The State and Boxes at Blackfriars', *S.P.*, LVIII (1966), 163–86.

25 This might be deduced from *The New Inn* as the Host is the last to exit at the end of Act IV and the first to appear at the beginning of Act V; see also Michael Hattaway, *Elizabethan Popular Theatre* (London, 1982), p. 62.

26 Modernised from the text printed in *H.& S.*, XI, 346–7.

27 Bentley, IV, 622.

28 *T.*, p. ix.

29 *H.& S.*, II, 189.

30 ll. 5–15; see also n.25 above.

31 Day, *Works*, ed. Bullen (London, 1881), p. 214.

32 See the prefatory matter to *E.M.O.*, *Sej.* and *S.S*; also J. A. Barish, 'Jonson and the Loathèd Stage' in W. Blissett *et al.* edd., *In Celebration of Ben Jonson* (Toronto, 1973), pp. 27–54.

33 *G.*, V, 296.

34 Robert Wild, Poem in *Nova Fert Animus* (Broadside of 1679), cited *H.& S.*, IX, 546.

35 See Armstrong (n. 21 above) and Clifford Leech, *Shakespeare's Tragedies* (London, 1950), pp. 174–5.

36 F. G. Fleay, *A Biographical Chronicle of the English Drama* (London, 1891), I, 324–57 and 385.

37 This was first suggested by Oliver Lodge, 'A Ben Jonson Puzzle', *T.L.S.*, 13 September 1947, p. 465.

38 *M.L.*, Ind. 35.

39 *H.& S.*, IX, 252.

40 E. Arber ed., *A Transcript of the Registers of the Company of Stationers of London 1554–1640 A.D.* (London, 1875–94), IV, 217.

41 Fleay, I, 331.

42 The history of the Jonson folios is discussed by William P. Williams, 'Chetwin, Crooke, and the Jonson Folios', *S.B.*, XXX (1977), 75–95.

43 The collation is (*)^8 A^{2}B–F^{8}G^8 (G^7 + H^2). The two additional leaves (H^2) were inserted before blank G8. 60 leaves unnumbered. Title, (*)1 (verso blank). 'The Dedication to the Reader', (*)2. 'The Argument', (*)3v. 'The Persons of the Play. With some short Characterisme of the chiefe Actors', (*)8v. 'The Prologue', A2v. Text headed 'Act I.Scene I' with HT, B1. 'Epilogue', G7v. 'Another Epilogue', H1. Verses headed 'The iust indignation the Author tooke at the vulgar censure of his Play, by some malicious spectators, begat this following Ode to himselfe', H1v. Catchwords: (*)–A, Ferret [Ferret.] B–C, And [And,] C–D,

Hos. D–E, Call E–F, Of F–G, Should H2V, *The end.*

44 Authors usually attended the press in person to correct proofs – see R. B. McKerrow, *An Introduction to Bibliography for Literary Students* (Oxford, 1927), pp. 205–7.

45 See W. W. Greg, *The Shakespeare First Folio* (Oxford, 1955), Note 5, p. 173.

46 See W. W. Greg, *A Bibliography of the English Printed Drama to the Restoration* (London, 1939–59), III, 1081, and D. F. McKenzie, 'The Printer of the Third Volume of Jonson's *Workes* (1640)', *S.B.*, XXV (1972), 177–8.

47 Allardyce Nicoll, *A History of the English Drama, 1660–1900* (Cambridge, 1952), I, 353.

48 *H.& S.*, IX, 157.

49 Scholarly opinion on Herford and Simpson's work is reviewed by T. H. Howard-Hill, 'Towards a Jonson Concordance: A Discussion of Texts and Problems', *R.O.R.D.*, XV–XVI (1972–3), 17–32.

50 *H.& S.*, VI, 386–90.

51 See *Engl.Gr.*, II.ix (*H.& S.*, VIII, 551–2), and *H.& S.*'s discussion, II, 431–5.

52 Jonson probably needs much more glossing for the modern reader than does Shakespeare. The setting of this play in an inn implies a vocabulary rich in the names of familiar and domestic implements and customs. At the other end of the linguistic spectrum his vocabulary contains a far larger proportion of Latinisms than does that of Shakespeare. Unfortunately the implications of this for a comparative study of the two dramatists – and of Milton – cannot be pursued here.

53 *M.L.*, Ind. 108–9.

54 *M.L.*, Chorus II.37–8; the words occur in an essay attributed to Donatus, 'De Tragoedia et comoedia', frequently included in Renaissance editions of Terence.

55 See Richard Perkins, 'Topographical Comedy in the Seventeenth Century', *E.L.H.*, III (1936), pp. 270–90, and Theodore Miles, 'Place-Realism in a Group of Caroline Plays', *R.E.S.*, XVIII (1942), pp. 428–40. John Drakakis suggests privately to me interesting comparisons between this and other aspects of *The New Inn* with Marmion's *Holland's Leaguer*, performed in 1631.

56 There is an interesting account of this aspect of the play by Harriett Hawkins, 'The Idea of a Theater in Jonson's *The New Inn*', *Ren.D.*, IX (1966), 205–26; cf. *Disc.*, 1093–6. For a wider context, see the opening chapters of Peter N. Skrine, *The Baroque* (London, 1978).

57 Dryden, 'An Essay of Dramatick Poesie', in *The Works of John Dryden*, edd. S. H. Monk *et al.* (Berkeley, 1956–), XVIII, 57.

58 See, for example, Lamb's selection of 'beautiful' but undramatic passages from the play in his *Specimens of English Dramatic Poets*, in *Works*, ed. W. MacDonald (London, 1903), I, 168–71. The same line of argument is used by modern critics who have not warmed to the play: see *H.& S.*, II, 194; Wallace A. Bacon, 'The Magnetic Field: the Structure of Jonson's Comedies', *H.L.Q.*, XIX (1956), 121–53; J. J. Enck, *Jonson and the Comic Truth* (Madison, 1957), pp. 219ff.; Jonas Barish, *Ben Jonson and the Language of Prose Comedy* (Cambridge Mass., 1960), p.

241; C. G. Thayer, *Ben Jonson, Studies in the Plays* (Norman, Oklahoma, 1963), pp. 198–232.

59 H. C. Agrippa, *Three Books of Occult Philosophy*, tr. J. F. (London, 1651), p. 132. For Agrippa's influence on Dürer see Erwin Panofsky, *The Life and Art of Albrecht Dürer* (Princeton, 1955), pp. 168–70. The best general discussion of humour theory is that of R. Klibansky, E. Panofsky and F. Saxl, *Saturn and Melancholy* (London, 1964).

60 See ch. ix, 'Love as a Dramatic Theme', in Clifford Leech, *Shakespeare's Tragedies* (London, 1950).

61 There was a great surge in the numbers of new baronets and peers in the year or so before the play: see Stone, ch. iii, 'The Inflation of Honours'.

62 See J. H. Hexter, 'The Education of the Aristocracy in the Renaissance', in his *Reappraisals in History* (London, 1961), pp. 45–70.

63 For their meanings, see the notes to 'Persons'.

64 See W. E. Houghton, 'The English Virtuoso in the Seventeenth Century', *J.H.I.*, III (1942), 51–93 and 190–219.

65 This is the account we have of him at II.iv.16ff. The reference to Fly as a 'fellow gipsy' at V.v.127, however, suggests if we read it literally that Jonson had forgotten these lines – see Arg. 118n.

66 Nashe, *Summer's Last Will and Testament*, ll. 1193–4, in *Works*, ed. McKerrow, III, 271.

67 A useful piece of contemporary social criticism is to be found in a sermon by Edmund Cobbes: 'everie one is so farre fallen in love with himselfe, either for his person, qualities, or apparell, which are so excellent in their owne eyes, that a poore mans wife will bee as fine as a gentlemans, and in all places we shall see pride ruffle in Rustickes, for every one will be in the fashion how ever they come by it; the servant can hardly bee knowne from the Master, and the maide from the Mistres, not scarce any man's estate can be distinguished by his apparell . . .' *Mundanum Speculum, or, The Worldlings Looking Glasse* (London, 1630), p. 193; see also E. B. Partridge, 'The Symbolism of Clothes in Jonson's Last Plays', *J.E.G.P.*, LVI (1957), 396–409.

68 Brome imitated Jonson's title in his *The New Academy or The New Exchange* (1635?) and *The Damoiselle or The New Ordinary* (1638).

69 Felltham, 'An Answer to the Ode . . .', Appendix I, ll. 22–5.

70 R. G. Moulton, *The Ancient Classical Drama* (Oxford, 1898), p. 256.

71 *Ben Jonson's Dotages* (Lexington, 1967), pp. 76–103. Champion calls his chapter on the play 'Abortive Court Satire'.

72 'A Guide to *The New Inn*', *E.C.*, XX (1970), 311–25. Duncan's subtle and perceptive argument is reductively attacked by Richard Levin, 'The New *New Inn* and the Proliferation of Good Bad Drama', *E.C.*, XXII (1972), 41–7.

73 Gayton, *Pleasant Notes upon Don Quixot* (London, 1654), p. 271.

74 Doran, *Endeavors of Art* (Madison, 1954), p. 172.

75 The point is perceptively developed by Anne Barton in '*The New Inn* and the problem of Jonson's Late Style', a chapter of a forthcoming book on Jonson, of which she generously sent me a copy. See also ch. viii of Mary Chan, *Music in the Theatre of Ben Jonson* (Oxford, 1980), which develops analogies between the dramatic structure of this play and that of Jonson's masques.

76 Macrobius, *Somnium Scipionis*, I.ii; see also Wm. Rossky, 'Imagination in the English Renaissance: Psychology and Poetic', *Studies in the Renaissance*, V (1958), 47–73; and G. R. Hibbard, 'Ben Jonson and Human Nature' in Blissett (see n. 32 above), pp. 55–81, who argues that 'all the plays including *Catiline* that Jonson wrote between 1603 and 1616 are concerned with deception in some form or another'. 'Phant'sie' is a key word in *V.D.*

77 *The Arte of English Poesie* (London 1589), pp. 14–15 (Macpherson, 147).

78 An alternative view of these two parts is given by Duncan: 'The contrast throughout is between a committed idealist prone to disappointment and a committed ironist dedicated to good cheer. In interpreting the play it is not absolutely necessary to accept that Jonson was writing about himself, but the theory becomes more attractive as we read, noting that the two characters move from mutual distrust to interest in one another and finally to an ironically-conceived alliance' (see n. 72 above).

79 See W. A. Neilson, *The Origins and Sources of the Court of Love* (Harvard Studies and Notes in Philology and Literature, VI), 1899.

80 See Frank Kermode, 'The Banquet of Sense', in his *Renaissance Essays* (London, 1971), pp. 84–115. Jonas Barish, 'Feasting and Judging in Jonsonian Comedy', *Ren.D.*, V (1972), 3–35, notes that the play consists of a feast within a feast within a feast: Jonson's festive repast (see Prologue), the Host's meal of wit and Lovel's philosophical banquet. See also Donald K. Anderson, 'The Banquet of Love in English Drama (1595–1642)', *J.E.G.P.*, LXIII (1964), 422–32.

81 See C. L. Barber, *Shakespeare's Festive Comedy* (Cleveland, 1963), pp. 24ff; Stuart Clark, 'Inversion, Misrule and the Meaning of Witchcraft', *Past and Present*, No. 87 (1980), 98–127.

82 Cf. Earle Fowler, *Spenser and the Courts of Love*, (Menasha, Wis., 1921).

83 See J. Rycher ed., *Les Arrets d'Amour de Martial d'Auvergne* (Paris, 1951).

84 John Stevens, *Music and Poetry in the Early Tudor Court* (London, 1961), p. 166; J. Finkelpearl, *John Marston of the Middle Temple* (Cambridge, Mass., 1969), pp. 46–61; and extracts from revels of 1635/6 presided over by 'the Prince de l'Amour' are reprinted by Leslie Hotson, *Shakespeare's Sonnets Dated* (Oxford, 1949), pp. 239–44.

85 See Neilson, p. 266.

86 Stevens, p. 163.

87 For an account of the movement see Kathleen M. Lynch, *The Social Mode of Restoration Comedy* (New York, 1926), pp. 43–106.

88 James Howell, *Familiar Letters*, ed. J. Jacobs (London, 1890), pp. 317–18.

89 E. B. Partridge, *The Broken Compass* (New York, 1958), p. 194.

90 See n. 16 above.

91 A. H. Upham, *The French Influence in English Literature* (New York, 1908), p. 314.

92 Davenant, *The Dramatic Works* (London, 1872–4), II, 52.

93 In late 1632 the Queen and her ladies were much involved in rehearsing their parts in a long Platonic pastoral drama, Walter Montague's *The Shepherd's Paradise*.

94 In this connection it is important to remember that Pru is a chamber-

maid, a lady's companion, and not simply, as Partridge infers, a domestic
drudge.

95 Beaumont and Fletcher, *Works*, edd. Glover and Waller (Cambridge,
    1905–12), I, xxxix.

96 *Ibid.*, I, xxiv.

97 *1H4*, V.iv.20–1; see Paul A. Jorgensen, 'Valor's Better Parts: Back-
    grounds and Meanings of Shakespeare's Most Difficult Proverb',
    Shak.S., IX (1976), 141–58; a late example occurs in *Paradise Lost*,
    I.645; the topic is placed in a wide historical perspective in Mervyn
    James's extremely well-documented *English Politics and the Concept of
    Honour 1485–1642, Past and Present*, Supplement 3 (1978). See also
    Baldwin Maxwell, 'The Attitude toward the Duello in later Jacobean
    Drama', *P.Q.*, LIV (1975), 104–16.

98 *H.& S.*, I, 18 and XI, 577.

99 Partridge again reads the scene differently: the scene reveals 'precisely
    the comic disproportion between the great mythical heroes who acted
    and Lovel who lectures. There is fine irony, too, in Lovel's becoming
    "angry valiant" immediately after discoursing on how mean it is to have
    angry valour about anything. If Lovel is taken simply as a straight-
    forward hero, as Herford takes him, he fails as all of Jonson's "good"
    people fail. Jonson could not do at all what Shakespeare could do
    surpassingly well: make a Viola or a Benedick absurd and attractive and
    decent and believable. Jonson's absurd people are almost never attract-
    ive, and his decent people are rarely believable. But Lovel is meant to be
    ridiculous, whatever good sense he speaks. He remains comic, in fact,
    exactly because the good sense he speaks reveals the great disparity
    between the ideal life he describes and the actual life he lives in the New
    Inn' (*The Broken Compass*, pp. 194–5).

100 Coleridge, *Shakespearean Criticism*, ed. Raysor (London, 1960), I, 199.

101 See the Preface to the 1602 ed. of *Il Pastor Fido*; tr. in W. F. Staton and
    W. E. Simeone edd., *Sir Richard Fanshawe's Translation of Il Pastor Fido*
    (Oxford, 1964), p. 177.

102 Doran, p. 204.

103 In Appendix XXXII, '*The Widow* and *The New Inn*', *H.& S.* (X,
    338–20) examine the alleged similarities between the conclusions of the
    two plays and conclude that the former (attributed in the main to
    Middleton) shows no sign of Jonson's hand.

104 Northrop Frye argues in *A Natural Perspective* (New York, 1965), pp.
    14ff., that the plot of *The New Inn* is preposterously complicated and
    compares it unfavourably with *Cymbeline* which, he says, 'is so close to
    folk tale that the manipulating of the action is at least not a breach of
    decorum'. By contrast 'In *The New Inn* the action is so manipulated that
    it betrays Jonson's illusionist principles'. It could be argued that the
    'plot' of *The New Inn* is in fact as nearly derived from folk tale as that of
    Cymbeline and that Frye underestimates the excellence of the realism of
    Jonson's play.

105 A. H. Sackton, *Rhetoric as Dramatic Language in Ben Jonson* (New York, 1948), seems to me to miss the point when he argues (p. 158): 'This is Jonsonian hyperbole gone to seed. It has the extravagances of the language of *Volpone* without its irony. The audience is expected to accept this language as an expression of strong, natural feeling.'

106 For a good discussion of this point see D. F. McKenzie, '*The Staple of News* and the Late Plays', in Blissett (n. 32 above), pp. 83–128.

THE NEW INN

or *The Light Heart*

3–4. *Or . . . Heart*] Double titles had been used from about 1600; see W. J. Lawrence, 'The Double Title in Elizabethan Drama', in his *Those Nut-Cracking Elizabethans* (London, 1935), pp. 175–93.

6–7. *acted . . . play'd*] 'Acting' was originally used for the 'action' or gestures of the orator, 'playing' for the art of the common stage; see Shakespeare, *Tit.*, V.ii.18n. (New Arden), and A. Gurr, 'Elizabethan Action', *S.P.*, LVIII (1966), 144–56; cf. *Pers.* 1.

9. *squeamishly*] coldly, disdainfully (*O.E.D.*, 1).

16–17. me . . . superbi] altered from Horace's 'Verum age et his, qui se lectori credere malunt, / Quam spectatoris fastidia ferre superbi' (*Epistulae*, II.i.214). Jonson's version means 'I prefer to entrust myself to a reader, rather than to bear the disdain of a scornful spectator.' John Drakakis informs me that Shakerley Marmion took over Jonson's version for the epigraph on the title-page of his play *A Fine Companion* (London, 1633).

The Dedication, To The Reader

IF thou be such, I make thee my patron and dedicate the piece to thee; if not so much, would I had been at the charge of thy better literature. Howsoever, if thou canst but spell and join my sense, there is more hope of thee than of a hundred fastidious impertinents who were there present the first day, yet never made piece of their prospect the right way. 'What did they come for, then?' thou wilt ask me. I will as punctually answer: 'To see, and to be seen. To make a general muster of themselves in their clothes of credit, and possess the stage

5

TO THE READER] The dedication to a reader rather than to a nobleman may reflect Jonson's bad temper with the noble Blackfriars audience. For general studies see *Sh.Eng.*, II, 182ff. and 'The Dedication of Early English Plays' in W. J. Lawrence, *Speeding up Shakespeare* (London, 1937), pp. 63–88.

2–3. *would . . . literature*] I wish I could have supervised your reading.

3. *if . . . spell*] Cf. the opening of Heminge and Condell's epistle to F1 of Shakespeare, 'From the most able, to him that can but spell'. Jonson, like Chapman and Donne, customarily distinguished between those who could and those who could not understand his works; cf. *H. & S.*'s note to *Cat., To the Reader*.

join] construe (*O.E.D.*, III.14).

5. *impertinents*] presumptuous spectators (*O.E.D.*, sb.B2).

6. *made . . . prospect*] formed a proper and coherent view of the play ('prospect' = mental view or scene (*O.E.D.*, II.6,7) 'piece' = a distinct whole (*O.E.D.*, sb.3e)); cf. the 'perspective' (painting) of *U.V.*, ii.9–11; and Jonson's 'best piece of poetry', *U.V.*, xlv.10.

8. *To see . . . seen*] translated from Ovid, *Ars Amatoria*, l.99: 'Spectatum veniunt, veniunt spectentur ut ipsae'. Jonson quoted the phrase often (*S.W.*, IV.i.60; *S.N.*, Ind. 9; *Und.*, lxxv.20) and customarily denigrated those who came merely to see and not to hear and mark (see *B.F.*, Ind. 65n.); the passage is related to the satire on clothing and fashion that runs through the play.

8–10. *general . . . play*] With this military metaphor cf. *Und.*, xliv (*c.* 1626), where Jonson satirises the growing indifference of the aristocracy to real military service; and see Clifford Leech, 'Pacificism in Caroline Drama', *Durham University Journal*, XXXI (1939), 126–36.

9. *clothes of credit*] unpaid for. The general characteristics of this

against the play. To dislike all, but mark nothing. And by their 10
confidence of rising between the acts, in oblique lines, make
affidavit to the whole house of their not understanding one
scene.' Armed with this prejudice, as the stage-furniture or
arras-cloths, they were there, as spectators, away. For the faces
in the hangings and they beheld alike. So I wish they may do 15
ever. And do trust myself and my book rather to thy rustic
candour than all the pomp of their pride and solemn ignorance
to boot. Fare thee well, and fall to. Read.

BEN JONSON.

But first, the argument.

---

unreceptive audience resemble those Dekker describes in *The Guls Horne-booke*, ch. vi (*N.D.*, II, 246ff.); *cf. E.M.O.*, II.vi.52.

possess] seize, occupy.

10. *dislike*] disapprove of (*O.E.D.*, 2).

mark] 'take note of' and 'aim at' – continuing the military metaphor.

11. *confidence*] impudence (*O.E.D.*, 4).

rising . . . acts] The practice was common and infuriated contemporary dramatists: cf. *D.is A.*, I.v.31–4: 'To day, I go to the *Black-fryers Play-house*, / Sit i' the view, salute all my acquaintance, / Rise vp between the *Acts*, let fall my cloake, / Publish a handsome man, and a rich suite', and see Cowley's *Love's Riddle* (1633), III.i. The example of those on the stage might be followed by the rest of the audience who would leave with them (see Chapman, *All Fools*, Prol., and John Day, *The Ile of Gulls*, in *The Works of John Day*, ed. A. H. Bullen (London, repr. 1963), p. 214).

in . . . lines] from the sides of the stage (continuing the perspective conceit from l. 6).

12. *understanding*] Jonson often puns on the literal meaning ('stand under') in his inductions. Here the word contrasts with 'rising' (l.11).

13. *as*] in the same way as.

14. *arras-cloths*] painted cloths hung against the tiring-house façade; cf. *C.R.*, Ind. 148–52.

16. *rustic*] simple, unsophisticated (*O.E.D.*, 4b).

17. *solemn*] customary, carefully observed (*O.E.D.*, 3c); cf. *E.M.I.*, Ded.

The Argument

THE Lord Frampul, a noble gentleman, well educated and
bred a scholar in Oxford, was married young to a virtuous
gentlewoman, Sylly's daughter of the South, whose worth
thought he truly enjoyed, he never could rightly value; but as
many green husbands (given over to their extravagant delights   5
and some peccant humours of their own) occasioned in his
over-loving wife so deep a melancholy by his leaving her in the
time of her lying-in of her second daughter, she having
brought him only two daughters, Frances and Laetitia; and,
out of her hurt fancy, interpreting that to be a cause of her   10
husband's coldness in affection, her not being blessed with a
son, took a resolution with herself after her month's time and

---

THE ARGUMENT] An outline of the play or 'plot' was sometimes
submitted to the players before composition for their approval. This example,
the slack syntax of which indicates rapid composition, may as W. J. Lawrence
suggests (*Speeding up Shakespeare*, London, 1937, p. 113), be of this type.
Other Stuart plays with 'Arguments' include Rowley's *All's Lost by Lust*
(1619, printed 1633) and Nabbes's *Hannibal and Scipio* (1635). Alternatively,
a copy of the argument was sometimes handed to the chief personage present
at a performance (see Kyd, *Sp.Tr.*, IV.iv.10.1 (Revels) and Jonson, *N.T.*,
l.7n.) For a general account of Jonson's prefatory matter designed for readers
rather than spectators see J. A. Barish, 'Jonson and the Loathèd Stage' in W.
Blissett *et al.* edd., *A Celebration of Ben Jonson* (Toronto, 1973) pp. 27–53.

    3. *Sylly's . . . South*] cognate with Sealey, Selly, Cely, etc. The name means
'pitiful' or 'defenceless' and is indicative of personality. For the construction
see *Engl.Gr.*, II.ii.37–41; Partridge, *Accidence*, § 12.d.2.

    5. *green*] youthful, immature (*O.E.D.*, 7 & 8).

    extravagant] 'excessive', but also contains the etymological sense of
wandering; cf. Shakespeare, *Ham.*, I.i.154.

    6. *peccant*] morbid, unhealthy (*O.E.D.*, 3).

    12. *after . . . time*] 'A reference to the office in the prayer-book entitled "The
Thanksgiving of Women after Child-birth; commonly called, The Church-
ing of Women." The direction reads: "The woman, *at the usual time after her
delivery*, shall come into the church decently apparelled," etc.' (T.). At this
time the ceremony was controversial: see Keith Thomas, *Religion and the*

thanksgiving ritely in the church, to quit her home with a vow
never to return, till by reducing her lord she could bring a
wished happiness to the family.   15

He in the mean time returning and hearing of this departure
of his lady, began, though over-late, to resent the injury he had
done her; and out of his cock-brained resolution entered into as
solemn a quest of her. Since when neither of them had been
heard of. But the eldest daughter Frances, by the title of Lady   20
Frampul, enjoyed the state, her sister being lost young, and is
the sole relict of the family.

Act I.

Here begins our comedy.

This lady, being a brave, bountiful lady, and enjoying this
free and plentiful estate, hath an ambitious disposition to be   25
esteemed the mistress of many servants, but loves none. And
hearing of a famous New Inn that is kept by a merry host called
Goodstock, in Barnet, invites some lords and gentlemen to
wait on her thither, as well to see the fashions of the place as to
make themselves merry with the accidents on the by. It   30
happens there is a melancholic gentleman, one Master Lovel,

Decline of Magic (Harmondsworth, 1973), p. 69.

13. *ritely*] with all due rites; cf. *Alc.*, II.iii.174n. (Revels).

14. *reducing*] bringing back (Lat. *reduco*); cf. *Volp.*, Epist. Ded. 105.

17. *resent*] regret (*O.E.D.*, 2b); cf. I.v.73.

18. *cock-brained*] 'Palsgrave, 1530, f. 208a, "Cockbraynde, light fole
hardy . . ."' (*H. & S.*); cf. I.v.66.

resolution] mental aberration caused by the dissolution of morbid humours
(*O.E.D.*, 3a).

21. *state*] estate.

22. *relict*] survivor (*O.E.D.*, 3).

24. *brave*] fine, finely arrayed.

26. *servants*] professed lovers (*O.E.D.*, 4b); the usage dates from Chaucer
and was to be much used in the Platonic love literature of the 1630's. Lady
Frampul sees herself as queen of a Court of Love.

28. *Barnet*] a market town in Hertfordshire, 11 miles north-north-west of
London, notorious as a place of assignations.

30. *accidents*] happenings.

on the by] incidental, on the side, in passing (*O.E.D.*, 'by' sb.2b); cf. *Cat.*,
III.377.

31. *melancholic*] Aristotle argued (*Problems*, 953a) that all men who are

hath been lodged there some days before in the inn, who,
unwilling to be seen, is surprised by the lady and invited by
Prudence, the lady's chambermaid, who is elected governess of
the sports in the inn for that day, and installed their sovereign.   35
Lovel is persuaded by the host and yields to the lady's
invitation, which concludes the first act. Having revealed his
quality before to the host.

[Act 2.]

Prudence and her lady express their anger conceived at the
tailor, who had promised to make Prudence a new suit and   40
bring it home, as on the eve, against this day. But he failing of
his word, the lady had commanded a standard of her own best
apparel to be brought down, and Prudence is so fitted. The
lady being put in mind that she is there alone without other
company of women, borrows, by the advice of Pru, the host's   45
son of the house, whom they dress with the host's consent, like
a lady, and send out the coachman with the empty coach, as for
a kinswoman of her ladyship's, Mistress Laetitia Sylly, to bear
her company; who attended with his nurse, an old charwoman
in the inn, dressed oddly by the host's counsel, is believed to be   50

38.1 Act 2.] *This ed.; In the second Act. O.*   49. charwoman] *This ed.;* chare-
woman O; Chair-woman *F3.*   50. counsel] *W;* councell *O;* Council *F3.*

---

outstanding in philosophy, poetry or the arts are melancholy; Jonson satirised
the fashionable humour in *E.M.I.*
    33. *surprised*] taken unawares.
    34. *chambermaid*] not simply, as E. B. Partridge asserts in his account of the
play (*The Broken Compass*), a servant but a gentlewoman – like Maria in
Shakespeare's *Tw.N.* (I.iii.51); for a satirical portrait see Overbury's
character of 'A Chamber-Mayde'.
    37–8. *Having . . . host*] The syntax suggests that this was an afterthought.
    38. *quality*] nobility, occupation (*O.E.D.,* 4 & 5).
    40. *new suit*] See Arg. 79–80n. below.
    41. *as*] an intensive (*O.E.D.,* 34a).
    against] in preparation for.
    42. *standard*] suit (*O.E.D.,* sb.28).
    46–8. *host's . . . Sylly*] See Arg. 3n.
    48. *Laetitia*] See *Pers.* 21n.
    49. *charwoman*] Jonson's 'chare-woman' was the usual seventeenth-
century spelling and reflects the word's derivation from 'chare' or chore
(*O.E.D.,* 5).
    50. *oddly*] nobly (*O.E.D.,* 3).

a lady of quality, and so received, entertained, and love made to
her, by the young Lord Beaufort, etc. In the mean time the fly
of the inn is discovered to Colonel Glorious, with the militia of
the house below the stairs in the drawer, tapster, chamberlain,
and ostler, inferior officers, with the coachman Trundle,   55
Ferret, etc. And the preparation is made to the lady's design
upon Lovel, his upon her, and the sovereign's upon both.

[Act 3.]

Here begins, at the third act, the epitasis,
or business of the play.

Lovel, by the dexterity and wit of the sovereign of the sports,   60
Prudence, having two hours assigned him of free colloquy and
love-making to his mistress, one after dinner, the other after
supper, the court being set, is demanded by the Lady Frampul
what love is, as doubting if there were any such power or no.
To whom he, first by definition and after by argument   65
answers, proving and describing the effects of love so vively as
she, who had derided the name of love before, hearing his
discourse, is now so taken both with the man and his matter as
she confesseth herself enamoured of him and, but for the
ambition she hath to enjoy the other hour, had presently   70

---

52. *fly*] See *Pers.* 55 and note.

56. *made to*] *O.E.D.* records ('make', vb.94) examples of this construction
only from early Scots.

58. *epitasis*] According to Evanthius whose notes on comedy were printed
with Donatus' influential commentary on Terence, comedies had three parts:
the protasis, or beginning of the action, the epitasis where is witnessed 'the
growth and progress of the confusions as I may say of the knot of the whole
misunderstanding', and the catastrophe which is 'the turning round of things
to happy issues, made clear to all by a full knowledge of the actions.' These
divisions were very widely known in the sixteenth century and influenced the
development of comedies like *The New Inn* where great emphasis is placed on
recognition. See Guarini, *Il Pastor Fido*, Preface to 1602 ed.; Scaliger,
Poetices, I.ix; Dryden, *Essay of Dramatic Poesy*, ed. Ker, p. 45; and L.
Salingar, *Shakespeare and the Traditions of Comedy* (Cambridge, 1974), pp.
84ff. Cf. *E.M.O.*, III.viii.102, and *M.L.*, Chorus I.1–13.

63. *demanded*] formally asked.

65. *by definition . . . argument*] See III.ii.90 and IV.iv.88ff. 'An Argument
is a waie to prove how one thing is gathered by another to shewe that thing
whiche is doubtfull by that whiche is not doubtfull', T. Wilson, *The Rule of
Reason* (1551), ed. R. S. Sprague (Northridge Cal., 1972), p. 56.

66. *vively*] clearly, vividly; cf. *M.of Q.*, l.83 Jonson's note.

C

declared herself; which gives both him and the spectators
occasion to think she yet dissembles, notwithstanding the
payment of her kiss, which he celebrates. And the court
dissolves upon a news brought of a new lady, a newer coach,
and a new coachman called Barnaby.   80

Act 4.

The house being put into a noise with the rumour of this new
lady, and there being drinking below in the court, the colonel,
Sir Glorious, with Bat Burst, a broken citizen, and Hodge
Huffle, his champion, she falls into their hands and being
attended but with one footman, is uncivilly entreated by them,   85
and a quarrel commenced, but is rescued by the valour of
Lovel; which beheld by the Lady Frampul from the window,
she is invited up for safety, where coming and conducted by
the host, her gown is first discovered to be the same with the
whole suit which was bespoken for Pru, and she herself, upon   90
examination, found to be Pinnacia Stuff, the tailor's wife, who
was wont to be preoccupied in all his customers' best clothes
by the footman her husband. They are both condemned and
censured, she stripped like a doxy and sent home a-foot. In the

76. *declared herself*] revealed her true feelings.

79–80. *news . . . Barnaby*] indicative of the satire on modishness that runs
through the play; cf ll.40 and 102.

82. *court*] yard of the inn, a figure of the Court of Love above.

83. *Bat*] an abbreviated form of 'Bartholomew'. *See B.F.,* I.v.126 (Revels).
broken] bankrupt (see II.i.10n.).

84. *champion*] a parody of the king's champion who had as his coronation fee
a gilt cup of wine (*O.E.D.*).

85. *entreated*] treated.

87. *window*] one of the arches or boxes which ran across the upper level of
the tiring-house; cf. *Poet.,* IV.ix.margin: '*Shee* [Julia] *appeareth above, as at
her chamber window*'; also *D.is A.,* II.vi.margin. Further examples are given in
T. J. King, *Shakespearean Staging, 1599–1642* (Cambridge Mass., 1971), pp.
42–3. The fight in fact takes place off stage – see IV.iii.1ff.

92. *preoccupied*] a bawdy quibble; cf. Shakespeare, *2H4.,* II.iv.138ff., 'as
odious as the word "occupy"; which was an excellent good word before it was
ill sorted'; *Und.,* xlii.39–42; *Disc.,* 1546; *C.R.,* V.ii.52–3; *M.L.,* V.iii.25–8.
See A. W. Read, 'An Obscenity Symbol', *American Speech,* IX (1934), 270–6.

105. *doxy*] 'These doxies be broken and spoiled of their maidenhead by the
upright men, and then they have their name of doxies and not afore' (Th.
Harman, *A Caveat . . . for Common Cursetors* (London, 1567), ch.xx).

a-foot] probably tied to the back of a cart as a whore although Jonson, as at l.
87 above, has not remembered the text accurately since at IV.iii.98 she is sent
off 'in a cart'.

interim the second hour goes on, and the question at suit of the   95
Lady Frampul is changed from love to valour; which ended, he
receives his second kiss, and, by the rigour of the sovereign,
falls into a fit of melancholy worse or more desperate than the
first.

[Act 5.]

The fifth and last act is the catastrophe or knitting up of all,   100
where Fly brings word to the host of the Lord Beaufort's being
married privately in the new stable to the supposed lady, his
son; which the host receives as an omen of mirth; but
complains that Lovel is gone to bed melancholic, when
Prudence appears dressed in the new suit, applauded by her   105
lady, and employed to retrieve Lovel. The host encounters
them with this relation of Lord Beaufort's marriage, which is
seconded by the Lord Latimer and all the servants of the
house. In this while Lord Beaufort comes in and professes it,
calls for his bed and bride-bowl to be made ready; the host   110
forbids both, shows whom he hath married, and discovers him
to be his son, a boy. The lord Bridegroom confounded, the
nurse enters like a frantic bedlam, cries out on Fly, says she is
undone in her daughter who is confessed to be the Lord
Frampul's child, sister to the other lady, the host to be their   115
father, she his wife. He finding his children, bestows them one
on Lovel, the other on the Lord Beaufort, the inn upon Fly

117. suit,] *G;* suit *O.*

---

95. *at . . . of*] No instances of this phrase without the definite article as here
are recorded in *O.E.D.*

100. *catastrophe*] See Arg. 58n.

102. *new stable*] See Arg. 79–80.

106. *retrieve*] recover like a wounded game bird; cf. *S.N.*, III.i.48.
encounters] confronts.

109. *professes*] acknowledges (*O.E.D.*, II.2).

110. *bride-bowl*] or bride-cup (V.iv.29) was handed round at weddings;
'bride-bowl' is not recorded in *O.E.D.*

111. *discovers*] reveals.

113. *bedlam*] 'An inmate of Bethlehem Hospital, London,.or of a lunatic
asylum . . . *spec.* one of the discharged, but only half-cured patients of the
former, who were licensed to beg' (*O.E.D.*).
cries out on] complains loudly of.

118. *gipsy*] Real gipsies were often reviled as by Dekker in *Lanthorne and*

who had been a gipsy with him; offers a portion with Prudence
for her wit, which is refused; and she taken by the Lord
Latimer to wife for the crown of her virtue and goodness. And   120
all are contented.

Candle-Light (*N.D.*, III, 259ff.). Jonson seems, however, to mean just a
canting rogue – see I.v.62ff., V.v.97 and 128; cf. *E.M.I.*, IV.iii.121. After
Jonson's *G.M.* (1621) the race was romanticised in literature and there was a
run of plays with nobles disguised as gipsies including Fletcher and
Massinger's *The Beggar's Bush* (1622), Middleton(?) and Rowley's *The
Spanish Gipsy* (1623) and Brome's *A Jovial Crew* (1641).

  118. *portion*] dowry.

  offers . . . with] Abbott, § 194.

The Scene: Barnet.
The Persons of the Play.
With some short characterism of the chief actors.

GOODSTOCK, the HOST (played well) alias the LORD FRAMPUL. He
pretends to be a gentleman and a scholar neglected by the
times, turns host and keeps an inn, the sign of the Light
Heart in Barnet; is supposed to have one only son, but is
found to have none but two daughters, Frances, and   5
Laetitia, who was lost young, etc.
LOVEL, a complete gentleman, a soldier, and a scholar, is a

Heading. *The Scene: Barnet*] Jonson sometimes posted the title and locality
of his plays on the stage, although in this play an inn sign was substituted
(I.i.2n.); see *C.R.*, Ind. 41; *Poet.*, Ind. 3 and 28; *M.L.*, Ind. 74–5; cf. Kyd,
Sp.Tr., IV.iii.17–18 (Revels); see Chambers, III, 126–7, 154. (See Introduction, n. 55.)

characterism . . . actors] Jonson prefixed a similar document to *E.M.O.* so it
is not necessary to interpret what follows as an attempt to explain the play
after its failure. Ford's play of the same year, *The Broken Heart*, contains a list
of 'The Names of the Speakers fitted to their Qualities'.

1. *GOODSTOCK*] This character may be a figure of the author – see
V.v.93–100n. This conjecture is supported by some lines describing Jonson
in an anonymous poem in *The Great Assizes* (1645), p.9: 'For sterne aspect,
with *Mars* hee might compare, / But by his belly, and his double chinne, / Hee
look'd like the old Hoste of a *New Inne*' (printed in *H.& S.*, XI, 498), and by
Suckling's complimentary verses in 'A Sessions of the Poets': 'And therefore
Apollo call'd him back agen, / And made him mine host of his own new Inne'
(printed in *H.& S.*, XI, 500).

played well] possibly by John Lowin or Joseph Taylor who are mentioned
in Alexander Gill's satirical verses on *M.L.*: 'Let Lowine Cease, and Taylore
feare to Touch, / The Loathed stage; for thou has made ytt such' (printed in
H.& S., XI, 348, ll. 61–2).

FRAMPUL] or frampold, sour-tempered, cross, peevish; see IV.iv.292
and *T.of T.*, II.iv.18; but Jonson may well have been thinking of the word's
meaning when applied to horses: 'fiery, mettlesome, spirited' (*O.E.D.*, 2).

3. *turns*] The sense would be clearer if Jonson had written 'has turned'.

7. *LOVEL*] The name is illuminated by I.vi.95, 'But is your name Love-ill,
sir, or Love-well?'; his Christian name, Herbert (III.ii.20), means 'bright-
warrior' (from O.H.G. *Heriberht*, 'bright army').

complete gentleman] possibly an allusion to H. Peacham's courtesy book for
virtuosi, *The Compleat Gentleman* (1622).

57

melancholy guest in the inn; first quarrelled, after much
honoured and beloved by the host. He is known to have been
page to the old Lord Beaufort, followed him in the French   10
wars, after a companion of his studies, and left guardian to
his son. He is assisted in his love to the Lady Frampul by the
Host and the chambermaid, Prudence. He was one that
acted well too.

FERRET, who is also called STOAT and VERMIN, is Lovel's   15
servant, a fellow of a quick, nimble wit, knows the manners
and affections of people, and can make profitable and timely
discoveries of them.

FRANK, supposed a boy and the Host's son, borrowed to be
dressed for a lady, and set up as a stale by Prudence to catch   20
Beaufort or Latimer, proves to be LAETITIA, sister to
Frances, and Lord Frampul's younger daughter, stolen by a
beggar-woman, shorn, put into boy's apparel, sold to the
Host, and brought up by him as his son.

NURSE, a poor charwoman in the inn with one eye that tends the   25
boy, is thought the Irish beggar that sold him, but is truly
the LADY FRAMPUL, who left her home melancholic and

---

8. *melancholy*] for similar characters see L. Babb, *The Elizabethan Malady*
(East Lansing, Mich., 1951), pp. 160–5.

quarrelled] reproved, criticised (*O.E.D.*, 5).

10. *Beaufort*] 'The castle of Beaufort came into the possession of the house
of Lancaster by the marriage of Blanche, daughter of Robert I of Artois, to
Edmund of Lancaster in 1276. John of Gaunt gave the name to his children by
his third wife, Catherine Swynford, because they were born there' (Sugden);
see V.v.68ff.; the family was destroyed by the Wars of the Roses (see Stone, p.
263).

10–11. *French wars*] Between 1589 and 1595 Elizabeth dispatched five
expeditions to northern France to assist the Huguenot cause in the wars of
religion; see I.vi.120.

12. *assisted*] accompanied.

15. *FERRET . . . STOAT*] See I.ii.3; cf. *B.F.*, II.ii.70 (although the Revels
editor is of the opinion that there Jonson wrote 'stot', a steer or heifer). The
names suggest a lean actor.

17. *affections*] dispositions (*O.E.D.*, sb.4).

18. *discoveries*] disclosures (*O.E.D.*, 2).

19. *FRANK*] The name indicates character; see II.ii.20ff.

20. *stale*] decoy (*O.E.D.*, sb.3.1b); 'he that faceth the man, is the Stale',
Dekker, *N.D.*, III., 155; cf. *C.is A.*, V.viii.7n.

21. *LAETITIA*] means joyfulness or gladness, see II.ii.56–7; a figure of
that name had appeared in *Beauty*, ll. 198ff. As D. J. Gordon pointed out she
was Euphrosyne, third of the three Graces – see *J.W.C.I.*, VI (1943), 134.

25. *with one eye*] symbolising her ignorance of her husband's presence.

jealous that her lord loved her not, because she brought him
none but daughters, and lives, unknown to her husband, as
he to her.   30

FRANCES, supposed the LADY FRAMPUL, being reputed his sole
daughter and heir, the barony descending upon her, is a lady
of great fortunes and beauty, but phantastical; thinks
nothing a felicity but to have a multitude of servants and be
called mistress by them, comes to the inn to be merry, with a   35
chambermaid only, and her servants, her guests, etc.

PRUDENCE, the chambermaid, is elected sovereign of the sports
in the inn, governs all, commands, and so orders as the Lord
Latimer is exceedingly taken with her, and takes her to his
wife in conclusion.   40

LORD LATIMER and

LORD BEAUFORT are a pair of young lords, servants and guests to
the Lady Frampul, but as Latimer falls enamoured of
Prudence, so doth Beaufort on the boy the Host's son, set up
for Laetitia, the younger sister, which she proves to be   45
indeed.

SIR GLORIOUS TIPTO, a knight and colonel, hath the luck to think

---

28. *jealous*] suspicious.

33. *phantastical*] a slave to 'phant'sie' or love – see I.iv.17, I.v.51 etc.

36. *servants*] See Arg. 26n.

37. *PRUDENCE*] originally Cecily – see textual introduction and 2 Epil. 8.
H.& S. note the reference to 'Secretarie *Sis*' of *Und.*, ii.8.25, and compare
'secretary Pru' of I.vi.25, V.iv.14. Possibly she represents wisdom more
pragmatic than that suggested by Cecily (heavenly) and complements
Laetitia. Tennant suggests, 'This name may have been chosen with reference
to the chambermaid's upbraiding her mistress for lack of circumspection
(II.i.45ff.).' Prudence, Frances, Sisley, Mary and Peg are among names given
to the wenches in *G.M.*, ll. 814ff.; there is a milkmaid called Cecily in Nabbe's
Tottenham Court (1633) who bears certain resemblances to Jonson's
character.

chambermaid] See Arg. 34n.

38. *orders*] comports herself – *O.E.D.* does not record the verb used
intransitively; the present form may be reflexive with the pronoun suppressed
(*O.E.D.*, vb.2c).

41. *LATIMER*] means interpreter; from O.Fr. *latimier*, 'Latin speaker'.
Tennant finds him interpreting at IV.iv.28, 122 and 177; cf. *M.L.*, Ind.
145–6: 'I have heard the Poet affirme that to be the most unlucky *Scene* in a
Play, which needs an interpreter'.

42. *BEAUFORT*] the libertine foil to the platonic Lovel.

43. *enamoured of . . . on*] 'Jonson has both constructions' (*H.& S.*).

47. *SIR GLORIOUS TIPTO*] from Lat. *gloriosus*, 'vain-glorious, brag-
ging'; to go on tiptoes meant to bear oneself proudly – see Shakespeare, *H5*,

well of himself, without a rival, talks gloriously of anything,
but very seldom is in the right. He is the lady's guest and her
servant too; but this day utterly neglects his service, or that   50
him. For he is so enamoured on the Fly of the inn and the
militia below stairs with Hodge Huffle and Bat Burst, guests
that come in, and Trundle, Barnaby, etc., as no other society
relisheth with him.

FLY is the parasite of the inn, visitor-general of the house, one   55
that had been a strolling gipsy but now is reclaimed to be
inflamer of the reckonings.

PIERCE, the drawer, knighted by the Colonel, styled SIR PIERCE
and young ANON, one of the chief of the infantry.

JORDAN, the chamberlain, another of the militia and an officer,   60

55, 71. Barnaby] *W;* Barnabe *O.*   57. visitor-general] *G;* visiter *generall O.*

IV.iii.42; see also *Und.*, xiii.143–8, on 'dwarfs of honour' who rise upon their
toes – a passage related to Seneca, *Epistulae*, cxi. 3, on the true philosopher's
not needing to walk on tiptoe, and cf. Nashe's name for Harvey, Timothie
Tiptoes (*Works*, I, 276).

Colonel] The rank dated only from the late sixteenth century and the first
colonel in English drama appears in Middleton's *A Fair Quarrel* (1614).
Colonels were subordinate only to generals.

48. *without a rival*] *H.& S.* cite Cicero *Ad Quintum Fratrem*, III.viii.4, and
Horace, *Ars Poetica*, ll. 443–4.

50–1. *neglects . . . him*] fail in his attentions to the lady, or rather she ignores
him; this does not catch the tone or business of II.vi; see especially l. 93.

54. *relisheth with*] gratifies.

55. *FLY*] See the Host's account of him, II.iv.10ff. *H.& S.* cite Brome *The
Sparagus Garden*, I.iii (1640, B4v) where Sir Hugh Moneylacks is taunted, 'I
heard . . . that you play the fly of the new Inne there; and sip with all
companies.' Anne Barton (see Introduction, n. 75) compares the flies that
infest the chamber of Phantastes in Spenser's House of Alma, *The Faerie
Queene*, II.ix.51.

parasite] Cf. Mosca, 'fly' (It.) the parasite in *Volp.*; the parasite was a stock
character in classical comedies; see E. Welsford, *The Fool* (London, 1935),
ch.i.

visitor] inspector; see *E.M.O.*, V.x.8n.

56. *gipsy*] See Arg. 118n.

57. *inflamer . . . reckonings*] Cf. the description of tricks in Dekker, *Guls
Horn-booke*, vi (*N.D.*, II, 259–60).

58–9. *PIERCE . . . ANON*] fitting names for a tapster who had to broach
barrels and whose call to waiting customers was 'anon' – see Shakespeare,
L.L.L., IV.ii.82n. (Arden), and *1H4*, II.iv.26ff.

59. *infantry*] servant boys; cf. *T.V.*, l. 177.

60. *JORDAN*] a chamberpot – the word may derive from the bottles in

commands the *tertia* of the beds.
JUG, the tapster, a thoroughfare of news.
PECK, the ostler.
BAT BURST, a broken citizen, an in-and-in man.
HODGE HUFFLE, a cheater, his champion.   65
NICK STUFF, the lady's tailor.
PINNACIA STUFF, his wife.
TRUNDLE, a coachman.
BARNABY, a hired coachman.
STAGGERS, the smith, TREE, the saddler, only talked on.   70
[FIDDLERS
SERVANTS.]

64. thoroughfare] *This ed.;* Through-fare *O.*

---

which pilgrims brought back water from the river; it is the first name of
Knockem in *B.F.*

Chamberlain] His office is described in Milton's poem 'On the University
Carrier' (1631); Death came to Hobson 'In the kind office of a chamberlain,
/Show'd him his room where he must lodge that night,/Pull'd off his boots,
and took away the light'; but this chamberlain fancies himself as a lover – see
IV.i.6–7 and 24–5.

61. tertia] from Sp. *tercio*, 'a regiment of the Spanish infantry of the
16–17th c. . . . hence, a body of foot forming a main division of an army'
(*O.E.D.*); see III.i. 6–10.

63. *PECK*] a measure for dry goods such as the oats supplied for horses.

64. *BAT BURST*] See Arg. 84n. Bat may have to do with bat-fowling, the
catching of birds by night when at roost; cf. Dekker, *The Bel-man of London*
(*N.D.*, III, 131), 'Sometimes . . . this *Card-cheating* . . . is called *Batt
fowling*, and then ye setter is the Beater'. Burst meants bankrupt; cf. *S.N.*,
I.ii.72.

in-and-in] 'In-and-in was a gambling game, played by three persons with
four dice, each person having a box. It was the usual diversion at ordinaries
and places of inferior resort. It is described in the *Compleat Gamester*, (ed.
1680, p. 117): ". . . *in* was, when there was a doublet, or two dice alike out of
the four; *in and in* when there were either two doublets or all four dice alike,
which swept all the stake"' *H.& S.* (citing Nares); cf. *T.of T.*, IV. Interloping
Scene, 3–9.

65. *HODGE HUFFLE*] Hodge is a by-form for Roger, a familiar name for
a rustic clown; 'huffle' means to swell or bluster.

66. tailor] Tailors were proverbial for their dishonesty – see Chapman,
May-Day, II.i.569–73, for being thin like Starveling in Shakespeare's
M.N.D. (cf. Tilley, T23: 'Nine (or three) tailors make a man'), and for being
lecherous – see *E.H.*, I.ii.68ff. (Revels).

67. *PINNACIA STUFF*] A pinnace was a go-between, bawd, or
prostitute; see *B.F.*, II.ii.73; *D.is A.*, I.vi.58; and Dekker and Webster's
Northward Hoe, V.i.444, 'Ile board your Pynnis while 'tis hotte'. For 'Stuff'
(woven fabric) see Florio, 'As we say good stuffe, that is a good wholesome

plum-cheeked wench', ('Bona-roba' in *Queen Anna's New World of Words*, London, 1611); and cf. Shakespeare, *Per.*, IV.ii.18 and *Und.*, xv.57–8; *B.F.*, IV.v.47n. (Revels). IV.i.5ff. suggests that in contrast to her diminutive husband she was gross.

68. *TRUNDLE*] See II.ii.55n.

70. *STAGGERS*] because drunken; it is also the name of a disease that afflicts horses and cattle.

TREE] from the tree or framework of a saddle.

only . . . on] See IV.i.8ff.

The Prologue

You are welcome, welcome all, to the New Inn;
Though the old house, we hope our cheer will win
Your acceptation: we ha' the same cook
Still, and the fat, who says you sha' not look
Long for your bill of fare, but every dish   5
Be served in i' the time, and to your wish;
If anything be set to a wrong taste,
'Tis not the meat there but the mouth's displaced;
Remove but that sick palate, all is well.
For this the secure dresser bade me tell,   10
Nothing more hurts just meetings than a crowd,
Or, when the expectation's grown too loud,

1ff.] For similarities to the prefatory matter of *The Emperor of the East* (1631) see Massinger, *P.& P.*, III, 400; Carew's verse epistle to the reader of Davenant's *The Wits* (1634) is also very similar to Jonson's Prologue.

2. *old house*] the Blackfriars Theatre, taken over by the King's Men in 1608–9. The King's Men were preparing to occupy the remodelled Cockpit-in-Court at Whitehall. They first performed there on 5 November 1630 (Bentley, I, 28).

3–4. *cook . . . fat*] Jonson weighed twenty stone – see *Und.*, liv.12; cf. Mirth's portrait of Jonson in *S.N.*, Ind. 61ff.: 'Yonder he is within (I was i' the Tiring-house a while to see the Actors drest) rowling himselfe vp and downe like a tun, i' the midst of 'hem, and spurges, neuer did vessel of wort, or wine work so! His sweating put me in minde of a good Shrouing dish . . . a stew'd Poet!'

9. *sick palate*] Cf. the 'cunning palates' in the Prologue to *S.W.*, l. 10. There are very similar sentiments about the fickle tastes of Caroline audiences in the Prologues to Shirley's *St Patrick for Ireland* (1637) and Nabbe's *Tottenham Court* (1638).

10. *secure*] confident.
dresser] Dekker is disparagingly referred to as a 'dresser' (i.e. reviser and collaborator) in *Poet.*, III.iv.322, V.iii.220; cf. *Satiromastix*, I.ii.408. However, here the word means one who prepares food.

11. *just meetings*] regular, right (*O.E.D.* 'just' adj.3b) or an analogy with *juste bataille*, 'regular battle' (?).

12. *loud*] pressing, urgent (*O.E.D.*, 2b).

That the nice stomach would ha' this or that,
And being asked, or urged, it knows not what;
When sharp or sweet have been too much a feast,   15
And both out-lived the palate of the guest.
Beware to bring such appetites to the stage,
They do confess a weak, sick, queasy age;
And a shrewd grudging too of ignorance,
When clothes and faces 'bove the men advance.   20
Hear for your health, then; but at any hand,
Before you judge, vouchsafe to understand,
Concoct, digest. If, then, it do not hit,
Some are in a consumption of wit
Deep, he dares say – he will not think that all –   25
For hectics are not epidemical.

---

13. *nice*] delicate, fastidious.

15. *have*] For plural forms after 'or' or 'nor' constructions, cf. Epil. 24; *B.F.*, I.iii.69; *K.Ent.*, ll. 579–80.

15–16. *When . . . guest*] Cf. *Disc.*, 409–11: '. . . the only decay, or hurt of the best mens *reputation* with the people, is, their wits have out-liv'd the peoples palats. They have been too much, or too long a feast.'

18. *confess*] reveal, disclose.

19. *shrewd*] grievous, sore (*O.E.D.*, 6).

grudging] symptom of an approaching or disappearing illness.

21. *at any hand*] in any case; cf. *Poet.*, V.iii.541.

23. *concoct*] digest, ruminate on.

hit] hit the mark, succeed (*O.E.D.*, vb.13).

24. *consumption*] See l. 26n.

26. *hectics*] the fever which accompanies consumption or other wasting diseases and is attended with flushed cheeks and hot dry skin; cf. *E.M.O.*, I.iii.76.

epidemical] universal, found everywhere.

Act I

[Enter] HOST *[and]* FERRET.

[Host]. I am not pleased, indeed, you are i' the right;
    Nor is my house pleased, if my sign could speak,
    The sign o' the Light Heart. There you may read it;
    So may your master too, if he look on't.
    A heart weighed with a feather, and out-weighed too: 5
    A brain-child o' mine own and I am proud on't!
    And if his worship think here to be melancholy
    In spite of me or my wit, he is deceived;
    I will maintain the rebus 'gainst all humours
    And all complexions i' the body of man –   10
    That's my word – or i' the isle of Britain!
Ferret. You have reason, good mine host.
Host.   Sir, I have rhyme too.
    Whether it be by chance or art,
    A heavy purse makes a light heart.

Act I Scene i] *This ed.;* THE/NEW INNE. / Act I. Scene I. *O (O uses Arabic numerals for scene headings throughout.)*
12. *Ferret*] *Fer. Oc; not in Ou.*   reason,] *G;* reason *O.*   13–14. Whether it

---

2. *sign*] The inn-board and perhaps a bush (see I.ii.28n.) must have hung on stage throughout the action; it presumably had two sides to bear the two rebuses; compare the sign of the Pig's Head that hangs over Ursula's booth in *B.F.*, III.ii.59.1 (Revels).

3. *Light*] meaning both happy and frivolous.

9. *rebus*] an enigmatic representation of a name or word by pictures or figures that suggest the syllables of which it is made up; perhaps from *non verbis sed rebus* ('not by words but by things'); the devices were common in the Lords Mayor's pageants; cf. *Alc.*, II.vi.6ff., Shakespeare and Fletcher, *The Two Noble Kinsmen*, III.v.117–19.

12. *reason . . . rhyme*] Tilley (R98) records examples from 1529, although the first coupling of rhyme and reason recorded in *O.E.D.* is 1664.

14. *A . . . heart*] Tilley, P655.

There 'tis expressed: first by a purse of gold,   15
A heavy purse; and then two turtles, makes;
A heart with a light stuck in't, a light heart!
Old Abbot Islip could not invent better,
Or Prior Bolton with his bolt and ton.
I am an innkeeper, and know my grounds   20
And study 'em; brain o' man, I study 'em!
I must ha' jovial guests to drive my ploughs,
And whistling boys to bring my harvest home,
Or I shall hear no flails thwack. Here your master
And you ha' been this fortnight drawing fleas   25
Out of my mats and pounding 'em in cages

be by chance or art, / A heavy purse makes a light heart!] *Oc;* Whether it be by
chance or art, a heauy purse makes a light heart. *Ou.*   16. makes;] *This ed.;*
makes, *O.*   25. fortnight] *F3;* fornight *O.*

---

16. *makes*] mates; turtle-doves were celebrated for their constancy.

18–19. *Abbot ... ton*] 'See Camden, *Remaines ... Concerning Britaine,* 1605,
pp. 147–8: "It may seeme doubtfull whether *Bolton* Prior of Saint *Bartholomew* in *Smithfield,* was wiser when hee invented for his name a bird-bolt
through a Tunne, or when hee built him an house vppon *Harrow Hill,* for
feare of a great innundation after a great coniunction in the watry Triplicitie.
[See Lillywhite, *London Signs,* 3816.] *Islip* Abbot of *Westminster,* a man most
favored by king *Henry* the seaventh, had a quadruple devise for his single
name; for somewhere hee sette vppe in his windowes an eie with a slip of a
tree, in other places one slipping boughs in a tree, in other places *I* with the
saide slip; and in some places one slipping from a tree with the worde Islip"'
(*H.& S.*).

20. *grounds*] principles.

24ff.] a conventional satire on the vanity of sciences and on *virtuosi*; cf.
Nashe, 'Who but a Foppe will labour to anatomize a Flye', *Works,* I, 260. The
speech is symmetrical with Lovel's protestations at IV.iv.269ff. There is a
similar satire on vain experiments in *D.is A.,* 1–13. Jonson may, however, be
referring to attempts to bring out the great work of Thomas Moffett,
Insectorum sive Minimorum Animalium Theatrum, which lay unpublished
until 1634. (Moffett's *Silkworms* had appeared in 1599.) The Epistle
Dedicatory by T. Mayerne to Dr Wm. Paddy, the King's Chief Physician,
vividly describes the dissection of insects and urges him to take it up.

24. *flails*] Cf. the phrase 'to be threshed with your own flail' – to be treated as
you have treated others (*O.E.D.,* 1b).

25. *fleas*] 'Fleas breed principally of straw or mats, where there hath been a
little Moisture', Bacon, *Sylva,* § 696 (*Works,* II, 558).

26. *mats*] made of a coarse fabric of plaited rushes, sedges, straws etc. and
known as 'Bedfordshire mats' – see *Sh.Eng.,* II, 124.

pounding] impounding.

cages] Cf. the 'tormentor for a flea', *B.F.,* II.iv.7; this was a flea-trap. See

Cut out of cards, and those roped round with pack-thread
Drawn thorough bird-lime, a fine subtlety!
Or poring through a multiplying-glass
Upon a captived crab-louse, or a cheese-mite,   30
To be dissected as the sports of nature
With a neat Spanish needle! Speculations
That do become the age, I do confess!
As measuring an ant's eggs with the silk-worm's,
By a fantastic instrument of thread,   35
Shall give you their just difference, to a hair!
Or else recovering o' dead flies with crumbs
(Another quaint conclusion i' the physics)
Which I ha' seen you busy at, through the key-hole –
But never had the fate to see a fly   40

Enter LOVEL.

Alive i' your cups or once heard, 'Drink, mine host',
Or such a cheerful chirping charm come from you.

---

35. fantastic] This ed.; phantastique O.   40–40.1 fly / *Enter* LOVEL.] *This
ed.;* flye – Ent. Louel. O.

---

the Revels editor's note and compare Webster, *The Duchess of Malfi*,
IV.ii.127 (Revels).
   28. *bird-lime*] a sticky substance spread on twigs to catch birds.
   29. *multiplying-glass*] magnifying-glass.
   31. *sports of nature*] Lat. *lusus naturae*, see Pliny, *Nat. Hist.*, XIV. 42;
Moffett uses the phrase: '[Insectos] nemo suspicit: quod nulli sint obvia,
miréque tenuia; quasi verò lusus lascivientis ebriaeque Naturae essent; atque
ea duntaxat in immanibus illus & horrendis belluis sobrie egisset' (*Theatrum*,
Sig.*1v). But Jonson may have known the phrase from the *Oratio de Lusibus
Naturae* in Dornavius' *Amphitheatrum Sapientiae* (Hanover, 1619), a copy of
which he owned (McPherson, 52).
   32. *neat*] bright (*O.E.D.*, 2).
   Spanish needle] Spanish steel was the best in the world although 'Spanish
needles' had been made in England from the time of Mary; cf. III.i.179; *D.is
A.*, I.i.58n.; Sugden, p. 480.
   34. *As*] as if (Abbott, § 107).
   with] in relation to (Abbott, § 193).
   35. *fantastic*] quaint, ingenious, characteristic of the 'phantasy' or
imagination.
   38. *conclusion*] experiment (*O.E.D.*, 8).
   40–1. *fly . . . cups*] probably 'a cheerful chirping charm', a familiar demon
used to win at dice; cf. *Alc.*, I.ii.80–90.

ACT I SCENE ii

[*Lovel.*] What's that? what's that?

Ferret.   A buzzing of mine host

    About a fly! A murmur that he has.

Host. Sir, I am telling your stoat here, Monsieur Ferret

    (For that I hear's his name) and dare tell you, sir,

    If you have a mind to be melancholy and musty,   5

    There's Footman's Inn at the town's end, the stocks,

    Or Carrier's Place at sign o' the Broken Wain,

    Mansions of state! Take up your harbour there;

    There are both flies and fleas, and all variety

    Of vermin for inspection or dissection.   10

Lovel. We ha' set our rest up here, sir, i' your Heart.

Host. Sir, set your heart at rest, you shall not do it –

    Unless you can be jovial. Brain o' man,

    Be jovial first and drink, and dance, and drink!

    Your lodging here, and wi' your daily dumps,   15

    Is a mere libel gain my house and me;

    And, then, your scandalous commons –

Lovel.   How, mine host?

Host. Sir, they do scandal me, upo' the road here.

0.1.] *Lovet. Ferret. Host. O.*   18. here.] *This ed.; here O.*

---

5. *melancholy*] Lovel probably stood with crossed arms, the traditional pose for melancholics; see T. W. Craik, 'Reconstruction of Stage Action', *The Elizabethan Theatre*, V (1975), 87; and cf. *Philaster*, II.iii.55n. (Revels).

6. *Footman's . . . stocks*] jail for footpads; cf. S. Rowlands, *The Knave of Harts*, 1612, C3v: 'His fearefull enemie is *Hue* and *Cry*, / Which at the heeles so hants his frighted ghost, / That he at last in foot-mans Inne must host' (cited *H.& S.*). Stocks were usually set up by a public road at the entrance to a town.

8. *harbour*] lodging.

11. *set . . . up*] taken up permanent quarters; cf. *C.is A.*, I.iii.10n.; *E.M.O.*, V.xi.52.

12. *it —*] O's colon at the end of this line suggests a break in the actor's speaking.

12–13. *heart . . . jovial*] The host opposes his own sanguine humour associated with Jove and the heart to Lovel's melancholic humour associated with Saturn and the spleen.

16. *mere*] absolute.

gain] O prints this word in italics and between inverted commas: presumably Jonson (or the printer) wanted to draw attention to the Host's use of this obsolete preposition (no examples in *O.E.D.* after 1529).

A poor quotidian rack o' mutton, roasted
Dry to be grated! and that driven down   20
With beer and butter-milk mingled together,
Or clarified whey instead of claret!
It is against my freehold, my inheritance,
My *magna charta, cor laetificat*,
To drink such balderdash, or bonny-clabbee!   25
Gi' me good wine, or catholic or christian,
Wine is the word that glads the heart of man,
And mine's the house of wine. 'Sack', says my bush;
'Be merry, and drink sherry': that's my posy!
For I shall never joy i' my Light Heart   30
So long as I conceive a sullen guest,
Or anything that's earthy!

Lovel.   Humorous host!

Host. I care not if I be.

Lovel.   But airy also,

29. posy] *This ed.;* poësie *O.*

---

19. *quotidian*] ordinary.
rack] neck.

22. *clarified whey*] purified or separated whey, which is referred to in
Philaster, II.ii.41, as a 'duller of the vital spirit' (semen, according to the
Revels ed.).

24. charta] the common medieval Latin spelling, often used in the
seventeenth century.
cor laetificat] from Psalm civ.15; *Et vinum laetificet cor hominis*, 'And wine
that maketh glad the heart of man'.

25. *balderdash*] 'John Taylor, *Drinke and Welcome*, 1637, B3: "Indeede
Beere, by a Mixture of Wine, it enjoyes approbation amongst some few (that
hardly understand wherefore) but then it is no longer Beere, but hath lost
both Name and Nature, and is called *Balderdash* . . ."' (*H.& S.*).

bonny-clabbee] or bonny-clabber, from Irish *bainne*, 'milk', *claba*, 'thick', is
'nothing else but Milk that has stood till it sower, and become of thick slippery
substance' (T. Tyron, *Wisdom's Dictates*, 1691, cited *O.E.D.*); cf. *I.M.*, l. 87.

26. *catholic*] coming from a Roman Catholic country, a realm of anti-
Christ.

28. *Sack*] various kinds of white wine from Spain.
bush] a bunch of ivy hung up as the sign of a tavern.

29. *posy*] a syncopated form of 'poesy' – Jonson's dieresis draws attention to
the word's etymology and not its pronunciation – a motto inscribed on the
inside of a ring.

32–3. *earthy . . . airy*] Earth, a 'sullen' or heavy element, was associated with
melancholy or Saturnine (l. 40) humours, air with a cheerful or Jovial
temperament; for 'airy' see *O.E.D.*, 6c, which records a meaning of 'cheerful'
only in 1644.

Not to defraud you of your rights, or trench
Upo' your privileges or great charter,   35
(For those are every ostler's language now)
Say, you were born beneath those smiling stars
Have made you lord and owner of the Heart,
Of the Light Heart in Barnet; suffer us
Who are more saturnine t' enjoy the shade   40
Of your round roof yet.
Host.   Sir, I keep no shades
Nor shelters, I – for either owls or reremice.

ACT I SCENE iii

[*Ferret.*] He'll make you a bird of night, sir.

Enter FRANK.

Host.   Bless you, child. –

[*To them.*] You'll make yourselves such.

The Host speaks to his child o' the by.

Lovel.   That your son, mine host?
Host. He's all the sons I have, sir.
Lovel.   Pretty boy!
Goes he to school?
Ferret.   O lord, sir, he prates Latin
And 'twere a parrot or a play-boy.
Lovel.   Thou –   5

42. I –] *This ed.; I: O.   0.1.] Ferret. Host. Lovel. O.   1.1. Enter* FRANK.]
*This ed.; printed before The Host in O.   2.1] This ed.; printed after l. 2 in
O.   2. That] This ed.; 'That O.*

34–5. *trench Upo'*] encroach on.

36. *ostler's language*] Cf. Overbury's complaints against ostlers that are
above themselves (*Characters*).

41. *round*] good, solid.

shades] sequestered places; cf. Shakespeare, *Mac.*, IV.iii.1.

42. *reremice*] bats; cf. III.i.174. Owls and bats were both associated with
Saturn: see H. C. Agrippa, *Three Books of Occult Philosophy*, tr. J.F.
(London, 1651), p. 56.

1–2. *bird . . . such*] Ferret characteristically lowers the tone of the
conversation with the reference to procuring; the Host turns the tables by
invoking the phrase's other meaning, a thief.

2.1. o' the by] aside.

5. *'twere*] for 'he were'; Partridge, *Syntax*, § 20.

Commendst him fitly.

Ferret.   To the pitch he flies, sir;

He'll tell you what is Latin for a looking-glass,

A beard-brush, rubber, or quick-warming-pan.

Lovel. What's that?

Ferret.   A wench, i' the inn-phrase, is all these:

A looking-glass in her eye,   10

A beard-brush with her lips,

A rubber with her hand,

And a warming-pan with her hips.

Host. This, in your scurril dialect. But my son

Knows no such language.

Ferret.   That's because, mine host,   15

You do profess the teaching him yourself.

Host. Sir, I do teach him somewhat. By degrees,

And with a funnel, I make shift to fill

The narrow vessel; he is but yet a bottle.

Lovel. O let him lose no time, though.

Host.   Sir, he does not.   20

Lovel. And less his manners,

Host.   I provide for those too.

Come hither, Frank, speak to the gentleman

In Latin. He is melancholy. Say,

'I long to see him merry, and so would treat him'.

Frank. Subtristis visu'es esse aliquantulum patri,   25

---

14. son] *conj. F. Cunningham;* Inne *O.*   15. *Ferret.*] *This ed.; F. O.*

---

play-boy] a boy trained at school to act in Latin plays: cf. *S.N.*, Intermean III.46.

Thou —] Presumably *O*'s dash indicates a hesitation on the part of Lovel who momentarily catches Ferret's intimation of Frank's true gender.

6. *pitch*] the highest point (of a bird of prey's flight).

8. *rubber*] towel.

quick-warming-pan] 'quick' means 'living'; Tennant cites Ray, *English Proverbs*, 1678: 'A Scotch *warming pan, i.e.* A wench. The story is well known of the Gentleman travelling in Scotland, who desiring to have his bed warmed, the servant-maid doffs her clothes, and lays her self down in it a while'; cf. Tilley, W71 and see V.ii.33; *Und.*, lvii.27.

14. *son*] *O* has 'Inne' and Jonson missed the misprint. The compositor may have misread manuscript 'sone', with long s.

18. *with a funnel*] Cf. *Disc.*, 1794; the figure is adapted from Quintilian, I.ii.27–8.

21. *And . . . manners*] continuing Lovel's injunction from l. 20.

25–6. Substristis . . . Pulchrè] 'You present a somewhat sorrowful

Qui te laute excipere, atque etiam tractare gestit.
Lovel.   *Pulchrè.*
Host. Tell him, 'I fear it bodes us some ill luck,
      His too reservedness'.
Frank.   *Veretur pater,*
      Ne quid nobis mali ominis apportet iste
      Nimis praeclusus vultus.
Lovel.   *Bellè.* A fine child!
      You wou' not part with him, mine host?
Host.   Who told you
      I would not?
Lovel.   I but ask you.
Host.   And I answer:
      To whom? for what?
Lovel.   To me, to be my page.
Host. I know no mischief yet the child hath done,
      To deserve such a destiny.
Lovel.   Why?
Host.   Go down, boy,   35
      And get your breakfast. –   [*Exeunt* FRANK *and* FERRET.]
                        Trust me, I had rather
      Take a fair halter, wash my hands, and hang him
      Myself, make a clean riddance of him, than –
Lovel.   What?
Host. Than damn him to that desperate course of life.
Lovel. Call you that desperate, which by a line   40

---

26. *atque etiam*] *H.& S.; etiam ac O.*

appearance to my father who desires to welcome you cheerfully and so treat
you. *Lovel.* Excellent.' Cf. Terence, *Andria*, l. 447: 'subtristis visust esse
aliquantillum mihi'.

26. atque etiam] *H.& S.*'s emendation for Jonson's *etiam ac.* Jonson
probably wrote *excipere ac tractare*, added an *etiam* (possibly while proof-
reading), and forgot to substitute *atque* for *ac.*

28–30. Veretur . . . Bellè] 'My father fears lest that too reserved face might
bring us some ill omen.*Lovel.* Prettily spoken.' Cf. *S.of N.*, IV.iv.64.

36.1 Exeunt . . . Ferret] Ferret's words at l. 150 below indicate that Jonson
wanted the Host and Lovel to have the stage to themselves for the ensuing
dialogue.

39ff.] For the decline of the traditional chivalric education, see *Sh.Eng.*, I,
33–5 and 209; J. H. Hexter, 'The Education of the Aristocracy in the
Renaissance', in his *Reappraisals in History* (London, 1961), pp. 45–70;
E.M.O., I.i.38. Anne Barton has suggested (privately) a comparison with a
piece of nostalgia in a play studded with reminiscences of Jonson's works, *The*

Of institution from our ancestors
Hath been derived down to us, and received
In a succession for the noblest way
Of breeding up our youth in letters, arms,
Fair mien, discourses, civil exercise,   45
And all the blazon of a gentleman?
Where can he learn to vault, to ride, to fence,
To move his body gracefuller, to speak
His language purer, or to tune his mind
Or manners more to the harmony of nature   50
Than in these nurseries of nobility?

Host. Ay, that was when the nursery's self was noble,
And only virtue made it, not the market,
That titles were not vented at the drum
Or common outcry; goodness gave the greatness   55
And greatness worship. Every house became
An academy of honour, and those parts –

51. nobility?] *G;* nobility?– *O.*   53. market] *F3;* mercate *O.*

Variety by William Cavendish, Duke of Newcastle (London, 1649), pp. 39ff.
It was acted about 1640 by the King's Men at the Blackfriars.

41. *institution*] law, custom (*O.E.D.*, 6).

42. *derived*] conveyed (*O.E.D.*, 4).

45. *mien*] bearing, carriage, demeanour.

46. *blazon*] record of virtues. (*O.E.D.*, 4).

48–9. *gracefuller . . . purer*] Partridge, *Accidence*, § 64.

51–3. *nurseries . . . virtue*] Cf. 'the sacred noursery/Of Vertue' in the proem
to *The Faerie Queene*, VI.

53. *market*] Jonson usually spelt this 'mercate' like Lat. *mercator*, 'merchant'; see *T.of T.*, II.i.23n.; cf. II.vi.126n. and 170n.

54. *That*] when (Abbott, § 284).

vented . . . drum] offered for sale after public proclamation; cf. *Volp.*,
IV.ii.29; *Alc.*, II.ii.86–7; *S.N.*, IV.iii.21ff.; *Disc.*, 1277. The reference is to the
habit of offering peerages for sale instituted by King James; see Stone, ch. iii,
'The Inflation of Honours'; Massinger, *The City Madam*, I.i.22–3n.
(*P.& P.*, V, 227).

55. *outcry*] auction.

57. *academy of honour*] Jonson's name appears as one of eighty four
'essentials' in proposals that Edmond Bolton made to James from 1617 until
the latter's death in 1625 for the founding of 'an Academ Roial or College of
Honor'. Verses by Sir John Beaumont to Buckingham (Harl. MS 6143) refer
to an 'Academ of Honor'. See E. M. Portal, 'The Academ Roial of King James
I', *Proc.Br.Acad.*, VII (1915–16), 189–208; there is a satirical reference to the
Academy in Massinger's *The Picture*, II.ii.16–20; cf. the false academy in *D.is
A.*, II.viii.19–22.

parts —] *O*'s dash presumably indicates a pause as the Host considers his

We see departed in the practice now
Quite from the institution.

Lovel.   Why do you say so?
Or think so enviously? Do they not still   60
Learn there the centaurs' skill, the art of Thrace,
To ride? Or Pollux' mystery, to fence?
The Pyrrhic gestures, both to dance and spring
In armour, to be active for the wars?
To study figures, numbers, and proportions,   65
May yield 'em great in counsels, and the arts
Grave Nestor and the wise Ulysses practised?
To make their English sweet upon their tongue
As rev'rend Chaucer says?

Host.   Sir, you mistake:
To play Sir Pandarus, my copy hath it,   70
And carry messages to Madam Cressid;
Instead of backing the brave steed o' mornings,
To mount the chambermaid; and for a leap

---

pun; cf. I.iii.109n.

57–9. *parts . . . institution*] 'those qualities and courtesies now bear no
resemblance to their originals'.

61. *centaurs' . . . Thrace*] The Centaurs lived in fact in Thessaly, but Thrace
was famous for its horses. Cf. IV.iii.1–2; *Und.*, liii.4–6; and Chapman, *The
Widow's Tears*, III.i.224.

62. *Pollux'*] He was renowned for boxing, so 'fence' has its wider meaning
of defensive fighting.

63. *Pyrrhic*] 'The war-dance of the ancient Greeks, in which the motions of
actual warfare were gone through, in armour, to a musical accompaniment'
(*O.E.D.*); see Plato, *Laws*, VII.815.

64. *active . . . wars*] Cf. *Und.*, xliv, on the nobility's lack of interest in
military service.

65. *figures . . . proportions*] here rhetorical and not mathematical terms.

66. *yield*] make (*O.E.D.*, II.9).

67. *Nestor*] was famed in Homer for his age, wisdom and eloquence.

Ulysses] famed for tact and cunning; cf. *Disc.*, 361: '*Vlysses* in *Homer*, is
made a long-thinking man, before hee speaks'.

69. *Chaucer*] a reference to the Friar in the General Prologue to *The
Canterbury Tales*: 'Somewhat he lipsed, for his wantownesse, / To make his
Englissh sweete upon his tonge' (ll. 264–5) ed. F. N. Robinson (London,
1957); see also *L.R.*, l. 49; *U.V.*, xxxiii.14; other references to Chaucer are at
II.iv.23, II.v.36–7 III.ii.219.

70. *play . . . Pandarus*] act as bawd.

72. *backing*] riding.

73. *chambermaid*] here a servant and not a lady's maid like Pru; see Arg. 34n.

O' the vaulting-horse, to ply the vaulting-house;
For exercise of arms, a bale of dice   75
Or two or three packs of cards to show the cheat
And nimbleness of hand; mistake a cloak
From my lord's back, and pawn it; ease his pockets
Of a superfluous watch, or geld a jewel
Of an odd stone or so; twinge three or four buttons   80
From off my lady's gown: these are the arts
Or seven liberal deadly sciences
Of pagery, or rather paganism,
As the tides run. To which if he apply him,
He may, perhaps, take a degree at Tyburn   85
A year the earlier, come to read a lecture
Upon Aquinas at St Thomas a Waterings,
And so go forth a laureat in hemp circle!

74. ply] *O;* play *1716.*

---

74. *vaulting-horse*] used for gymnastics and for courtship displays; see *C.R.*, II.i.63–6; *E.M.O.*, III.ix.50; Webster, *The White Devil*, II.ii.37.1ff; and Nathaniel Richards, *The Tragedy of Messalina* (1635), ll. 438–9. Cf. Donne, *The Progresse of the Soule*, depicting one who was 'First that could make love faces, or could doe/ The valters sombersalts, or us'd to wooe/ With hoiting gambolls, his owne bones to breake/ To make his mistresse merry' (ll. 464–7).

vaulting-house] brothel, (*O.E.D.*, 'vaulting' 2.3a). Coleridge remarked: 'The punlet, or pun-maggot, or pun intentional, "horse and house", is below Jonson. The *jeu-de-mots* just below – Read . . . Waterings – had a learned smack in it to season its insipidity' (p. 189).

75. *bale*] 'The set of dice for any special game . . . usually three' (*O.E.D.*).

76. *cheat*] a common term in thieves' cant for the art or proceeds of villainy; see Th. Harman's *A Caueat . . . for Common Cursetors,* 1567.

77. *mistake*] steal; cf. III.i.92 and *B.F.*, II.ii.101n.

79–80. *geld . . . stone*] steal from a costly ornament: stone was common bawdy for testicle.

80. *twinge*] pinch, tweak.

82. *seven . . . sciences*] a conflation of the seven deadly sins and seven liberal arts; cf. *C.R.*, II.ii.92.

84. *As . . . run*] as times are now.

85. *degree at Tyburn*] Until 1783 Tyburn was the place of public execution for Middlesex. The gallows stood in the angle formed by the Edgware Road and Oxford Street. 'Degree' is a quibble on the sense of 'step' (*H.& S.*): i.e., mount the steps of the gallows.

87. *St Thomas a Waterings*] the place of execution for Surrey, at the second milestone on the road to Canterbury which was taken by pilgrims to Thomas à Becket's shrine (cf. Chaucer, Gen. Prol. 826). Jonson alludes to St Thomas Aquinas (punning on *aqua*, 'water') as a suitable learned topic for a lecture.

88. *hemp circle*] formed by the hangman's rope. Such jests were common.

Lovel. You're tart, mine host, and talk above your seasoning,
        O'er what you seem: it should not come, methinks,   90
        Under your cap, this vein of salt and sharpness,
        These strikings upon learning now and then!
        How long have you, if your dull guest may ask it,
        Drove this quick trade, of keeping the Light Heart,
        Your mansion, palace here, or hostelry?   95
Host. Troth, I was born to somewhat, sir, above it.
Lovel. I easily suspect that. Mine host, your name?
Host. They call me Goodstock.
Lovel.   Sir, and you confess it,
        Both i' your language, treaty, and your bearing.
Host. Yet all, sir, are not sons o' the white hen;   100
        Nor can we, as the songster says, come all
        To be wrapped soft and warm in Fortune's smock,
        When she is pleased to trick, or trompe mankind.
        Some may be coats, as in the cards; but then
        Some must be knaves, some varlets, bawds, and ostlers;   105
        As aces, deuces, cards o' ten, to face it
        Out i' the game which all the world is.
Lovel.   But

106. deuces] *This ed.;* duizes *O.*

---

89. *tart . . . seasoning*] 'your talk is sharper than my first taste suggested'.
90–1. *come . . . cap*] occur to you.
92. *strikings*] touches, smacks.
94. *Drove*] practised (*O.E.D.*, 'drive' IV.19).
96. *somewhat*] something; Partridge, *Syntax,* § 70.
98. *confess*] reveal (*O.E.D.*, 1b); cf. Shakespeare, *Ham.,* III.i.5.
99. *treaty*] discussion, discourse.
100. *sons . . . hen*] Tilley, S632; from Juvenal, *Sat.,* xiii.141; 'gallinae filius albae'; cf. Fr. 'le fils de la poule blanche' meaning to be born fortunate (seemingly because eggs of a white hen were held in higher estimation than others.)
102. *Fortune's smock*] Cf. *Alc.,* III.v.12; and 'lapped in his mother's smock' (Tilley, M1203).
103. *trompe*] from Fr. *tromper,* 'deceive', punning with 'trump', take a trick at cards.
104. *coats*] playing-cards with 'coated' figures (kings, queens, or knaves); after *c.* 1688 corrupted to court [cards].
105. *varlet*] attendant, or an alternative designation for 'knave' in cards; cf. *E.M.I.,* IV.ix.70; *S.N.,* IV.i.30.
106–7. *cards . . . is*] A card of ten had the same value as court cards and so makes a bold show in a game. Cf. Shakespeare, *Shr.,* II.i.396–7: 'A vengeance of your crafty withered hide: / Yet I have fac't it with a card of ten.'

It being i' your free will (as 'twas) to choose
What parts you would sustain, methinks a man
Of your sagacity, and clear nostril, should　　　　110
Have made another choice than of a place
So sordid as the keeping of an inn:
Where every jovial tinker, for his chink,
May cry, 'Mine host, to crambe! Give us drink!
And do not slink, but skink, or else you stink!'　　　　115
Rogue, bawd, and cheater, call you by the surnames
And known *synonyma* of your profession.

Host. But if I be no such, who then's the rogue,
In understanding, sir, I mean? Who errs,
Who tinkleth then, or personates Tom Tinker?　　　　120
Your weasel here may tell you I talk bawdy,
And teach my boy it; and you may believe him;
But, sir, at your own peril, if I do not,
And at his too, if he do lie and affirm it.
No slander strikes, less hurts, the innocent.　　　　125
If I be honest, and that all the cheat
Be of myself, in keeping this Light Heart,
Where I imagine all the world's a play:

---

109. *parts*] introduces the theatrical metaphor developed below; see Harriett Hawkins, 'The Idea of a Theater in Jonson's *The New Inn*', *Ren.D.* IX (1966), 205–26. Cf.II.i.39.

110. *sagacity . . . nostril*] Lat. *sagacitas* refers particularly to keeness of scent; cf. the *emunctae naris* of Horace, I. *Serm.*, iv.8. For Jonson's use of 'hawking and hunting languages' see *E.M.I.*, I.i.41–2n. and cf. *Poet.*, Apol.Dial. 208n.

113. *jovial tinker*] Cf. the reference to the ballad of 'The Jovial Tinker' in *T.of T.*, I.iv.42; and see Simpson, p. 713.

chink] money.

114. *crambe*] or crambo, a tavern game in which one player gives a word or line or verse which each of the others has to cap with a fresh rhyme; cf. *D.is A.*, V.viii.110; *T.of T.*, IV.i.99; *F.I.*, l. 322; Dekker, *N.D.*, II, 19.

115. *skink*] draw liquor.

116–17.] These lines are very similar to *S.N.*, I.ii.138–9.

116. *call*] follows the 'may' of l. 114.

117. synonyma] The Graeco-Latin plural was often used; see *O.E.D.*, 'synonym' 1β.

120. *tinkleth*] makes jingles, as in crambo; cf. *F.I.*, l. 291.

Tom Tinker] Tinkers were commonly portrayed as knaves – see Overbury's character.

126. *that*] if (Abbott, § 285).

128. *play*] Cf. *Disc.*, 1093ff., 'De Vita humana'.

The state and men's affairs, all passages
Of life, to spring new scenes, come in, go out,   130
And shift and vanish; and if I have got
A seat to sit at ease here, i' mine inn,
To see the comedy; and laugh and chuck
At the variety and throng of humours
And dispositions that come justling in   135
And out still, as they one drove hence another –
Why, will you envy me my happiness?
Because you are sad and lumpish? Carry a loadstone
I' your pocket to hang knives on, or jet rings
T' entice light straws to leap at 'em; are not taken   140
With the alacrities of an host! 'Tis more
And justlier, sir, my wonder why you took
My house up, Fiddlers' Hall, the seat of noise
And mirth, an inn here, to be drowsy in
And lodge your lethargy in the Light Heart;   145
As if some cloud from court had been your harbinger,
Or Cheapside debt-books, or some mistress charge,
Seeing your love grow corpulent, gi' it a diet
By absence – some such mouldy passion!

138. lumpish?] *This ed.;* lumpish; *O.*   140. light] *O;* young *G.*   148. gi' it]
O; gave it *G.*

---

129. *passages*] what passes or is done (*O.E.D.*, III.13).

130. *spring . . . scenes*] cause to appear new painted backdrops of the kind
used in masques etc.

131. *shift*] undergo transmutation, change.

132. *sit . . . inn*] a popular proverb – Tilley, E42; cf. Shakespeare, *1H4*,
III.iii.78. It was a capital offence (known as 'hamesucken') to assault a man in
his own dwelling (the general meaning of 'inn').

133. *chuck*] chuckle, laugh inwardly.

136. *as*] as if (Abbott, § 107).

138. *lumpish*] low-spirited.

138–40. *Carry . . . at 'em*] harmless if futile amusements; jet rings were
popular for their property of attracting light objects by static electricity; cf.
E.M.I., II.iv.35n.; *G.M.*, ll. 932–3.

143. *Fiddlers Hall*] Cf. the halls of the guilds, Grocers', Drapers', Merchant
Taylors' etc., to which their members resorted and also Ruffin's (or Ruffian's)
Hall, the site of duels and brawling – *E.H.*, I.i.21–2n. (Revels).

146.] as if some trouble at court had been the forerunner of your arrival
here.

147. *Cheapside debt-books*] Cheapside was London's market-place; account
books in which debts were recorded.

charge] a verb with 'gi' it a diet' as complement.

Lovel. [*Aside.*] 'Tis guessed unhappily.

[*Enter* FERRET.]

Ferret.   Mine host, you're called.   150
Host. I come, boys.   [*Exit* HOST.]
Lovel.   Ferret, have not you been ploughing
 With this mad ox, mine host, nor he with you?
Ferret. For what, sir?
Lovel.   Why, to find my riddle out.
Ferret. I hope you do believe, sir, I can find
 Other discourse to be at, than my master,   155
 With hosts and ostlers.
Lovel.   If you can, 'tis well.
 Go down and see who they are come in, what guests,
 And bring me word.   [*Exit* FERRET.]

ACT I SCENE iv

Lovel.   O love, what passion art thou!
 So tyrannous and treacherous! First, t' enslave,
 And then betray all that in truth do serve thee!
 That not the wisest, nor the wariest creature
 Can more dissemble thee, than he can bear   5
 Hot burning coals in his bare palm or bosom;
 And less conceal or hide thee than a flash
 Of inflamed powder, whose whole light doth lay it
 Open to all discovery, even of those
 Who have but half an eye, and less of nose!   10
 An host to find me! Who is, commonly,
 The log, a little o' this side the sign-post;
 Or, at the best, some round-grown thing, a jug,

155. my] *Oc;* o'my *Ou.*
0.1.] *Lovel. O.*

151–3. *ploughing . . . out*] Cf. Samson, whose riddle was revealed to the
Philistines by his wife, in Judges xiv.18: 'If ye had not ploughed with my
heifer, ye had not found out my riddle'; see also *S.W.*, V.i.96; the mad ox is a
cuckold joke.

5. *dissemble*] pretend not to see, ignore (*O.E.D.*, 3a).
10. *but . . . eye*] See *Pers.* 25n.
11ff.] For a conventional and less flattering portrait, see Overbury,
Characters, 'An Host'.
13–14. *jug . . . beard*] like a 'Bellarmine', a drinking-jug with a bearded face,

Faced with a beard, that fills out to the guests,
And takes in fro' the fragments o' their jests!   15
But I may wrong this out of sullenness,
Or my mistaking humour? Pray thee, phant'sie,
Be laid again; and, gentle melancholy,
Do not oppress me. I will be as silent
As the same lover should be, and as foolish.   20

ACT I SCENE V

[*Enter*] HOST.

[*Host*.] My guest, my guest, be jovial, I beseech thee.
I have fresh golden guests, guests o' the game,
Three coachfull! Lords and ladies, new come in!
And I will cry them to thee, and thee to them,
So I can spring a smile but in this brow,   5
That, like the rugged Roman alderman,
Old Master Gross surnamed Agelastos,
Was never seen to laugh but at an ass.

---

18. gentle melancholy] *This ed.;* Gentle-Melancholy *O.*   19. silent,] *Oc;*
silent, *Enter Host. Ou.*
o.1.] *This ed.;* Host. Ferret. Lovel. *O.*   2. I have] *F3;* I'have *O.*   4. and]
This ed.; 'and *O.*   7. Agelastos; *untransliterated in O.*   8. at] *O;* as *F3.*

---

caricaturing Cardinal Bellarmine, opponent of the reformers; cf. *B.F.*,
IV.iv.189n.
    16. *wrong this*] do wrong to the host.
    16–17. *I . . . humour*] Melancholic humour was supposed to invade the
fantasy and 'forge monstrous fictions' (T. Bright, *A Treatise of Melancholie*
(1586), p. 102); cf. Burton, *The Anatomy of Melancholy* (1621), pp. 121–2;
E.M.I., II.iii.6off.; Overbury, *Characters*, 'A Melancholy Man'; Webster,
The White Devil, IV.i.101–2 (Revels).
    17. *mistaking*] misjudging.
    phant'sie] fancy; Jonson spells this word thus and in the modern way (e.g.
III.i.138).

    2. *guests . . . game*] gamesome, bent on sport; but cf. *B.F.*, IV.v.94, where
the phrase refers to whores.
    4. *cry*] announce (as if for sale, *O.E.D.*, 5b).
    5. *So*] provided that.
    6–8. *Roman . . . ass*] Jonson is referring to Marcus Licinius Crassus,
grandfather of the triumvir, who was Praetor in 127/6 B.C. 'Alderman' was
commonly used to translate many Roman designations of rank (*O.E.D.*, 1b)
and Jonson translates *crassus* as 'Gross'. 'Marcus Crassus . . . laughed but

Enter FERRET.

Ferret. Sir, here's the Lady Frampul.

Lovel.   How!

Ferret.   And her train:
Lord Beaufort and Lord Latimer, the Coronel   10
Tipto, with Mistress Pru, the chambermaid,
Trundle, the coachman –

Lovel.   Stop! Discharge the house,
And get my horses ready; bid for the groom
Bring 'em to the back gate.   [*Exit* FERRET.]

Host.   What mean you, sir?

Lovel. To take fair leave, mine host.

Host.   I hope, my guest,   15
Though I have talked somewhat above my share,
At large, and been i' the altitudes, th' extravagants,
Neither myself nor any of mine have gi'n you
The cause to quit my house thus on the sudden.

Lovel. No, I affirm it, on my faith. Excuse me   20
From such a rudeness; I was now beginning
To taste and love you, and am heartily sorry
Any occasion should be so compelling
To urge my abrupt departure thus. But –
Necessity's a tyrant, and commands it.   25

Host. She shall command me first to fire my bush,

8.1.] *printed after Agélastos in O.*   11. Tipto] *G; Tipto' O.*   Pru] *W; Cis
O.*   25. *tyrant*] *F3; Tyran O.*

---

once in his life; that one exception did not prevent his being called *agelastos*
('unsmiling') as Lucilius has it' (Cicero, *De Finibus*, V.92, tr. H. Rackham,
Loeb ed.). '. . . the saying . . . applies – one at which . . . Crassus laughed for
the one and only time in his life: "Like lips, like lettuce," the reference being
to an ass eating thistles,' (St Jerome, Epistle VII, 5, in *Letters*, tr. C. C.
Mierow, London, 1963). 'Like lips like lettuce' was proverbial (Tilley, L.
326) and cf. II.vi.19. The tale is also referred to in a play of the same year,
Ford's *The Lover's Melancholy*, I.ii.42ff. *H.& S.* note that in Jonson's day
Greek words were pronounced by accent not by quantity (note to *C.R.*,
Persons).

    10. *Coronel*] the early French form of 'colonel', which prevailed until the
mid-seventeenth century; but see II.v.71.

    11. *Pru*] See Introduction, p. 13; and cf. Tennant's note (*T.*, p. 176).

    12. *Discharge*] pay, settle with.

    17. *i' the altitudes*] above my station; cf. Fletcher, *The Laws of Candy*, II.i.:
'This Woman's in the altitudes, and he must be / A good Astrologer shall
know her Zodiack' (cited *H.& S.*).

    26. *bush*] See I.ii.28n.

Then break up house; or, if that will not serve,
To break with all the world; turn country bankrupt
I' mine own town, upo' the market-day,
And be protested for my butter and eggs   30
To the last bodge of oats and bottle of hay.
Ere you shall leave me, I will break my Heart;
Coach and coach-horses, lords and ladies, pack;
All my fresh guests shall stink! I'll pull my sign down,
Convert mine inn to an almshouse or a spital   35
For lazars or switch-sellers; turn it to
An academy o' rogues; or gi' it away
For a free school to breed up beggars in,
And send 'em to the canting universities,
Before you leave me!

Lovel.   Troth, and I confess.   40
I am loath, mine host, to leave you: your expressions
Both take and hold me. But, in case I stay,
I must enjoin you and your whole family
To privacy, and to conceal me; for
The secret is I would not willingly   45
See, or be seen to, any of this ging,
Especially the lady.

---

28. bankrupt] *G;* bankrupt. *O.*   29. market-day] *F3;* Mercat-day *O.*   33.
pack;] *H.& S.;* pack? *O.*   46. seen to,] *This ed.;* seene, to *O.*

---

30. *protested*] proclaimed for not honouring bills.
31. *bodge*] measure of oats etc., 'apparently about half a peck' (*O.E.D.*).
bottle] bundle, truss.
33. *pack*] send packing.
35. *spital*] retreat for the poor, especially those afflicted with venereal
disease; cf. *E.M.I.*, I.i.93.
36. *lazars*] lepers.
switch-sellers] the poorest of beggars who sold switches for use as whips or
whisks.
39. *canting*] 'This word canting seems to bee deriued from the latine *verbe*
(*canto*) which signifies in English, to sing, or to make a sound with words,
thats to say to speake. And very aptly may *canting* take his deriuatiō *a
cantando*, from singing, because amongst these beggerly consorts that can
play vpon no better instruments, the language of *canting* is a kinde of musicke,
and he that in such assemblies can *cant* best, is counted the best Musitian'
(Dekker, *N.D.*, III, 194).
43. *family*] household.
46. *to*] the usual preposition after 'be seen' (*O.E.D.*, 9b).
ging] gang, set; *E.M.I.*, II.ii.31.

Host.   Brain o' man,
    What monster is she, or cockatrice in velvet,
    That kills thus?
Lovel.   O good words, mine host. She is
    A noble lady, great in blood and fortune,   50
    Fair, and a wit! But of so bent a phant'sie
    As she thinks nought a happiness but to have
    A multitude of servants; and to get them,
    (Though she be very honest) yet she ventures
    Upon these precipices that would make her   55
    Not seem so to some prying, narrow natures.
    We call her, sir, the Lady Frances Frampul,
    Daughter and heir to the Lord Frampul.
Host.   Who?
    He that did live in Oxford first a student,
    And after married with the daughter of –
Lovel.   Sylly.   60
Host. Right; of whom the tale went to turn puppet-master.
Lovel. And travel with young Goose, the motion-man.
Host. And lie and live with the gipsies half a year
    Together, from his wife.
Lovel.   The very same:
    The mad Lord Frampul! And this same is his daughter,   65
    But as cock-brained as e'er the father was!

---

59 live] *W.;* love *O.*

48. *cockatrice*] or basilisk, a fabulous reptile said to be hatched by a serpent from a cock's egg and to kill by its mere glance; hence a monster or prostitute; cf. *E.M.O.*, I.ii.220; *Ep.*, xii.20; and Tilley, C495. It is discussed by Sir Thomas Browne, *Vulgar Errors*, III.vii.

51. *bent*] determined.

55. *precipices*] falls, descents.

59. *live*] I accept *W*'s reading for *O*'s 'love': there is no suggestion that Lord Frampul was promiscuous.

60. *Sylly*] Cf. Arg. 3 and II.vi.269.

61. *to turn*] a Latinate infinitive construction: 'that he turned'.

62. *young Goose*] 'A showman named Gosling, noticed in the *Diary* of Thomas Crosfield, Fellow of Queen's College, Oxford (ed. F. S. Boas, p. 71). He notes on 15 July 1634, among the "Spectacula Oxonij hoc anno", "Hierusalem in its glory, destruction . . . invented by Mr. Gosling, sometimes scholler to Mr Camden, Enginer" . . .' (*H.& S.*).

motion-man] mounter of shadow plays; see *T.of T.*, V.xn.; *E.M.O.* Ind. 163–4n.; *B.F.*, Act V.

66. *cock-brained*] rash, foolish; cf. Arg. 18n.

There were two of 'em, Frances and Laetitia,
But Laetice was lost young; and, as the rumour
Flew then, the mother upon it lost herself:
A fond weak woman, went away in a melancholy.   70
Because she brought him none but girls, she thought
Her husband loved her not. And he, as foolish,
Too late resenting the cause given, went after
In quest of her, and was not heard of since.
Host. A strange division of a family!   75
Lovel. And scattered, as i' the great confusion!
Host. But yet the lady, th' heir, enjoys the land.
Lovel. And takes all lordly ways how to consume it
As nobly as she can: if clothes and feasting
And the authorised means of riot will do it.   80
Host. She shows her extract, and I honour her for it.

ACT I SCENE vi

[*Enter* FERRET.]

[*Ferret.*] Your horses, sir, are ready, and the house
    Dis-
Lovel.   Pleased, thou thinkst?
Ferret.   I cannot tell; discharged
    I'm sure it is.
Lovel.   Charge it again, good Ferret,
    And make unready the horses: thou knowst how.

---

70. melancholy.] *This ed.;* melancholy, *O.*   80. it.] *This ed.;* it. *Ent. Fer. O.*
0.1.] *This ed.; Ferret. Lovel. Host. Prudence. Oc; Ferret, Lovel, Host, Cicelie.*
Ou.   3. I'm] *This ed.;* I'am *O.*   4. how.] *Oc;* how, *Ou.*

---

69. *lost herself*] became distracted.
73. *resenting*] regretting, repenting; cf. Arg. 17.
76. *the great confusion*] 'the confusion of tongues' at the tower of Babel. See
Genesis xi.9: 'Therefore is the name of it called Babel; because the Lord did
there confound the language of all the earth; and from thence did the Lord
scatter them abroad upon the face of all the earth' (Authorised Version).
Josephus develops this popular but false etymology of 'Babel' in *Antiq.*,
I.iv.3.
79ff.] See Stone, ch. x, 'Conspicuous Expenditure'.
80. *authorized*] sanctioned (ironical).
riot] revelry.
81. *extract*] extraction.
2. *discharged*] paid.

Chalk, and renew the rondels; I am now
Resolved to stay.   5

Ferret.   I easily thought so,
When you should hear what's purposed.

Lovel.   What?

Ferret.   To throw
The house out o' the window!

Ferret.   Brain o' man,
I shall ha' the worst o' that! Will they not throw
My household stuff out first? Cushions and carpets,   10
Chairs, stools, and bedding? Is not their sport my ruin?

Lovel. Fear not, mine host, I am not o' the fellowship.

Ferret. I cannot see, sir, how you will avoid it:
They know already, all, you are i' the house.

Lovel. Who know?

Ferret.   The lords: they have seen me and
enquired it.   15

Lovel. Why were you seen?

Ferret.   Because indeed I had
No medicine, sir, to go invisible:
No fern-seed in my pocket; nor an opal
Wrapped in a bay-leaf, i' my left fist,
To charm their eyes with.

---

17. medicine] *This ed.;* med'cine *O.*   19–20. fist, / To charm their] *O;* first
to charm / Their *G.*

---

5. *Chalk . . . rondels*] Scores were chalked up in ale-houses; a rondel
(according to Nares in a sense disallowed by *O.E.D.*) was a round sign for
shillings. See *H.& S.*'s note and Dekker, *N.D.*, III, 91.

6. *easily*] readily.

7–8. *throw . . . window*] proverbial (Tilley, H785) for riotous merry-making;
cf. Beaumont, *The Knight of the Burning Pestle* (ed. Hattaway), III.478.

10. *carpets*] usually at this time tapestry table-covers; see *S.W.*, IV.v. 257n;
Sh.Eng., II, 128.

17. *medicine*] drug.

18. *fern-seed*] 'Before the mode of reproduction of ferns was understood,
they were popularly supposed to produce an invisible seed, which was capable
of communicating its invisibility to any person who possessed it' (*O.E.D.*).
Cf. *E.M.O.*, IV.iii.33–4; Shakespeare, *1H4*, II.i.85–6.

18–20. *opal . . . with*] 'this stone optallius kepeth and saueth his eien that
hym beareth clere and sharpe and without greif. And dimmeth other mens
eyen that be about with a maner clowde and smyteth hem with a maner
blindness that is called Amentia so that they now not se nother take heede
what is doone to fore theyr eyen', *Bartholomeus de Proprietatibus Rerum*, tr.

D

Host.   He does give you reasons   20
    As round as Gyges' ring; which, say the ancients,
    Was a hoop-ring: and that is, round as a hoop!
Lovel. You will ha' your rebus still, mine host.
Host.   I must.
Ferret. My lady too looked out o' the window and called me.

        [*Enter* PRUDENCE.]

    And see where Secretary Pru comes from her,   25
    Employed upon some embassy unto you.
Host. I'll meet her, if she come upon employment.
    Fair lady, welcome, as your host can make you.
Pru. Forbear, sir, I am first to have mine audience
    Before the compliment. This gentleman   30
    Is my address to.
Host.   And it is in state.
Pru. My lady, sir, as glad o' the encounter
    To find a servant here, and such a servant
    Whom she so values; with her best respects,
    Desires to be remembered; and invites   35
    Your nobleness to be a part, today,
    Of the society and mirth intended
    By her and the young lords your fellow servants,
    Who are alike ambitious of enjoying

---

20. reasons] *O;* reasons, Sir, *G.*   22. as a hoop!] *Oc;* as a hoop! *En. Cic.*
Ou.   25. Pru.] *Oc;* Cis *Ou.*   her,] *Ou;* her, *Ent.* Pru. *Oc; G prints entrance
after l. 27.*   29, 32. Pru.] *This ed.; Pru Oc;* Cis *Ou.*   30. compliment] *W;*
complement *O.*

Trevisa, 1535, XVI.lxxiii (cited *H.& S.*); this passage is possibly a jibe at the
'bright stone that brings Invisibility' (*Und.*, xliii.24–5) of the Rosicrucians. A
description of their mysteries is found in Thomas Vaughan's 'The Fraternity
of the Rosy Cross' (1652) in *The Works of Thomas Vaughan*, ed. A. E. Waite
(London, 1919), pp. 343–76. Cf. I.vi.127n., II.vi.67n.
   21. *Gyges' ring*] The story of the shepherd who found on the finger of an
enormous corpse a ring that conferred invisibility is told in Plato, *Republic*,
II.359–60. Cf. Tilley, R132, and *E.M.O.*, IV.iii.33–4.
   22. *hoop-ring*] consisted of a plain band.
   25. *rebus*] See I.i.9n.
   25. *Secretary*] confidante.
   29. *audience*] Pru comes as ambassador – see l. 26 above.
   31. *in state*] to do with government, official (*O.E.D.*, 32).
   33. *servant*] lover; see Arg. 26n.
   39. *ambitious*] desirous (*O.E.D.*, 2).

The fair request; and to that end have sent   40
Me their imperfect orator to obtain it.
Which if I may, they have elected me,
And crowned me with the title of a sovereign
Of the day's sports devisèd i' the inn,
So you be pleased to add your suffrage to it.   45

Lovel. So I be pleased, my gentle mistress Prudence?
You cannot think me of that coarse condition
T' envy you anything.

Host.   That's nobly said,
And like my guest!

Lovel.   I gratulate your honour,
And should, with cheer, lay hold on any handle   50
That could advance it. But for me to think
I can be any rag or particle
O' your lady's care, more than to fill her list –
She being the lady that professeth still
To love no soul or body but for ends   55
Which are her sports; and is not nice to speak this,
But doth proclaim it, in all companies –
Her ladyship must pardon my weak counsels
And weaker will, if it decline t' obey her.

Pru. O, Master Lovel, you must not give credit   60
To all that ladies publicly profess,
Or talk o' th' volley unto their servants:
Their tongues and thoughts oft-times lie far asunder.
Yet, when they please, they have their cabinet-counsels
And reserved thoughts, and can retire themselves   65
As well as others.

Host.   Ay, the subtlest of us!
All that is born within a lady's lips –

46. Prudence] *Oc;* Cicely *Ou.*   47 condition] *Oc;* disposition *Ou.*   59. it]
O; I *W.*   67. born] *This ed.;* borne *O.*

---

45. *suffrage*] consent.
48. *envy*] grudge.
49. *I . . . honour*] I rejoice in the honour done to you.
50. *handle*] occasion, opportunity.
56. *nice*] reluctant.
62. *o' th' volley*] without consideration (Fr. *à la volée*); cf. *S.N.* IV.i.24.
64. *cabinet-counsels*] counsel given privately; Charles I had, however, recently instituted the cabinet council, the forerunner of the cabinet.
65. *retire*] remove (*O.E.D.*, 6).

Pru. Is not the issue of their hearts, mine host.
Host. Or kiss, or drink afore me.
Pru.   Stay, excuse me;
    Mine errand is not done. Yet if her ladyship's   70
    Slighting or disesteem, sir, of your service
    Hath formerly begot any distaste
    Which I not know of, here I vow unto you
    Upon a chambermaid's simplicity,
    Reserving still the honour of my lady,   75
    I will be bold to hold the glass up to her,
    To show her ladyship where she hath erred,
    And how to tender satisfaction;
    So you vouchsafe to prove but the day's venture.
Host. What say you, sir? Where are you? Are you within?   80
                [*Strikes Lovel on the breast.*]
Lovel. Yes. I will wait upon her and the company.
Host. It is enough, Queen Prudence. I will bring him;
    And o' this kiss.   [*Kisses her. Exit* PRUDENCE.]
           I longed to kiss a queen!
Lovel. There is no life on earth but being in love!
    There are no studies, no delights, no business,   85
    No intercourse, or trade of sense, or soul,
    But what is love! I was the laziest creature,
    The most unprofitable sign of nothing,
    The veriest drone, and slept away my life
    Beyond the dormouse, till I was in love!   90
    And now I can outwake the nightingale,
    Outwatch an usurer, and outwalk him too,

80.1. *Strikes . . . breast.*] G.   83. *Kisses . . .* PRUDENCE.] G.

---

69. *Or*] either.
  Or . . . me] 'This is a familiar expression, employed when what the speaker is just about to say is anticipated by another of the company' (*G*.).
  72. *distaste*] offence.
  73. *not know*] 'do' was sometimes omitted before 'not' (see Abbott, § 305).
  75. *Reserving*] preserving.
  77.] As Queen of the court, Pru combines the roles of sovereign and judge.
  79. *prove*] try.
  80. *Are . . . within?*] The jest occurs also in *Conv.Drum.*, ll. 557–8; *D.is A.*, I.v.2. It was delivered as the Host knocked on Lovel's chest.
  83. *o'*] on, i.e. after.
  86. *trade*] way, method (*O.E.D.*, 3).
  88. *sign*] mere semblance (*O.E.D.*, 8b).
  92. *Outwatch . . . too*] Cf. *F.I.*, ll. 53–4.

Stalk like a ghost that haunted 'bout a treasure,
And all that phant'sied treasure, it is love!

Host. But is your name Love-ill, sir, or Love-well?   95
I would know that.

Lovel.   I do not know't myself
Whether it is. But it is love hath been
The hereditary passion of our house,
My gentle host, and, as I guess, my friend.
The truth is I have loved this lady long   100
And impotently, with desire enough,
But no success: for I have still forborne
To express it in my person to her.

Host.   How then?

Lovel. I ha' sent her toys, verses and anagrams,
Trials o' wit, mere trifles she has commended,   105
But knew not whence they came, nor could she guess.

Host. This was a pretty riddling way of wooing!

Lovel. I oft have been too in her company;
And I looked upon her, a whole day; admired her;
Loved her, and did not tell her so; loved still,   110
Looked still, and loved; and loved, and looked, and sighed;
But as a man neglected I came off,
And unregarded –

Host.   Could you blame her, sir.
When you were silent and not said a word?

Lovel. O but I loved the more; and she might read it   115
Best in my silence, had she been –

Host.   As melancholic
As you are. Pray you, why would you stand mute, sir?

112. off] *F3;* of *O.*   117. Pray] *G;* 'Pray *O.*

---

93. *ghost . . . treasure*] a common practice; cf. III.ii.11–12n. and see Stith
Thompson, *Motif-Index of Folk-Literature,* N.570ff.

94. *treasure*] The correct reading may be 'pleasure', 'treasure' having been
caught by the compositor from the line above.

96. *Love-ill . . . Love-well*] Cf. the way in which *L'Astrée* (see III.ii.205) is
structured about the words *aimer, amer, animer.* See Peter N. Skrine, *The
Baroque* (London, 1978), p. 47.

97. *Whether*] which (of the two).

101. *impotently*] without restraint, passionately; (*O.E.D.,* 2).

104. *toys*] trifles of verse or prose (*O.E.D.,* 7).

105. *trials*] samples (*O.E.D.,* 10).

112. *came off*] left the field.

114. *not said*] Abbott, § 305.

Lovel. O thereon hangs a history, mine host.

    Did you ever know, or hear of the Lord Beaufort,
    Who served so bravely in France? I was his page   120
    And, ere he died, his friend! I followed him
    First i' the wars and, i' the times of peace,
    I waited on his studies, which were right.
    He had no Arthurs, nor no Rosicleers,
    No Knights o' the Sun, nor Amadis de Gauls,   125
    Primalions, and Pantagruels, public nothings;
    Abortives of the fabulous dark cloister,
    Sent out to poison courts and infest manners:
    But great Achilles', Agamemnon's acts,
    Sage Nestor's counsels, and Ulysses' sleights,   130

---

118. *thereon . . . history*] Cf. the proverb 'thereby hangs a tale', Tilley, T48.

120. *France*] Many English noblemen fought in the French wars of religion.

124ff.] all heroes of chivalric romances despised by Jonson and many others; see *E.M.O.*, II.iii.67–8, *E.H.*, V.i.32–4n. (Revels) and *Und.*, xliii.29–31, where he claims his library contained no '*Amadis de Gaule* / Th' *Esplandians, Arthur's, Palmerins*, and all / The learned Librarie of *Don Quixote.*' Cf. Beaumont, *The Knight of the Burning Pestle, passim*, and Burton on the ignorance of the English gentry, *Anatomy*, I.II.iii.15.

124–5. *Rosicleers . . . Sun*] Rosicleer was brother to the Knight of the Sun, hero of Ortuñez de Calahorra's *Espejo de Principes y Caualleros*, one of the romances owned by Don Quixote and translated into English by Margaret Tyler and others as *The Mirror of Knighthood* (1578–1601); cf. *C.R.*, III.v.31.

125. *Amadis de Gauls*] *c.* 1508. The most famous of the Iberian romances; the English translation by Antony Munday appeared in parts 1590–1618; cf. *S.W.*, IV.i.56; *Alc.*, IV.vii.40.

126. *Primalions*] The *Second Book of the Emperor Palmerin, in which are recounted the noble and valorous deeds of Primaleon and Polendus his sons . . .* (1512).

Pantagruels] Although Jonson seems to have been acquainted with Rabelais's writings (see IV.iv.344n. and Huntingdon Brown, *Rabelais in English Literature* (Cambridge Mass., 1933), pp. 31–94), the reference is to the sixteenth century English Gargantuan chapbooks; cf. *E.M.I.*, II.ii.25; *C.is A.*, IV.ix.3.

126. *public nothings*] Cf. Nashe in *The Anatomie of Absurditie* on 'the fantasticall dreames of those exiled Abbie-lubbers, from whose idle pens proceeded those worne out impressions of the feyned no where acts . . .' (*Works*, I, 11).

127–8.] the Rosicrucian tracts that purported to come from the cloister of Christian Rosencreutz (fabulous = founded on error). It is described in the *Fama Fraternitatis*, reprinted in F. A. Yates, *The Rosicrucian Enlightenment* (London, 1972), pp. 238–51. Jonson inveighed against the Rosicrucians in *F.I.*, ll. 34ff., and cf. II.vi.67; *S.N.*, III.ii.99; *Und.*, xliii.72–5.

Tydides' fortitude, as Homer wrought them
In his immortal phant'sie for examples
Of the heroic virtue. Or as Virgil,
That master of the epic poem, limned
Pious Aeneas, his religious prince,   135
Bearing his aged parent on his shoulders,
Rapt from the flames of Troy, with his young son:
And these he brought to practice and to use.
He gave me my first breeding, I acknowledge,
Then showered his bounties on me, like the Hours   140
That open-handed sit upon the clouds,
And press the liberality of heaven
Down to the laps of thankful men! But then
The trust committed to me at his death
Was above all, and left so strong a tie   145
On all my powers as time shall not dissolve
Till it dissolve itself, and bury all:
The care of his grave heir and only son!
Who being a virtuous, sweet, young, hopeful lord,
Hath cast his first affections on this lady.   150
And though I know and may presume her such,
As, out of humour, will return no love;
And therefore might indifferently be made
The courting-stock for all to practise on,
As she doth practise on all us, to scorn: 155

---

131. *Tydides*] Diomedes, son of Tydeus.

135. *Pious*] Lat. *pius*, dutiful, conscientious – Virgil's stock epithet for Aeneas.

137. *Rapt*] seized.

140–3. *Hours . . . men*] Cf. *1 Theob.*, 1–3; '*aboue, ouer the porch, sate the three Howers, vpon clouds, as at the ports of Heauen*'. The Hours, Eunomia, Dike and Eirene, daughters of Jupiter and Themis, presided over the changes of the seasons and kept watch at the gates of heaven; see Hesiod, *Theog.*, l. 901. Cf. *Und.*, lxxiv. 16–18. Coleridge remarked on this line: 'Like many other similar passages in Jonson, this is *eidos palepòn ideîn* a sight which it is difficult to make one's self see, – a picture my fancy cannot copy detached from the words' (Coleridge, p. 190).

146. *dissolve*] loosen.

149. *hopeful*] promising.

152. *humour*] See Introduction, p. 19.

153. *indifferently*] without prejudice (*O.E.D.*, 2).

154. *courting-stock*] an idol or object of courtship; cf. *C.R.*, V.iv.608.

155.] as she practises her scorn on us.

Yet, out of a religion to my charge,
And debt professed, I ha' made a self-decree,
Ne'er to express my person, though my passion
Burn me to cinders.

Host.   Then you're not so subtle
Or half so read in love-craft as I took you.   160
Come, come, you are no phoenix: an' you were,
I should expect no miracle from your ashes.
Take some advice: be still that rag of love
You are; burn on till you turn tinder.
This chambermaid may hap to prove the steel   165
To strike a spark out o' the flint, your mistress,
May beget bonfires yet; you do not know
What light may be forced out, and from what darkness.

Lovel. Nay, I am so resolved, as still I'll love,
Though not confess it.

Host.   That's, sir, as it chances;   170
We'll throw the dice for it: cheer up.

Lovel.   I do.   [*Exeunt.*]

166. spark] *Oc;* sparkle *Ou, F3.*

---

156. *religion*] scruple of conscience (Latinism).

158. *express*] reveal.

161–2. *phoenix . . . ashes*] The phoenix burnt itself up on the altar at Heliopolis; the next day a young phoenix arose from the ashes.

163–4. *rag . . . tinder*] Tinder was often made from partially charred linen.

171.] 'I hardly know where to find a more admirable first act of a comedy than this. *Si sic*' – Dyce (MS).

Act II

[*Enter*] LADY [FRAMPUL *and*] PRUDENCE [*pinning her lady's gown on herself.*]

[*Lady F.*] Come, wench, this suit will serve: dispatch, make
    ready.
    It was a great deal with the biggest for me,
    Which made me leave it off after once wearing.
    How does it fit? Will't come together?
Pru.   Hardly.
Lady F. Thou must make shift with it. Pride feels no pain.   5
    Girt thee hard, Pru. Pox o' this errant tailor,
    He angers me beyond all mark of patience.
    These base mechanics never keep their word
    In anything they promise.
Pru.   'Tis their trade, madam.
    To swear and break: they all grow rich by breaking   10
    More than their words; their honesties and credits

0.1. *pinning . . . herself*] *This ed.*   6. errant] *W;* errand *O.*

---

2. *with the biggest*] too big (*O.E.D.*, 'with', 15b); cf. *E.M.I.*, I.v.165n;
presumably the suit was made too big by Stuff to accommodate his enormous
wife.

4. *Hardly*] with difficulty.

5. *Pride . . . pain*] Tilley, P575.

6. *Girt . . . hard*] pull hard on the belt or girdle. 'Girt' is a form of 'gird'.

    errant] punning on a confused etymology, 'straying' and 'erring'. From the
phrase 'thief errant' or 'arrant thief', it came to mean 'notorious', 'rascally'.

7. *mark*] limit (*O.E.D.*, sb.1.1b).

10. *break*] quibbling throughout the passage on break = turn bankrupt; cf.
Dekker on 'Politick Bankruptisme', *N.D.* II, 17–30.

11–12. *honesties . . . off*] '*Cf.* Earle's description of a shop-keeper (*Character
Writings*): "His conscience was a thing that would have laid upon his hands,
and he was forced to put it off, and make great use of honesty to profess
upon"' (cited *T.*).

Lady F. And worst, it seems; which makes 'em do't so
    often.
    If he had but broke with me, I had not cared,
    But with the company, the body politic –   15
Pru. Frustrate our whole design, having that time,
    And the materials in so long before!
Lady F. And he to fail in all, and disappoint us!
    The rogue deserves a torture –
Pru.   To be cropped
    With his own scissors.
Lady F.   Let's devise him one.   20
Pru. And ha' the stumps seared up with his own cering-
    candle!
Lady F. Close to his head, to trundle on his pillow!
    I'll ha' the lease of his house cut out in measures.
Pru. And he be strangled with 'em?
Lady F.   No; no life
    I would ha' touched, but stretched on his own yard   25
    He should be a little, ha' the strappado.
Pru.   Or an ell of taffeta
    Drawn thorough his guts by way of clyster, and fired
    With *aqua-vitae.*
    Are still the first commodity they put off.

21. cering-] *This ed.;* searing *O.*   27. clyster] *This ed.;* glister *O.*

---

12. *put off*] dispose of by sale (*O.E.D.*, 'put' 45j., records this sense only
from 1639).

18. *disappoint*] punning on appoint = accoutre.

19–29.] Cf. the imagined poetic justice for a barber in *S.W.*, III.v.69ff.

19. *cropped*] have his ears lopped off, a common mutilation.

21. *seared up . . . candle*] punning on sear up = cauterise, and cere = to wax or
dress material.

22. *trundle*] roll.

23. *measures*] measuring tapes.

24. *he*] a grammatical error for 'him' – the pronoun is the object of 'have' in
l. 23.

25. *yard*] measuring rod.

26. *strappado*] a form of torture in which the victim's hands were tied across
his back and then secured to a pulley. After being hoisted from the ground he
was let fall half way with a jerk to break his arms and dislocate his joints. Cf.
Shakespeare, *1H4*, II.iv.232n. (Arden); *Volp.*, IV.vi.32.

27. *clyster*] enema; for Jonson's sadism and anal eroticism see Edmund
Wilson, 'Morose Ben Jonson' in *The Triple Thinkers* (1952).

28. aqua-vitae] alcohol or brandy.

Lady F.   Burning i' the hand
  With the pressing-iron cannot save him.

Pru.   Yes.
  Now I have got this on, I do forgive him   30
  What robes he should ha' brought.

Lady F.   Thou art not cruel,
  Although strait-laced I see, Pru!

Pru.   This is well.

Lady F. 'Tis rich enough, but 'tis now what I meant thee!
  I would ha' had thee braver than myself,
  And brighter far. 'Twill fit the players yet   35
  When thou hast done with it, and yield thee somewhat.

Pru. That were illiberal, madam, and mere sordid
  In me, to let a suit of yours come there.

Lady F. Tut, all are players and but serve the scene, Pru;
  Dispatch; I fear thou dost not like the province, 40
  Thou art so long a-fitting thyself for it.
  Here is a scarf to make thee a knot finer.

Pru. You send me a-feasting, madam.

Lady F.   Wear it, wench.

Pru. Yes; but with leave o' your ladyship, I would tell you

28–9. *Burning . . . him*] Imprisonment or branding on the hand could be substituted for the death penalty for those who could plead benefit of clergy, i.e. could read.

29. *pressing-iron*] smoothing-iron.

31. *cruel*] a common pun on cruel=severe, just (*O.E.D.*, 4) and crewel=worsted, worn by those who could not afford silk; cf. *Alc.*, I.i.173; Shakespeare, *Lr.*, II.iv.7.

33. *strait-laced*] punning on tight stays and precise morality; cf. *B.F.*, I.v.198; Middleton, *The Family of Love*, V.iii.192–3, 'a crew of narrow-ruffed, strait-laced, yet loose-bodied dames'; Chapman, *The Widow's Tears*, II.iii.25–6n. (Revels).

34. *braver*] more splendid.

35. *players*] It was the custom for the rich to give their costumes to their retainers who often sold them to the players; see Chambers, II, 365; cf. *Und.*, xv.106ff.; Donne, Satire IV, l. 180.

37. *illiberal*] ill-bred.
mere] absolutely.
sordid] menial, ignoble.

40. *province*] duty, office (*O.E.D.*, II.7).

42. *scarf*] Scarves were made of light material, tasselled at the ends, and cast across the face to prevent sunburn.
knot] ornamental bow (*O.E.D.*, 2).

This can but bear the face of an odd journey. 45
Lady F. Why, Pru?
Pru. A lady of your rank and quality,
To come to a public inn, so many men,
Young lords, and others i' your company,
And not a woman but myself, a chambermaid!
Lady F. Thou doubtst to be overlaid, Pru? Fear it not, 50
I'll bear my part, and share with thee i' the venture.
Pru. O but the censure, madam, is the main:
What will they say of you or judge of me,
To be translated thus 'bove all the bound
Of fitness or decorum?
Lady F. How now, Pru!
Turned fool upo' the sudden, and talk idly
I' thy best clothes? Shoot bolts and sentences
To affright babies with? As if I lived
To any other scale than what's my own,
Or sought myself, without myself, from home? 60
Pru. Your ladyship will pardon me my fault:
If I have overshot, I'll shoot no more.
Lady F. Yes, shoot again, good Pru; I'll ha' thee shoot,
And aim, and hit; I know 'tis love in thee,
And so I do interpret it.
Pru. Then, madam, 65
I'd crave a farther leave.
Lady F. Be it to license,
It sha' not want an ear, Pru. Say, what is it?
Pru. A toy I have, to raise a little mirth

---

45. *bear . . . of*] look like.
50. *overlaid*] punning on overlade(n) and overlie = have intercourse with (*O.E.D.*, 'overlie' 2b).
51. *bear*] sustain (a role) and expose (bawdy).
52. *main*] chief concern; cf. Shakespeare, *Ham.*, II.ii.56.
54. *translated*] transformed.
57. *bolts*] arrows; an oblique allusion to the proverb 'A fool's bolt is soon shot' (Tilley, F515).
sentences] *sententiae* or maxims.
59. *scale*] degree.
60. *sought . . . without myself*] 'Persius, *Sat.*i.7, "nec te quaesiveris extra": 'without' = outside. So Ben's scholar Field in *A Woman is a Weathercock*, I.i. (1612, B2): "I loue that Poet / That gaue vs reading, not to seeke our selues/ Beyond our selues"' (*H.& S.*).
68. *toy*] piece of fun (*O.E.D.*, 2).

To the design in hand.

Lady F.   Out with it, Pru,
   If it but chime of mirth.

Pru.   Mine host has, madam,   70
   A pretty boy i' the house, a dainty child,
   His son, and is o' your ladyship's name too, Francis,
   Whom if your ladyship would borrow of him,
   And give me leave to dress him as I would,
   Should make the finest lady and kinswoman,   75
   To keep you company, and deceive my lords
   Upo' the matter with a fountain o' sport.

Lady F. I apprehend thee, and the source of mirth
   That it may breed; but is he bold enough,
   The child, and well assured?

Pru.   As I am, madam,   80
   Have him in no suspicion more than me.

[*Enter* HOST.]

Here comes mine host; will you but please to ask him,
   Or let me make the motion?

Lady F.   Which thou wilt, Pru.

ACT II SCENE ii

[*Host.*] Your ladyship and all your train are welcome.

Lady F. I thank my hearty host.

Host.   So is your sovereignty:
   Madam, I wish you joy o' your new gown.

Lady F. It should ha' been, my host, but Stuff, our tailor
   Has broke with us; you shall be o' the counsel.   5

Pru. He will deserve it, madam. My lady has heard
   You have a pretty son, mine host; she'd see him.

Lady F. Ay, very fain; I prithee let me see him.

0.1.] *Host. Lady. Prudence. Franke. O.*   8. him] *This ed.;* him, *Oc;* him, host
Ou.

---

70. *chime of*] agree with, although *O.E.D.* records this sense (8) only from
1690.

77. *fountain*] spring or source (*O.E.D.*, 1d).

78. *apprehend*] understand.

83. *motion*] proposal.

4–5. *Stuff . . . counsel*] let us put you in the secret that Stuff has failed us.

Host. Your ladyship shall presently. [*Goes to the door.*] Ho!
Pierce. [*Within.*]   Anon.
Host. Bid Frank come hither, Anon, unto my lady. –   10
    It is a bashful child, homely brought up
    In a rude hostelry. But the Light Heart,
    It is his father's, and it may be his.

            [*Enter* FRANK.]

    Here he comes. – Frank, salute my lady.
Frank.   I do
    What, madam, I am designed to by my birthright;   15
    As heir of the Light Heart, bid you most welcome.
Lady F. And I believe your 'most', my pretty boy,
    Being so emphased by you.
Frank.   Your ladyship,
    If you believe it such, are such to make it.
Lady F. Prettily answered! Is your name Francis?
Frank.   Yes.   20
Lady F. I love mine own the better.
Frank.   If I knew yours,
    I should make haste to do so too, good madam.
Lady F. It is the same with yours.
Frank.   Mine then acknowledgeth
    The lustre it receives by being named after.
Lady F. You will win upon me in compliment.
Frank.   By silence.   25
Lady F. A modest and a fair well-spoken child.
Host. Her ladyship shall have him, sovereign Pru,
    Or what I have beside: divide my Heart
    Between you and your lady. Make your use of it:
    My house is yours, my son is yours. Behold,   30

---

9. *Goes ... door*] G.   Ho ... Anon.] *This ed.*; Ho Ser. Anone.
Oc.   10. Anon] *This ed.; Anone Oc;* anone *Ou.*   13. It is] *Oc;* Is *Ou.*   15.
designed to by] *Oc;* desin'd to doe, by *Ou.*   17. your] *O;* you *F3.*   20.
Yes.] *Oc; Yes* madame. *Ou.*   25. compliment] *G;* complement *O.*   26.
and a] *O;* and *F3.*

---

  9. *presently*] at once.
  10. *Anon*] Pierce the drawer, nicknamed Anon; see *Pers.* 58–9n.
  18. *emphased*] stressed; the only example in *O.E.D.*
  25. *win upon*] excel.
  28. *Heart*] punning on the name of his Inn.

I tender him to your service. Frank, become
What these brave ladies would ha' you. Only this,
There is a charwoman i' the house, his nurse,
An Irish woman I took in a beggar,
That waits upon him; a poor, silly fool,   35
But an impertinent and sedulous one
As ever was: will vex you on all occasions,
Never be off, or from you, but in her sleep,
Or drink, which makes it. She doth love him so,
Or rather dote on him. Now, for her, a shape,   40
As we may dress her (and I'll help) to fit her
With a tuftaffeta cloak, an old French hood,
And other pieces, heterogene enough.

Pru. We ha' brought a standard of apparel down,
Because this tailor failed us i' the main.   45

Host. She shall advance the game.

Pru.   About it, then,
And send but Trundle hither, the coachman, to me.

Host. I shall [*Aside.*] But, Pru, let Lovel ha' fair quarter.

Pru. The best.   [*Exit* HOST.]

Lady F.   Our host, methinks, is very gamesome!

Pru. How like you the boy?

Lady F.   A miracle!

Pru.   Good madam,   50
But take him in and sort a suit for him;

---

48. *Aside.*] G.   49.1. *Exit* HOST.] G.

---

35. *silly*] defenceless.
fool] simpleton.
36. *impertinent*] meddlesome; cf. Ded.5; *M.L.*, I.v.45.
sedulous] persistent.
40. *shape*] stage costume (*O.E.D.*, 8b).
42. *tuftaffeta*] a rich taffeta with the pile in tufts; cf. *E.H.*, I.ii.16; *B.F.*,
IV.iv.149n. (Revels).
French hood] at this time a city and not a court fashion. 'The front band
[was] depressed over the brows and raised in folds over the temples. It could
thus be pulled down over the face as a disguise' (Sugden). Cf. *T.of T.*,
IV.v.95n.; *Alc.*, II.vi.32–3.
43. *heterogene*] *O.E.D.* records the longer form 'heterogeneous' only from
1624.
44. *standard*] suit (*O.E.D.*, 28a); see Arg. 42.
48. *quarter*] treatment (*O.E.D.*, 17b).
51. *sort*] select.

I'll give Trundle his instructions,
And wait upon your ladyship i' the instant.
Lady F. But, Pru, what shall we call him when we ha'
    dressed him?
Pru. My Lady Nobody, anything, what you will.   55
Lady F. Call him Laetitia, by my sister's name,
    And so 'twill mind our mirth too we have in hand.

Exit LADY FRAMPUL.

ACT II SCENE iii

[Enter] TRUNDLE.

[*Pru.*] Good Trundle, you must straight make ready the
    coach,
    And lead the horses out but half a mile
    Into the fields, whither you will, and then
    Drive in again with the coach-leaves put down
    At the back gate, and so to the back stairs,   5
    As if you brought in somebody to my lady,
    A kinswoman that she sent for. Make that answer
    If you be asked, and give it out i' the house so.
Trundle. What trick is this, good mistress secretary,
    You'd put upon us?
Pru.   Us! Do you speak plural?   10
Trundle. Me and my mares are us.
Pru.   If you so join 'em,
    Elegant Trundle, you may use your figures:
    I can but urge, it is my lady's service.

57. mind] *O;* mend *conj.* L. Theobald, *G.*
0.1. *Enter* TRUNDLE.] *G; Prudence. Trundle. O.*

---

55. *Nobody*] i.e. 'no body', an old joke; cf. Shakespeare, *Tp.*, V.iii.124–5;
associated with a ballad of John Nobody – see C. R. Baskerville, *The
Elizabethan Jig* (Chicago, 1929), pp. 47–8. It may have been suggested by the
coachman's name, for John Trundle, bookseller in the Barbican from
1603–26, used the sign of Nobody. He had published the anonymous play
Nobody and Somebody (c. 1606).
    56. *Laetitia*] See *Pers.* 21.
    57. *mind*] have in view, contribute to (*O.E.D.*, 7).
    4. *coach-leaves*] 'folding blinds of a coach-window' (*O.E.D.*).
    11. *join*] (1) construe (cf. Ded. 3); (2) harness (*O.E.D.*, I.i.b); (3) a laborious
équivoque involving the 'mares' of l. 11 and 'service' at l. 13.
    12. *figures*] figures of speech.

Trundle. Good Mistress Prudence, you can urge enough.
    I know you are secretary to my lady,   15
    And mistress steward.
Pru.   You'll still be trundling,
    And ha' your wages stopped now at the audit.
Trundle. 'Tis true, you are gentlewoman o' the horse too;
    Or what you will beside, Pru. I do think it
    My best to obey you.
Pru.   And I think so too, Trundle.   20
                    [*Exeunt* PRU *and* TRUNDLE.]

ACT II SCENE iv

[*Enter*] BEAUFORT [*and*] LATIMER.

[*Beaufort.*] Why, here's return enough of both our ventures,
    If we do make no more discovery.
Latimer.   What
    Then o' this parasite?
Beaufort.   O, he's a dainty one,
    The parasite o' the house.

[*Enter* HOST.]

Latimer.   Here comes mine host.
Host. My lords, you both are welcome to the Heart.   5
Beaufort. To the Light Heart, we hope.
Latimer.   And merry, I swear.
    We never yet felt such a fit of laughter
    As your glad Heart hath offered us sin' we entered.
Beaufort. How came you by this property?
Host.   Who? My Fly?

15. you] *F3;* you' *O.*   18. you] *G;* you' *O.*
0.1] *This ed.; Beaufort. Latimer. Host. O.*   4.1. *Enter* HOST.] *G.*   6. merry,]
Oc; merry *Ou;* marry *F3.*

---

16. *trundling*] 'revolving, with a suggestion of "getting off the track"'
(*H.& S.*).
17. *audit*] the hearing presided over by Pru.
18. *gentlewoman . . . horse*] The gentleman of the horse was in charge of a
nobleman's stables; cf. *Ep.*, xc; there is possibly a pun on 'whores' – cf. note to
l. 11 above.
2. *discovery*] exploration.
3. *parasite*] i.e. Fly; see Pers. 55.
9. *property*] instrument, tool (*O.E.D.*, 4).

Beaufort. Your Fly if you call him so.

Host.   Nay, he is that,   10
    And will be still.

Beaufort.   In every dish and pot?

Host. In every cup and company, my lords,
    A creature of all liquors, all complexions:
    Be the drink what it will, he'll have his sip.

Latimer. He is fitted with a name.

Host.   And he joys in't.   15
    I had him when I came to take the inn here,
    Assigned me over in the inventory
    As an old implement, a piece of household-stuff,
    And so he doth remain.

Beaufort.   Just such a thing
    We thought him.

Latimer.   Is he a scholar?

Host.   Nothing less;   20
    But colours for it, as you see, wears black,
    And speaks a little tainted fly-blown Latin
    After the School.

Beaufort.   Of Stratford o' the Bow:
    'For Lily's Latin is to him unknow'.

Latimer. What calling has he?

Host.   Only to call in,   25

15. he] *This ed.;* he' *O.*   24. unknow] *Oc;* vn-known *Ou.*   25, 31. has] *F3;*
has' *O.*   25. in,] *Oc;* in, still. *Ou;* in, still, *F3.*

---

13. *liquors*] punning on the fluids which determined the 'humours' or
complexions of the body.

16.] See Arg. 118n.

18. *household-stuff*] furniture.

20. *Nothing less*] scarcely.

23. *School*] the Schoolmen, medieval philosophers and theologians
(*O.E.D.*, 8).

23–4. *Stratford . . . unknow*'] usually Stratford-at-Bow, a suburb of London
4½ miles north-east of St Paul's. Jonson is echoing Chaucer's description of his
Prioress: 'And Frenssh she spak ful faire and fetisly, / After the scole of
Stratford atte Bowe, / For Frenssh of Parys was to hire unknowe.' (Gen. Prol.
124–6). Jonson obviously thought the lines were disparaging: for contrary
opinions see F. N. Robinson's note to these lines in his *Chaucer* (London,
1957).

24. *Lily's*] William Lily, first high-master of St Paul's School, wrote a Latin
grammar with John Colet that was used in schools for three and a half
centuries; cf. *T.of T.*, III.vii.72.

25–8. *call in . . . discipline*] a series of military puns: call in = withdraw and

    Inflame the reckoning, bold to charge a bill,
    Bring up the shot i' the rear, as his own word is.
Beaufort. And does it in the discipline of the house
    As corporal o' the field, *maestro del campo*?
Host. And visitor-general of all the rooms: 30
    He has formed a fine militia for the inn too.
Beaufort. And means to publish it?
Host.   With all his titles:
    Some call him Deacon Fly, some Doctor Fly,
    Some Captain, some Lieutenant; but my folks
    Do call him Quartermaster Fly, which he is.   35

                    ACT II SCENE V

                [Enter] TIPTO *[and]* FLY.

[Tipto.] Come, Quarter-master Fly.
Host.   Here's one already
    Hath got his titles.
Tipto.   Doctor!
Fly.   Noble colonel!

30. rooms] *Oc.;* roome *Ou.*   31. formed] *G;* 'formed *O.*   35. Quartermaster Fly] *O;* Quarter-master *conj. H.& S.*
0.1.] *This ed.; Tipto. Host. Flie. Beaufort. Latimer. O.*

---

shout in orders (*O.E.D.*, 'call' 29b & 4); inflame = set on fire and augment
(*O.E.D.*, 1 & 4b); bill = bill-man (bearer of an axe-like weapon) and account
(*O.E.D.*, 'bill' 1. 3 & 'bill' 2.6); shot = soldier armed with a firearm and tavern
reckoning (*O.E.D.*, III.21b & III.23 – cf. Shakespeare *1H4*, V.iii.30, and
Satiromastix, V.ii.329); discipline = military drill and order (*O.E.D.*, 3b & 5).
    29. *corporal . . . field*] 'a superior officer of the army in the 16th and 17th
centuries who acted as an assistant or a kind of aide-de-camp to the sergeant-
major' (*O.E.D.*).
    maestro del campo] quartermaster. The office was Roman and entailed
pitching and fortifying the camp, superintending arms and weapons. Campo
was schoolboy cant for the privy. For examples see Keith Thomas, *Rule and
Misrule in the Schools of Early Modern England* (Reading, 1976), p. 16, n. 68.
This meaning is not given in the *O.E.D.*
    30. *visitor*] inspector.
    31. *militia*] described in III.i.1–32.
    32. *publish*] bring to public notice (*O.E.D.*, 3b).
    Scene v.] 'Though it was hard upon old Ben, yet Feltham, it must be
confessed, was in the right in considering the Fly, Tipto, Bat. Burst, etc. of
this play mere dotages. Such a scene as this was enough to damn a new play;
and Nick Stuff is worse still, – most abominable *stuff* indeed' (Coleridge,
p. 190).

No doctor, yet a poor professor of ceremony
Here i' the inn, retainer to the host,
I discipline the house.

Tipto.   Thou readst a lecture   5
Unto the family here: when is thy day?

Fly. This is the day.

Tipto.   I'll hear thee, and ha' thee a doctor.
Thou shalt be one, thou hast a doctor's look,
A face disputative, of Salamanca.

Host. Who's this?

Latimer.   The glorious Colonel Tipto, host.   10

Beaufort. One talks upon his tiptoes, if you'll hear him.

Tipto. Thou hast good learning in thee, *macte* Fly.

Fly. And I say *macte* to my colonel.

Host. Well *macted* of 'em both.

Beaufort.   They are matched, i' faith.

Tipto. But, Fly, why *macte*?

Fly.   *Quasi magis aucte,*   15
My honourable colonel.

Tipto.   What, a critic?

Host. There's another accession: critic Fly.

Latimer. I fear a taint here i' the mathematics.
They say lines parallel do never meet;
He has met his parallel in wit and schoolcraft.   20

Beaufort. They side, not meet, man; mend your metaphor
And save the credit of your mathematics.

---

3. yet a] *G;* Yet. A *O.*   5. lecture] *G;* lecture. *O.*   6. thy] *Oc;* the *Ou.*   7.
and ha'] *Oc;* and I'le ha' *Ou, F3.*   16. What,] *H.& S.;* What *O.*   21.
meet,] *H.& S.;* meet *O.*

---

9. *Salamanca*] Its university, founded early in the thirteenth century, was
one of the greatest in Europe.

12. macte] honoured (Lat.).

15. magis aucte] 'Priscian, *Institutiones Grammaticae,* v.66, "macte, id est
magis aucte" ("greater")' (*H.& S.*): a false etymology. *Mactus* derives from
the root *mak* as in *makár* 'blessed'. For other etymological conundrums see
C.R., IV.iii.; and Shakespeare, *L.L.L.,* IV.ii.85.

17. *accession*] addition (to your profession).

18. *taint*] 'hit' as in tilting.

20. *schoolcraft*] the first recorded use in the *O.E.D.*

21. *side*] presumably 'run parallel' and 'take up sides', but the joke is
laboured.

Tipto. But, Fly, how cam'st thou to be here, committed
    Unto this inn?

Fly.   Upon suspicion o' drink, sir,
    I was taken late one night here with the tapster   25
    And the under-officers, and so deposited.

Tipto. I will redeem thee, Fly, and place thee better
    With a fair lady.

Fly.   A lady, sweet Sir Glorious!

Tipto. A sovereign lady. Thou shalt be the bird
    To Sovereign Pru, queen of our sports, her fly,   30
    The fly in household and in ordinary;
    Bird of her ear, and she shall wear thee there,
    A fly of gold, enamelled, and a school-fly.

Host. The school, then, are my stables or the cellar
    Where he doth study deeply at his hours   35
    Cases of cups, I do not know how spiced
    With conscience, for the tapster and the ostler: as
    Whose horses may be cosened, or what jugs
    Filled up with froth. That is his way of learning.

Tipto. What antiquated feather's that that talks?   40

Fly. The worshipful host, my patron, Master Goodstock,
    A merry Greek, and cants in Latin comely,

24. *Fly.*] H.& S.; *Fly, O; om. F3.*

---

   23. *committed*] imprisoned.

   26. *deposited*] 'placed in safe keeping' and possibly 'laid' (as an egg –
although *O.E.D.* records this meaning only from 1692).

   29. *bird*] Cf. II.vi.59 and 69; V.i.1; bird meant young man or maiden (by
confusion with *burde* and perhaps bryde – see *O.E.D.*, Ic & d). Here it may
mean 'confidant', perhaps by analogy with the phrase 'a bird of one's own
brain', a secret. See l. 32 below.

   31. *in ordinary*] added to official designations = belonging to the regular
staff. An ordinary was also an eating house or tavern.

   33. *school-fly*] fly of the academy of the inn.

   35. *at*] Abbott, § 144.

   36–7. *cases . . . conscience*] punning on 'case' = pair and the phrase 'case of
conscience' (Lat. *casus conscientiae*). Cases of conscience 'were divided into
two classes, (1) those which concern a man's state before God, (2) those which
concern his actions in that state. It is mainly to the second of these, or cases of
conduct, that *Casuistry* is understood to refer' (*O.E.D.*). Cf. *B.F.*, I.iii.122,
and *Sej.*, V.202n.; for the phrase 'spiced conscience', see Chaucer, Gen.Prol.
526, and Massinger, *The Emperor of the East*, I.ii.88.

   39. *Filled . . . froth*] a common tavern trick; cf. *B.F.*, II.ii.97ff. (Revels).

   40. *feather*] Cf. the phrase 'a man of the first feather' = of showy parts.

   42. *merry Greek*] roisterer, boon companion; see T. J. B. Spencer, 'Greeks

    Spins like the parish-top.

Tipto.   I'll set him up, then.

    Art thou the dominus?

Host.   Factotum here, sir.

Tipto. Host real o' the house, and cap of maintenance?   45

Host. The lord o' the Light Heart, sir, cap-a-pie,

    Whereof the feather is the emblem, colonel,

    Put up with the ace of hearts.

Tipto.   But why in *cuerpo*?

    I hate to see an host, and old, in *cuerpo*.

Host. Cuerpo? What's that?

Tipto.   Light, skipping hose and doublet: 50

    The horse-boy's garb! Poor blank and half-blank *cuerpo*,

    They relish not the gravity of an host

---

and Merrygreeks' in R. Hosley ed., *Essays in Honour of Hardin Craig* (Columbia, 1962), pp. 223–33; *T.of T.*, IV. Interloping Scene, 23, and *H.& S.*'s note; *U.V.*, xi.38.

    cants] talks to elaborately; see I.v.39n.

    43. *parish-top*] 'A large top was kept in every parish to keep out-o'-work labourers out of mischief' (*Sh.Eng.*, II, 481); Shakespeare, *Tw.N.*, I.iii.38; *T.of T.*, III.vii.42–3.

    set him up] ready to be spun.

    44. *dominus . . . Factotum*] Cf. *U.V.*, xxxiv.64–5, of Inigo Jones, '*Dominus* ('Master') *Do-All*' (Factotum).

    45. *real*] royal.

    cap of maintenance] a symbol of official dignity borne, with a sword and mace, before the monarch or Lord Mayor.

    46. *cap-a-pie*] from head to foot (O.Fr.).

    47–8. *feather . . . hearts*] The Host presumably overheard Tipto designate him as a 'feather' and sardonically rejoins that he is the best card in the pack.

    48. *in* cuerpo] without a cloak or upper garment (Sp. *cuerpo*, body). Cf. Beaumont and Fletcher, *Love's Cure* (1606?): 'Boy; my Cloake and Rapier; it fits not a Gentleman of my rancke to walk the streets in *Querpo*' (II.i.2); Shakespeare, *Wiv.*, III.i. 46; and Appendix II, n. 3.

    50. *skipping*] vain, slight (although *O.E.D.* does not record exactly this meaning). Cf. the 'skipping king' of Shakespeare, *1H4*, III.ii.60, and the contemptuous use of a 'skipper' as applied to a youth (*O.E.D.*, sb.1.1b). Cf. *Poet.*, III.iv.299–300. Fletcher's version reads 'squirting' (mean, contemptible).

    51. *blank*] white, bare, simple.

    half-blank] 'a reference to parti-coloured hose, which Planché says had gone out of use nearly half a century before the date of this play' (*T.*). Parti-coloured costumes signified inconstant dispositions (Linthicum, pp. 20–2) and were the costumes of fools, disdained by other servants – see *E.M.I.*, II.iv.10.

    52. *relish*] partake of (*O.E.D.*, 1b).

Who should be king at arms and ceremonies
In his own house; know all to the gold-weights.
Beaufort. Why, that his fly doth for him here, your bird.   55
Tipto. But I would do it myself, were I my host,
      I would not speak unto a cook of quality,
      Your lordship's footman, or my lady's Trundle
      In *cuerpo*! If a dog but stayed below
      That were a dog of fashion, and well-nosed,   60
      And could present himself, I would put on
      The Savoy chain about my neck, the ruff
      And cuffs of Flanders, then the Naples hat,
      With the Rome hatband, and the Florentine agate,
      The Milan sword, the cloak of Genoa set   65
      With Brabant buttons, all my given pieces –
      Except my gloves, the natives of Madrid –

62. ruff] *F3;* ruffe; *O.*   65. Genoa] *This ed.; Genoa, O.*

---

53. *king at arms*] chief herald.

54. *to the gold-weights*] to the utmost scruple; cf. Fletcher, *The Wild Goose Chase* (1621): 'To one that weight her words and behaviours / In the gold weights of discretion' (I.iii.221–2).

59. *If . . . below*] if even a dog required attendance. 'Dog' was also used for a jovial man or gallant (*O.E.D.*, 3b).

60. *well-nosed*] keen scented, or 'of disguised appearance'.

61–7.] Cosmopolitan dress was a common object of satire; see *E.M.O.*, III.i.32n.

62. *Savoy chain*] Cf. Webster, *The White Devil*, 'my lord of Savoy, Knight of the Annunciation' (IV.iii.11–12). 'This was an order instituted by Amadeus VI in 1362 . . . The gold collar of the Order was specially massive' (Sugden).

62–3. *ruff . . . Flanders*] Outsize ruffs were favourite objects of satire – see *E.M.O.*, Ind. 111. Flanders was famous for its lace.

63. *Naples*] possibly made of the famous fustian of Naples, a kind of cotton velvet. 'In Cockayne's Trapolin [1658] II.i, T. says of his hat: "I think some N. devel made it, 'tis so high-crowned . . ."' (Sugden).

64. *hatband*] In Dekker's *Match mee in London* there is mention of 'rich Tuscan *hatbands*' and he speaks of vices having 'a Shopkeepers wealth in a Hat-band' (*N.D.*, III, 330); hatbands were made of a twisted cord of gold, silver or silk – see *E.M.O.*, Ind. 111n.

Florentine] Florence was famous for its settings of semi-precious stones.

65. *Milan*] 'Coryat noted the fame of Milan for "embroidering and making of hilts for swords and daggers . . . Their cutlers that make hilts are more exquisite in that art than any that I euer saw"' (*Crudities*, 1611, p. 102), cited *H.& S.*

66. *Brabant*] Belgium has always produced large quantities of buttons. Fletcher, however, substitutes 'Flemish buttons'.

67. *natives of Madrid*] i.e. made of Spanish leather and possibly 'titillated'

To entertain him in; and compliment
With a tame cony, as with a prince that sent it.

Host. The same deeds, though, become not every man: 70
What fits a colonel will not fit an host.

Tipto. Your Spanish host is never seen in *cuerpo*,
Without his *paramentos*, cloak, and sword.

Fly.   Sir,
He has the father of swords within, a long sword,
Blade Cornish, styled of Sir Rud Hudibras.   75

Tipto. And why a long sword, bully bird? Thy sense?

Fly. To note him a tall man, and a master of fence.

Tipto. But doth he teach the Spanish way of Don Lewis?

Fly. No, the Greek master he.

Tipto.   What call you him?

Fly.   Euclid.

71. What] *Oc;* That *Ou, F3, G;* That that *1716, W.*   73–5. Sir, / He . . .
sword, / Blade . . . Hudibras.] *Oc; Sir* he has the father / Of Swords, within a
long sword; Blade *cornish* stil'd / Of Sir *Rud Hughdibras Ou, F3.*   76. And
why] *Oc;* And with *Ou, F3.*

---

or elaborately perfumed; see *E.M.O.*, II.iv.93n.

68–9. *compliment . . . prince*] speak as courteously to a poor-spirited gull or
dupe as to a prince.

71. *colonel*] trisyllabic; cf. IV.ii.13.

73. paramentos] ornaments (It. and Sp. *paramento*).

74. *father . . . sword*] an old-fashioned two-handed sword which had been
superseded early in Elizabeth's reign by the rapier; see *S.W.*, II.v.109–11n.;
the remark gives a hint of the Host's noble lineage.

75. *Sir Rud Hudibras*] the son of the British king Leil, mythical founder of
Canterbury, Winchester and Shaftesbury. See Geoffrey of Monmouth, II.ix,
and Milton, *The History of Britain* (1670), pp. 16–17. Captain Ironsides in
The Magnetic Lady is called Rudhudibras several times (V.i.20 etc.).

76. *bully*] a term of endearment; cf. Shakespeare, *M.N.D.*, IV.ii.20.

77. *tall man*] tall here means valiant (cf. *E.M.I.*, IV.vii.125; Shakespeare
Wint. (New Arden), V.ii.164n.) but tallmen or highmen were loaded dice
(*E.M.O.*, III.vi.154–5n.).

78. *Don Lewis*] Don Luis Pacheco de Narvaez published his *Libro de las
Grandezas de la Espada* ('Book of the Glories of the Sword') at Madrid in 1600
and also edited Çarranza (see l. 87) whose pupil he was. These were the
leading authorities of the Spanish school.

79. *No*] Fly's contrast between the Spanish and 'Euclidian' schools betrays
his ignorance – they were identical.

Euclid] 'The Spanish system of swordsmanship . . . may be called the
Geometrical or Euclidian School of Fencing, based as it was upon the
theorems of geometry. The adversaries come on guard at the extremities of
the diameter of an imaginary circle, the length of the diameter being

Tipto. Fart upon Euclid, he is stale and antique!   80
　　Gi' me the moderns.
Fly.   Sir, he minds no moderns.
　　Go by, Hieronimo!
Tipto.   What was he?
Fly.   The Italian,
　　That played with Abbot Antony i' the Friars,
　　And Blinkinsops the bold.
Tipto.   Ay, marry, those
　　Had fencing names; what are become o' them?   85
Host. They had their times, and we can say they were.
　　So had Carranza his, so hath Don Lewis.

---

85. what are] *Oc;* what's *Ou, F3;* what is *G.*   87. hath] *Oc;* had *Ou, F3.*

---

determined by the two arms extended horizontally sword in hand' (*Sh.Eng.*,
II, 397). With this compare *E.M.I.*, IV.vii, where Bobadill describes the
Italian school of rapier duelling which had flourished in London in the 1590's;
cf. *Und.*, lix.7: 'I hate such measured, give me mettled! fire, / That trembles in
the blaze, but then mounts higher'; and Dekker's *The Wonder of a Kingdom*
(1631), I.i.
　　antique] accented, as usual in the period, on the first syllable.
　　82.] a late allusion to Kyd's *Sp.Tr*, III.xii,31. 'Perhaps no single passage in
Elizabethan drama became so notorious as this. It is quoted over and over
again as the stock phrase to imply impatience of anything disagreeable,
inconvenient, or old-fashioned' (Boas's ed. of *Sp.Tr*.); quotations are listed
by Claude Dudrap, '*La Tragedie espagnole* et la critique élisabéthaine' in J.
Jacquot ed., *Dramaturgie et Société* (Paris, 1968), II, 607–31; cf. *E.M.I.*,
I.v.47n. This Italian Hieronimo, or Jeronimo, was Master of Defence and
'usher' to Rocho Bonetti. He taught for his master in Blackfriars. See George
Silver's *Paradoxes of Defence* (1599) and *Sh.Eng.*, II, 395–6.
　　82–4. *Italian . . . bold*] For a description of a celebrated fight between
English and Italian fencing masters in the 1590's see Silver, *Paradoxes*, pp.
65–72. Abbot Antony was 'probably a fencer named Antony Abbot, the name
being inverted to suggest "Abbot of the Blackfriars"' (*H.& S.*). John
Blinkinsop, a Master of Defence, 'in 1579 played his master's prize at the
Artillery Gardens against six other masters, at four kinds of weapons'
(*Sh.Eng.*, II, 390). He is also heard of in 1580 at Cambridge (see *H.& S.*'s
note).
　　83. *played*] fenced.
　　Friars] Blackfriars.
　　85. *are become*] usually 'is'; see *O.E.D.*, 'become' 4.
　　87. *Carranza*] Jeronimo de Carranza, was author of *De la Filosofia de las
Armas* (1569) and the leading authority for the Spanish style of fencing that
was superseded at the end of Elizabeth's reign by the Italian. See *Sh.Eng.*, II,
397–8, and *E.M.I.*, I.v.113n.; Massinger, *The Guardian*, III.ii.50; Fletcher,
Love's Pilgrimage, V.vi.55ff.

Tipto. Don Lewis of Madrid is the sole master
    Now of the world!
Host.   But this o' the other world.
    Euclid demonstrates! He! He's for all.   90
    The only fencer of name now in Elysium.
Fly. He does it all by lines and angles, colonel,
    By parallels and sections, has his diagrams.
Beaufort. Wilt thou be flying, Fly?
Latimer.   At all; why not?
    The air's as free for a fly as for an eagle.   95
Beaufort. A buzzard! He is in his contemplation.
Tipto. Euclid a fencer, and in the Elysium!
Host. He played a prize last week with Archimedes,
    And beat him, I assure you.
Tipto.   Do you assure me?
    For what?
Host.   For four i' the hundred. Gi' me five,   100
    And I assure you again.
Tipto.   Host peremptory,
    You may be ta'en. But where, whence had you this?
Host. Upo' the road. A post that came from thence,
    Three days ago, here, left it with the tapster.
Fly. Who is indeed a thoroughfare of news,   105
    Jack Jug with the great belly, a witty fellow!
Host. Your bird here heard him.
Tipto.   Did you hear him, bird?
Host. Speak i' the faith of a fly.   [*Exit* HOST.]

89. world! . . . world.] *Oc;* world . . . world *Ou, F3.*   106. great] *Oc;*
broken *Ou, F3.*   108.1. *Exit* HOST.] *G.*

---

94. *At all*] to fly at all game; Tilley, G22.
96. *buzzard*] a stupid or worthless person – the buzzard, an inferior hawk,
was useless for falconry; cf. *E.M.I., Q,* I.i.51. Beaufort is referring to Tipto.
is . . . contemplation] is thinking hard.
98. *played a prize*] engaged in a prize-fight.
Archimedes] the ancient inventor and mathematician.
99. *assure*] (1) promise; (2) insure.
100. *four . . . hundred*] four per cent; for Jonson on insurance see *E.M.O.*
II.iii. 245n.
101. *peremptory*] obstinate, imperious; cf. *E.M.I.,* I.ii.26.
103. *post*] messenger.
thence] Elysium – continuing the baiting of Tipto.
108.1. Exit *HOST*] I follow *G.* in giving the Host an exit here. Line 138

Fly.   Yes, and he told us
  Of one that was the Prince of Orange's fencer.
Tipto. Stevinus?
Fly.   Sir, the same, had challenged Euclid   110
  At thirty weapons, more than Archimedes
  E'er saw, and engines: most of his own invention.
Tipto. This may have credit and chimes reason, this!
  If any man endanger Euclid, bird,
  Observe (that had the honour to quit Europe   115
  This forty year) 'tis he. He put down Scaliger!
Fly. And he was a great master.
Beaufort.   Not of fence, Fly.
Tipto. Excuse him, lord, he went o' the same grounds.
Beaufort. On the same earth, I think, with other mortals?
Tipto. I mean, sweet lord, the mathematics. *Basta!*   120
  When thou know'st more, thou wilt take less green
      honour.
  He had his circles, semicircles, quadrants –
Fly. He writ a book o' the quadrature o' the circle.
Tipto. *Cyclometría*, I read –
Beaufort.   The title only.

109. Orange's] *O;* Orange *G.*   111. At . . . weapons,] *Oc;* A . . . weapons
Ou.   115–6. (that . . . year)] *Oc;* that . . . yeare, *Ou, F3.*   121. less]*G;*
lesse, *O.*

---

below suggests that he has left the stage by then, presumably because he is
bored by the conversation. It could equally mean that he has simply moved
away from the group and that no exit is necessary.

110. *Stevinus*] Simon Stevinus (1548–1620) of Bruges, a mathematician,
physicist and inventor of a sluice system and a wagon fitted with sails; he
published nothing on fencing, nor was he known for that skill.

112. *engines*] machines or large weapons (*O.E.D.*, 5a).

113. *chimes*] sounds forth (*O.E.D.*, 1b).

115. *quit*] reward, *O.E.D.*, 10 (with reference to Stevinus); alternatively the
ignorant Tipto may be inferring that Euclid had died only forty years
previously.

116. *Scaliger*] J. J. Scaliger (1540–1609), the great Greek and Latin scholar.
His *Cyclometrica Elementa* (1594) has an appendix on the 'quadrature of the
circle'. His assertions were disputed by Sir Henry Savile whom Jonson
admired. Tipto's admiration of his mathematics is therefore ill-founded.

120. *Basta*] enough (It.).

121. *thou . . . honour*] you will be content only with more judicious acclaim.

124. *Cyclometría*] 'Jonson, as usual, scans by accent; cf. I.v.7n.' (*H.& S.*)
and Tipto has in fact the word wrong.

Latimer. And indice.

Beaufort.   If it had one: of that, *quaere*.   125
            What insolent, half-witted things these are!

Latimer. So are all smatterers, insolent and impudent.

Beaufort. They lightly go together.

Latimer.   'Tis my wonder
            Two animals should hawk at all discourse thus!
            Fly every subject to the mark, or retrieve –   130

Beaufort. And never ha' the luck to be i' the right!

Latimer. 'Tis some folk's fortune!

Beaufort.   Fortune's a bawd
            And a blind beggar; 'tis their vanity,
            And shows most vilely!

Tipto.   I could take the heart, now,
            To write unto Don Lewis into Spain,   135
            To make a progress to the Elysian fields
            Next summer –

Beaufort.   And persuade him die for fame,
            Of fencing with a shadow! Where's mine host?
            I would he had heard this bubble break, i' faith.

ACT II SCENE vi

[*Enter*] HOST [*with*] PRUDENCE [*richly dressed*], FRANK [*as a
            lady*], NURSE, [*and*] LADY [FRAMPUL].

Host. Make place, stand by, for the queen regent,

134. now,] *H.& S.;* now. *O;* now *F3.*
0.1.] *This ed.; Host. Tipto. Prudence. Beaufort. Latimer. Franke. Nurse. Lady.
Flie. Lovel. O.*

---

125. *indice*] *O.E.D.* cites no examples of the word used with the meaning
Latimer infers, 'prefatory matter'. This, however, is a meaning for 'index'
(*O.E.D.*, 5a). The *Cyclometrica* does in fact have a table of contents.
    quaere] imperative of Lat. *quaerere*; i.e. it is to be asked.

126. *insolent*] impertinently familiar (*O.E.D.*, 2).

127. *smatterers*] dabblers; cf. *Disc.*, 231–5.
    impudent] shameless, presumptuous.

128. *lightly*] commonly, often; cf. Shakespeare, *R3*, III.i.94.

129. *hawk at*] fly at.

130. *Fly . . . mark*] a metaphor from hawking (mark = quarry); 'attempt to
discourse learnedly on every subject'; cf. I.iii.110n. and B.F., II.iv.43.
    retrieve] recover sprung game; cf. Arg. 110.´

132–3. *Fortune's . . . beggar*] not in Tilley, although Jonson uses it in *T.of T.*,
II.v.38–9; *Cat.*, V.100; *Und.*, xliii.153; and cf. Shakespeare, *Macbeth*,
I.ii.14–15; *Ham.*, II.ii.232–3; Webster, *The White Devil*, I.i.4.

        gentlemen!
Tipto. This is thy queen that shall be, bird, our sovereign.
Beaufort. Translated Prudence!
Pru.   Sweet my lord, hand off:
        It is not now as when plain Prudence lived
        And reached her ladyship –
Host.   The chamber-pot.   5
Pru. The looking-glass, mine host: lose your house
            metaphor!
        You have a negligent memory indeed;
        Speak the host's language! Here's a young lord
        Will make't a precedent else.
Latimer.   Well acted, Pru.
Host. First minute of her reign! What will she do   10
        Forty years hence, God bless her!
Pru.   If you'll kiss,
        Or compliment, my lord, behold a lady,
        A stranger, and my lady's kinswoman.
Beaufort. I do confess my rudeness, that had need
        To have mine eye directed to this beauty.   15
Frank. It was so little as it asked a perspicil.
Beaufort. Lady, your name?
Frank.   My lord, it is Laetitia.
Beaufort. Laetitia! A fair omen, and I take it.
        Let me have still such Lettice for my lips.
        But that o' your family, Lady?
Frank.   Sylly, sir.   20

6. metaphor!] *G;* Metaphore? *O.*   7. You have] *H.& S.;* you'have *O.*

---

3. *Translated*] transformed; the word could apply specifically to a tailor altering a garment (*O.E.D.*, 4).

4. *It . . . lived*] echoes Kyd, *Sp.Tr.*, 'It is not now as when Andrea lived' (III.xiv.111); further citations in Dudrap (see II.v.82n.); cf. *S.N.*, I.iv.17.

6–8. *lose . . . language*] Pru accuses the Host of forgetting to play his part in a proper and decent manner.

6. *lose*] 'loose' (Jonson's spelling here) and 'lose' are interchangeable at this period.

house metaphor] tavern jest.

9. *Well . . . Pru*] 'The first hint of Lord Latimer's being "taken with her"' (*H.& S.*).

11. *Forty . . . hence*] Queen Elizabeth had reigned for forty-seven years.

16. *perspicil*] optic glass, telescope; cf. *S.N.*, I.i.6.

19. *Lettice . . . lips*] See I.v.6–8n. and III.ii.126n.

still] always.

Beaufort. My lady's kinswoman?

Frank.   I am so honoured.

Host. [*Aside to Lady Frampul.*] Already it takes!

Lady F.   An excellent fine boy.

Nurse. He is descended of a right good stock, sir.

Beaufort. What's this, an antiquary?

Host.   An antiquity

    By the dress, you'd swear! An old Welsh herald's
      widow: 25
    She's a wild Irish born, sir, and a hybrid,
    That lives with this young lady a mile off here,
    And studies Vincent against York.

Beaufort.   She'll conquer

    If she read Vincent. Let me study her.

Host. She's perfect in most pedigrees, most descents.   30

Beaufort. [*Aside.*] A bawd, I hope, and knows to blaze a coat.

Host. And judgeth all things with a single eye.

    [*Aside to Fly.*] Fly, come you hither. No discovery
    Of what you see to your Colonel Toe, or Tip, here,
    But keep all close, though you stand i' the way o'
      preferment,   35
    Seek it off from the road; no flattery for't,

---

22. *Aside . . . Frampul.*] G.   31. *Aside.*] G.   32.1. *Aside to Fly.*] G (*after l.
38*).

---

23. *good stock*] a hint as to Frank's true identity.

26. *hybrid*] mongrel, half-breed (Lat. *hibrida*).

28. *Vincent . . . conquer*] Augustine Vincent published *A Discouerie of
Errours In the . . . Catalogue of Nobility Published by Raphe Brooke, Yorke
Herald, 1619* (London, 1622). Vincent, who was Rouge Rose Pursuivant in
the College and then Windsor Herald, was deputy to Camden, Jonson's
friend (see *Sh.Eng.*, II, 82). Jonson owned a copy of Brooke (McPherson, 29).
'Conquer' translates Lat. *vinco*, giving a punning association with 'Vincent'.

31. *blaze*] blazon, i.e. describe or paint a heraldic device; but the word also
refers tortuously to venereal disease (perhaps suggested by 'descents' in the
above); Brome was to use the pun in *The Antipodes* (1638) where a suspicious
genealogist Blaze watches his wife Barbara turn libertine.

coat] Cf. a bawdy passage in Middleton's *Women Beware Women*: 'your cats
are always safe i'th' chimney-corner, / Unless they burn their coats'
(I.ii.106–7 and note (Revels)).

32. *single eye*] She has a patch on one eye – see V.v.76–8. Cf. Luke, xi.34:
'When thine eye is single, thy whole body also is full of light.'

36. *off from the road*] discreetly.

          No lick-foot, pain of losing your proboscis,
          My lickerish fly.
Tipto.   What says old velvet-head?
Fly. He will present me himself, sir, if you will not.
Tipto. Who? He present? What? Whom? An host? A groom?   40
          Divide the thanks with me? Share in my glories?
          Lay up; I say no more.
Host.   Then silence, sir,
          And hear the sovereign.
Tipto.   Ostlers to usurp
          Upon my Sparta or province, as they say?
          No broom but mine!
Host.   Still, colonel, you mutter!   45
Tipto. I dare speak out, as *cuerpo*.
Fly.   Noble colonel –
Tipto. And carry what I ask –
Host.   Ask what you can, sir,
          So't be i' the house.
Tipto.   I ask my rights and privileges;
          And though for form I please to call't a suit,
          I have not been accustomed to repulse.   50
Pru. No, sweet Sir Glorious, you may still command –
Host. And go without.
Pru.   But yet, sir, being the first,
          And called a suit, you'll look it shall be such

---

          37. *lick-foot*] servility (nonce word).
          37–8. *proboscis . . . lickerish*] 'A quibble: (1) literally *proboskís* "a means of
providing food"; (2) the sucking mouth of a fly . . .' (*H.& S.*). There is also a
bawdy sense from the context. Lickerish = fond of good food (as well as
lustful).
          38. *velvet-head*] The new antlers of deer are covered with down or 'velvet':
the reference can be to cuckoldry but here may be to a hat worn by the Host.
Cf. *Alc.*, I.ii.61; *E.M.I.*, III.iii.34–8.
          42. *Lay up*] go and lie down, i.e. what nonsense.
          44. *Sparta or province*] Sparta was renowned for the valour of its
inhabitants; cf. 'The Cuntrey's Censure' (see Appendix I): 'since thy crazy
muse doth now / To quit her Spartan province faintly know'. (ll. 7–8); cf.
II.i.40n. Contemporary references to Sparta may be pursued in T. J. B.
Spencer's Revels edition of Ford's *The Broken Heart* (Manchester, 1980),
pp. 21ff.
          45. *broom*] puns on *spártos* 'broom'. The joke derives from Aristophanes,
Birds, ll. 813–16.
          46. *as* cuerpo] elliptical for 'as I might to one in *cuerpo*'.
          53. *called*] i.e. having called.

As we may grant.
Lady F.   It else denies itself.
Pru. You hear the opinion of the court.
Tipto.   I mind   55
No court opinions.
Pru.   'Tis my lady's, though.
Tipto. My lady is a spinster at the law,
And my petition is of right.
Pru.   What is it?
Tipto. It is for this poor learned bird.
Host.   The fly?
Tipto. Professor in the inn here of small matters –   60
Latimer. How he commends him!
Host.   As to save himself in him.
Lady F. So do all politics in their commendations.
Host. This is a state-bird, and the verier fly!
Tipto. Hear him problematise.
Pru.   Bless us, what's that?
Tipto. Or syllogise, elenchise.
Lady F.   Sure, petards   65
To blow us up.
Latimer.   Some enginous strong words!
Host. He means to erect a castle i' the air,

66. enginous] G; inginous O.

---

57. *spinster*] 'As all unmarried women from a viscount's daughter downward came under this title, Tipto suggests that Lady Frampul was entitled to
no special privilege in a court of law' (*T.*). Cf. *E.M.O.*, V.xi.32n.
58. *petition . . . right*] an allusion to the Petition of Right framed by Coke
which achieved Charles's assent in 1628; cf. *M.L.*, III.iv.128–9.
61. *As . . . him*] as if Fly might redeem him from his disgrace.
62. *politics*] unscrupulous politicians.
commendations] prayers for the commendation of souls (*O.E.D.*, 6) picking
up the religious quibble in l. 61; also remembrances sent to great persons
(*O.E.D.*, 4).
63. *state-bird*] politician and see II.v.29n.
64. *problematise*] propound problems.
65. *syllogise*] argue by syllogisms.
elenchise] argue by Socratic question and answer – the only example of this
word cited in the *O.E.D.*
petards] small explosive devices, squibs.
66. *enginous*] (1) belonging to an engine (*O.E.D.*, 2) alluding to the 'petards'
above; and (2) deceitful, crafty (*O.E.D.*, 1). The text reads 'inginous' which is
unrecorded in *O.E.D.* Cf. *C.R.*, III.iii.40.
67. *castle i' the air*] a proverb since 1566 (Tilley, C126), but possibly a

And makes his fly an elephant to carry it.
Tipto. Bird of the arts he is, and Fly by name.
Pru. Buzz!
Host.   Blow him off, good Pru, they'll mar all else.   70
Tipto. The sovereign's honour is to cherish learning.
Pru. What, in a fly?
Tipto.   In anything industrious.
Pru. But flies are busy!
Lady F.   Nothing more troublesome,
          Or importune!
Tipto.   There's nothing more domestic,
          Tame, or familiar than your fly in *cuerpo*.   75
Host. That is when his wings are cut, he is tamed indeed,
          else
          Nothing more impudent and greedy; licking –
Lady F. Or saucy, good Sir Glorious.
Pru.   Leave your advocateship,
          Except that we shall call you orator Fly,
          And send you down to the dresser and the dishes.   80
Host. A good flap, that!
Pru.   Commit you to the steam!
Lady F. Or else condemn you to the bottles.
Pru.   And pots.
          There is his quarry.
Host.   He will chirp far better,

77. licking –] *G;* licking: *O.*

---

specific reference to an engraving in Theophilus Schweighardt's *Speculum Sophicum Rhodo-stauroticum* of 1618. This Rosicrucian tract is referred to in *N.W.*, ll. 209–12; and *F.I.*, l. 99: cf. I.v.18–20n. and I.vi.127n.

68. *make . . . carry it*] make too much of a trifle (Erasmus, *Adagia*, 359A, Tilley, F398). The history of the elephant and castle device familiar in pageants and on inn-signs may be pursued in R. Withington, *English Pageantry* (Cambridge, Mass., 1918), I, 66–70; for other references see *E. H.*, I.ii.144–5n. (*H.& S.*) and I.ii.163–4n. (Revels).

70. *Buzz*] Nonsense! With a play on 'Fly'; cf. Shakespeare, *Ham.*, II.ii.388–9; *C.R.*, V.iv.464n.

72ff.] Cf. Mosca on parasites, *Volp.*, III.i.1–33.

73. *busy*] meddlesome.

80. *dresser*] sideboard.

81. *flap*] 'put down'. 'Fly-flaps' were common household implements.

81–4. *steam . . . music*] a possible string of *double entendres*.

83. *quarry*] prey, object.

E

Your bird, below.

Lady F.   And make you finer music.

Pru. His buzz will there become him.

Tipto.   /   Come away.   85
Buzz in their faces: give 'em all the buzz,
Dor in their ears and eyes: hum, dor, and buzz!
I will statuminate and under-prop thee.
If they scorn us, let us scorn them – we'll find
The thoroughfare below, and *quaere* him;   90
Leave these relicts, Buzz; they shall see that I,
Spite of their jeers, dare drink, and with a fly.

                              [*Exeunt* TIPTO *and* FLY.]

Latimer. A fair remove at once of two impertinents!
Excellent Pru, I love thee for thy wit,
No less than state.

Pru.   One must preserve the other.   95

                    [*Enter* LOVEL.]

Lady F. Who's here?

Pru.   O Lovel, madam, your sad servant.

Lady F. Sad? He is sullen still and wears a cloud
About his brows; I know not how to approach him.

Pru. I will instruct you, madam, if that be all:
Go to him and kiss him.

Lady F.   · How, Pru?

Pru.   Go and kiss him,   100

92.1. *Exeunt* . . . FLY.] *G.*   95.1.] *G.*   97. sullen] *F3;* sollen *O.*

---

87. *Dor* . . . *buzz*] 'To give someone the dor' means to ridicule; cf. *E.M.I.*,
IV.viii.139; *Alc.*, I.ii.169–70. Jonson is also alluding to the dor-fly or bumble-
bee.

88. *statuminate*] prop up, support (Lat. *statumino*).

90. *thoroughfare*] i.e. Jug, described in *Pers.* as 'a thoroughfare of news'.
quaere] two syllables; obs. form of 'query'; cf. II.v.125n.

91. *relicts*] forsaken people (*O.E.D.*, 4a) or 'relics', i.e. left-overs (see
O.E.D., 'relic', 3).

93. *impertinents*] presumptuous fellows.

95. *state*] position, dignity.

96. *sad*] grave, serious.

98. *brows*] 'the seat of the facial expressions of joy, sorrow . . . etc.' (*O.E.D.*,
5b).

    I do command it.

Lady F.   Th'art not wild, wench?

Pru.   No,

    Tame and exceeding tame, but still your sovereign.

Lady F. Hath too much bravery made thee mad?

Pru.   Nor proud.

    Do what I do enjoin you. No disputing

    Of my prerogative with a front or frown;   105

    Do not detrect: you know th'authority

    Is mine, and I will exercise it swiftly

    If you provoke me.

Lady F.   I have woven a net

    To snare myself in. – Sir, I am enjoined

    To tender you a kiss: but do not know   110

    Why or wherefore, only the pleasure royal

    Will have it so, and urges – Do not you

    Triumph on my obedience, seeing it forced thus.

    There 'tis.   *[Kisses him.]*

Lovel.   And welcome. [*Aside.*] Was there ever kiss

    That relished thus, or had a sting like this,   115

    Of so much nectar, but with aloes mixed!

Pru. No murmuring nor repining, I am fixed.

Lovel. [*Aside.*] It had, methinks, a quintessence of either,

    But that which was the better drowned the bitter.

    How soon it passed away, how unrecovered!   120

    The distillation of another soul

    Was not so sweet; and till I meet again

    That kiss, those lips, like relish, and this taste,

    Let me turn all consumption, and here waste.

---

114. *Kisses him.*] G.   118. *Aside.*] G.   124. all] *F3;* all, *O.*

---

   101. *wild*] licentious (*O.E.D.*, 7b), demented; see IV.ii.91ff.

   103. *bravery*] splendour, finery (*O.E.D.*, 12).

   105. *front*] expression, look (*O.E.D.*, 3a).

   106. *detrect*] draw back, decline, refuse.

   113. *Triumph on*] be elated by.

   116. *aloes*] plants known for their bitter taste.

   117. *fixed*] firmly resolved (*O.E.D.*, 2).

   118. *quintessence*] the highest power of a natural body, superior to the four elements of which it is comprised. See *Alc.*, I.i.70n. (Revels).

   121. *distillation*] refined essence.

   124. *turn . . . consumption*] be consumed by ardour.

Pru. The royal assent is past, and cannot alter.   125
Lady F. You'll turn a tyrant.
Pru.   Be you not a rebel,
    It is a name alike-odious.
Lady F. You'll hear me?
Pru.   No, not o' this argument.
    Would you make laws, and be the first that break 'em?
    The example is pernicious in a subject,   130
    And of your quality, most.
Latimer.   Excellent princess!
Host. Just queen!
Latimer.   Brave sovereign!
Host.   A she-Trajan, this!
Beaufort. What is't? Proceed, incomparable Pru:
    I am glad I am scarce at leisure to applaud thee.
Latimer. It's well for you, you have so happy expressions.   135
Lady F. Yes, cry her up with acclamations, do,
    And cry me down; run all with sovereignty:
    Prince Power will never want her parasites.
Pru. Nor Murmur her pretences: Master Lovel,
    For so your libel here or bill of complaint,   140
    Exhibited in our high court of sovereignty
    At this first hour of our reign, declares
    Against this noble lady a disrespect
    You have conceived, if not received, from her.
Host. Received; so the charge lies in our bill.   145

126. tyrant] *1716;* Tyran *O.*

───

  126. *tyrant*] Jonson customarily wrote 'tyran' presumably because it was
closer to Lat. *tyrannus*; see *T.of T.*, II.iv.52 etc.; cf. I.iii.53n.
  127. *alike*-] a late example of this obsolete adverbial use.
  129. *Would . . . 'em?*] Cf. Tilley, L118, 'They that make laws must not break
them.'
  131. *of . . . quality*] in a man of your rank.
  132. *she-Trajan*] Trajan was Roman Emperor from A.D. 98–117 and famous
for the justness of his reign. After his reign emperors were saluted with the
phrase *Augusto felicior, melior Traiano* ('More fortunate than Augustus,
better than Trajan').
  134. *I am glad . . . thee*] Beaufort is wooing Frank; cf. l. 189.
  138. *Prince*] used for sovereigns of either sex (*O.E.D.*, 1b).
  139. *Murmur*] complaint, grumbling (*O.E.D.*, 2a).
  pretences] false claims (*O.E.D.*, 3b).
  140. *libel*] in civil law 'The writing or document of the plaintiff containing
his allegations and instituting a suit' (*O.E.D.*).

Pru. We see it, his learned counsel, leave your plaining.
    We that do love our justice above all
    Our other attributes, and have the nearness
    To know your extraordinary merit,
    As also to discern this lady's goodness,   150
    And find how loath she'd be to lose the honour
    And reputation she hath had, in having
    So worthy a servant, though but for few minutes,
    Do here enjoin –
Host.   Good!
Pru.   Charge, will, and command
    Her ladyship, pain of our high displeasure   155
    And the committing an extreme contempt
    Unto the court, our crown, and dignity –
Host. Excellent sovereign, and egregious Pru!
Pru. To entertain you for a pair of hours
    (Choose when you please, this day) with all respects   160
    And valuation of a principal servant,
    To give you all the titles, all the privileges,
    The freedoms, favours, rights she can bestow –
Host. Large, ample words, of a brave latitude!
Pru. Or can be expected, from a lady of honour   165
    Or quality, in discourse, access, address –
Host. [*Aside.*]   Good.
Pru. Not to give ear, or admit conference
    With any person but yourself; nor there,
    Of any other agrument but love,
    And the companion of it, genteel courtship.   170
    For which two hours' service you shall take
    Two kisses.
Host.   Noble!
Pru.   For each hour a kiss

153. minutes,] *This ed.;* minutes. *O;* minutes – *H.& S.*   166. Host.] *This ed.;* (Hos. *O.*   170. genteel] *This ed.;* gentile *O.*

---

146. *plaining*] complaining.

148. *nearness*] intimacy, friendship.

158. *egregious*] distinguished, renowned.

164. *latitude*] extent, scope.

166. *address*] courtship to a lady (*O.E.D.*, 9).

168. *there*] when you are present.

170. *genteel*] noble – without ironic implications; for Jonson's spelling after the Lat. *gentilis* see *C.R.*, Ind. 116n.; cf. I.iii.53n. and 126n. above.

To be ta'en freely, fully, and legally,
Before us, in the court here and our presence.

Host.   Rare!

Pru. But those hours past, and the two kisses paid,   175
The binding caution is, never to hope
Renewing of the time or of the suit
On any circumstance.

Host.   A hard condition!

Latimer. Had it been easier, I should have suspected
The sovereign's justice.

Host.   O you are servant,   180
My lord, unto the lady, and a rival:
In point of law, my lord, you may be challenged.

Latimer. I am not jealous!

Host.   Of so short a time
Your lordship needs not, and being done *in foro*.

Pru. What is the answer?

Host.   He craves respite, madam,   185
To advise with his learned counsel.

Pru.   Be you he,
And go together quickly.   [*Lovel and Host walk aside.*]

Lady F.   You are no tyrant?

Pru. If I be, madam, you were best appeal me.

Latimer. Beaufort –

Beaufort.   I am busy; prithee let me alone;
I have a cause in hearing too.   190

Latimer.   At what bar?

Beaufort. Love's court o' requests.

---

187. *Lovel . . . aside.*] G.   tyrant] G; Tyron O.

---

176. *caution*] 'Security given for the performance of some engagement' (*O.E.D.*, 1). Here Jonson may be referring to the first sort of surety in ecclesiastical law, the *cautio fidejussoria.* See E. Gibson, *Codex Juris Ecclesiastici Anglicani* (London, 1758 ed.), 1063.

182. *challenged*] objected to.

183. *I . . . jealous*] Latimer is taken with Pru.

183–4. *Of . . . needs*] the obs. constr. 'to need of' = have need of (*O.E.D.*, 6).

184. in foro] in open court; cf. *M.L.*, Ind. 83.

186. *advise*] consider, consult (*O.E.D.*, 3).

188. *appeal*] challenge, impeach (*O.E.D.*, 1).

191. *court of requests*] 'A former court of record, technically forming part of the king's council, held by the Lord Privy Seal, and the Masters of Requests for the relief of persons petitioning the king' (*O.E.D.*).

Latimer.   Bring't into the sovereignty;
 It is the nobler court, afore Judge Pru,
 The only learned mother of the law,
 And lady o' conscience, too!
Beaufort.   'Tis well enough
 Before this mistress of requests, where it is.   195
Host. Let 'em not scorn you. Bear up, Master Lovel,
 And take your hours and kisses. They are a fortune.
Lovel. Which I cannot approve, and less make use of.
Host. Still i' this cloud! Why cannot you make use of?
Lovel. Who would be rich to be so soon undone?   200
 The beggar's best is wealth he doth not know,
 And but to show it him inflames his want.
Host. Two hours at height?
Lovel.   That joy is too, too narrow
 Would bound a love so infinite as mine;
 And being past, leaves an eternal loss.   205
 Who so prodigiously affects a feast
 To forfeit health and appetite to see it?
 Or but to taste a spoonful, would forgo
 All gust of delicacy ever after?
Host. These, yet, are hours of hope.
Lovel.   But all hours following,   210
 Years of despair, ages of misery!
 Nor can so short a happiness but spring
 A world of fear with thought of losing it.
 Better be never happy, than to feel

---

192. *sovereignty*] power, jurisdiction (i.e. Pru's court).

194. *conscience*] The Court of Requests was also called the Court of Conscience: see *O.E.D.*, 'court' 11c; and Middleton, *A Mad World my Masters*, I.i.125.

198. *approve*] put to the test (*O.E.D.*, 8).

199. *cloud*] gloom.

203. *Two . . . height*] 'You are not tempted by two hours of the most intense love?'

 too, too] 'very common *c.* 1540–1660' (*O.E.D.*).

204. *bound*] contain.

206. *prodigiously affects*] immensely desires. *O.E.D.* records this colloquial use of 'prodigiously' only from 1664.

209. *gust*] taste.

 delicacy] delight, something that gratifies the palate or sensuality (*O.E.D.*, 12).

212. *spring*] start (*O.E.D.*, 21).

A little of it, and then lose it ever.   215
Host. I do confess it is a strict injunction;
      But then the hope is, it may not be kept.
      A thousand things may intervene. We see
      The wind shift often, thrice a day sometimes;
      Decrees may alter upon better motion   220
      And riper hearing. The best bow may start,
      And th' hand may vary. Pru may be a sage
      In law, and yet not sour; sweet Pru, smooth Pru,
      Soft debonair, and amiable Pru
      May do as well as rough and rigid Pru;   225
      And yet maintain her venerable Pru,
      Majestic Pru, and serenissimous Pru.
      Try but one hour first, and as you like
      The loose o' that, draw home and prove the other.
Lovel. If one hour could the other happy make,   230
      I should attempt it.
Host.   Put it on, and do.
Lovel. Or in the blest attempt that I might die!
Host. Ay, marry, there were happiness indeed,
      Transcendent to the melancholy meant.
      It were a fate above a monument   235
      And all inscription to die so; a death
      For emperors to énjoy, and the kings
      Of the rich East to pawn their regions for,

237. énjoy] *O;* envy *conj. H.& S.*

---

220. *motion*] legal application.
221. *hearing*] punning on its legal sense.
start] warp; cf. Tilley, B561.
222. *sage*] punning on 'sage', the herb.
223. *sour*] bitter, harsh.
226. *venerable*] respected.
227. *serenissimous*] 'most famous, a terme applyed to Kings' (Cockeram). This and Jonson's example are the only two recorded in *O.E.D.*
229. *loose . . . other*] loose = (1) upshot; (2) the act of discharging an arrow which suggests the quibble 'draw home', i.e. as far as it will go.
prove] try.
231. *put it on*] set forward, advance (*O.E.D.*, 'put' 46h).
do] act, exert yourself.
232–3.] the familiar bawdy quibble on 'die' (ejaculate).
234. *meant*] which you intended.
237. *énjoy*] accented on the first syllable as in *C.is A.*, 'To enjoy nothing vnderneath the sonne' (III.iii.32). But *H.& S.* conjecture 'envy'.

To show their treasure, open all their mines,
Spend all their spices to embalm their corps,   240
And wrap the inches up in sheets of gold,
That fell by such a noble destiny!
And for the wrong to your friend, that fear's away:
He rather wrongs himself, following fresh light,
New eyes to swear by. If Lord Beaufort change,   245
It is no crime in you to remain constant.
And upon these conditions, at a game
So urged upon you.
Pru.   Sir, your resolution –
Host. How is the lady affected?
Pru.   Sovereigns use not
To ask their subjects' suffrage where 'tis due,   250
But where conditional.
Host.   A royal sovereign!
Latimer. And a rare stateswoman. I admire her bearing
In her new regiment.
Host.   Come, choose your hours,
Better be happy for a part of time,
Than not the whole; and a short part, than never.   255
Shall I appoint 'em, pronounce for you?
Lovel.   Your pleasure.
Host. Then he designs his first hour after dinner,
His second after supper. Say ye? Content?
Pru. Content.
Lady F.   I am content.
Latimer.   Content.
Frank.   Content.
Beaufort. What's that? I am content too.
Latimer.   You have reason,   260

239. show] *H.& S.*, sow *O.*   246. constant,] *This ed.;* constant. *O.*

---

240. *corps*] obs. form of corpses; cf. III.ii.97.
241. *inches*] perhaps connected with *O.E.D.*, 3d, meaning 'stature' so that 'the inches' would be 'tall men'; or with a bawdy quibble.
244. *fresh light*] another love (cf. the phrase 'the light of one's eye' = loved one).
249. *affected*] inclined.
250. *suffrage*] support, approval.
253. *regiment*] office, function (*O.E.D.*, 2a).
257. *designs*] designates, appoints.

You had it on the by, and we observed it.

Nurse. Trot' I am not content: in fait' I am not.

Host. Why art not thou content, good Shelee-nien?

Nurse. He tauk so desperate, and so debausht,
  So bawdy like a courtier and a lord,   265
  God bless him, one that taketh tobacco.

Host.   Very well mixed!
  What did he say?

Nurse.   Nay, nothing to the purposh,
  Or very little, nothing at all to purposh.

Host. Let him alone, Nurse.

Nurse.   I did tell him of Serly
  Was a great family come out of Ireland,   270
  Descended of O'Neill, Mac Con, Mac Dermot,
  Mac Murrogh, but he marked not.

Host.   Nor do I;
  Good queen of heralds, ply the bottle and sleep.

              [*Exeunt.*]

---

271. O'Neill] *This ed.;* ONeale O.

---

261. *on the by*] not intentionally; cf. I.iii.1.1n.; *Cat.*, III.377n.

262ff.] For other examples of stage Irish see Captain Whit in *B.F.*, III.i; the *Irish Masque*; Captain Macmorris in Shakespeare, *H5*, III.ii; and Bryan in Dekker's *2 Honest Whore*; the type may be pursued in 'The Origin of Bulls' in W. J. Lawrence, *Speeding up Shakespeare* (London, 1937) pp. 144–58.

263. *Shelee-nien*] Cf. III.ii.8; IV.iv.341. 'Irish *Sile*, i.e. Celia, used also as the equivalent of Julia; *-nien, -neen* is the Irish *nighean*, a common form of *inghean*, "daughter". *Sheleen-nien Thomas* [*sic*] in IV.iv.234, V.v.28, and in our text of V.iii.3, is "Sile, Thomas's daughter"' (*H.& S.*).

264. *debausht*] drunken pronunciation of 'deboshed', a variant of 'debauched'.

266. *mixed*] inebriated, muzzy (?). *O.E.D.* records examples only from the nineteenth century.

269–72. *Serly . . . Mac Murrogh*] Jonson may have made up the names but some identification is possible.

269. *Serly*] Sorley Boy (*Somhairle Buidhe*, fair-haired Charles), chief of the Macdonnells, in fact come from Scotland. His family was slaughtered by Essex on the island of Rathlin in 1575. He submitted to Elizabeth in 1586.

271. *O'Neill*] probably Con Bacach, first Earl of Tyrone (1484?–1559?), a rebel who eventually became privy councillor of Ireland.

Mac Con] There was a Gaelic king, Conn of the Hundred Battles, who reigned about A.D. 150.

Mac Dermot] probably Diarmaid MacMurchada (Dermot MacMurrough) 1110?–71), a king of Leinster, who claimed sovereignty over all Ireland. A

Mac Dermot was chief of Moylurg in the reign of King John.

272. *Mac Murrough*] an Irish chief (1356–1417). 'The sept of which he was the head was so numerous and important that the name of "Cavanagh's country" was applied to districts occupied by them, which are now comprised in the counties of Carlow, Wexford, and Wicklow' (*D.N.B.*).

Act III

ACT III SCENE i

[*Enter*] TIPTO, FLY, [*and*] JUG.

[*Tipto.*] I like the plot of your militia well;
    It is a fine militia, and well ordered,
    And the division's neat! 'Twill be desired
    Only th'expressions were a little more Spanish:
    For there's the best militia o' the world!   5
    To call 'em *tertias* – *tertia* of the kitchen,
    The *tertia* of the cellar, *tertia* of the chamber,
    And *tertia* of the stables.
Fly.   That I can, sir,
    And find out very able, fit commanders
    In every *tertia*.
Tipto.   Now you are i' the right!   10
    As i' the *tertia* o' the kitchen, yourself
    Being a person elegant in sauces,
    There to command as prime *maestro del campo*,
    Chief master of the palate, for that *tertia*;
    Or the cook under you, 'cause you are the marshal,   15
    And the next officer i' the field to the host.

0.1.] *This ed.; Tipto. Flie. Iug. Peirce. Iordan. Ferret. Trundle. O.*   4. th'
expressions] *This ed.;* the'expressions *O.*   9. commanders] *G;* comman-
ders. *O.*

---

    1. *plot*] plan (*O.E.D.*, 5).
    4. *only*] The expected 'that' following is omitted.
    Spanish] Tipto's humour is to overvalue all things Spanish.
    6. *tertias*] Latinisation of Sp. *tercio*, a division of infantry.
    12. *elegant*] correct and delicate of taste, although *O.E.D.*, 6, records this
meaning only from 1667.
    13. maestro del campo] See II.iv.29n.
    15. *marshal*] officer of unspecified rank, often in charge of armies in the
field.

128

Then for the cellar, you have young Anon,
Is a rare fellow – what's his other name?

Fly. Pierce, sir.

Tipto.   Sir Pierce, I'll ha' him a cavalier.
Sir Pierce Anon will pierce us a new hogshead!   20
And then your thoroughfare, Jug here, his *alferez*:
An able officer. Gi' me thy beard, round Jug;
I take thee by this handle, and do love
One of thy inches! In the chambers, Jordan here:
He is the *don del campo* o' the beds.   25
And for the stables, what's his name?

Fly.   Old Peck.

Tipto. *Maestro del campo* Peck! His name is curt,
A monosyllabe, but commands the horse well.

Fly. O, in an inn, sir, we have other horse.
Let those troops rest a while. Wine is the horse   30
That we must charge with here.

Tipto.   Bring up the troops,
Or call, sweet Fly; 'tis an exact militia,
And thou an exact professor; Lipsius Fly
Thou shalt be called, and Jouse –

22. Gi' me] *F3;* giu'me *O.*

---

19. *cavalier*] horseman, knight (*O.E.D.*, 1).

21. *alferez*] ensign, standard-bearer (Sp.).

22. *beard*] like that on a bearded drinking-jug, see I.iv. 13–14n.

24. *inches*] stature; cf. II.vi.241n.

Jordan] chamber-pot (extending the conceit on 'Jug').

25. don . . . beds] Jordan vaunts his prowess as a lover – see IV.i.6–7 and 24–5; *don del campo* means 'gentleman of the field', not a specific rank.

27. *curt*] the first recorded use in *O.E.D.*

28. *monosyllabe*] spelt and pronounced (with five syllables) by Jonson after Gk. *syllabé*; cf. I.iii.53n.

29. *horse*] another horse/whores joke; cf. II.iii.18n.

31. *Bring . . . troops*] bring wine.

32. *exact*] accomplished (*O.E.D.*, 2).

33. *Lipsius Fly*] In Franciscus Scribanus' *Muscae Principatus* included in Dornavius' *Amphitheatrum Sapientiae* (Hanover, 1619; McPherson, 52) there is a reference (p. 120) to Lipsius' *Politicorum Libri Sex.* V.vi, which describes the necessity of money, provisions and arms for waging war. *H.&* S., however, refer to a note in Lipsius' *Antiquae Lectiones*, III.i, p. 83, explaining the use of *musca* in Plautus. The reference could scarcely be more obscure. Perhaps the joke is based simply on the resemblance between 'lips' and Lipsius as it is in Middleton, *The Changeling*, III.iii.179 (Revels).

34. *Jouse*] 'Lipsius's name was Joest, Juste, or Josse Lips; there may be a

[*Enter* FERRET *and* TRUNDLE.]

Jack Ferret, welcome,
Old trench-master, and colonel o' the pioneers,   35
What canst thou bolt us now: a cony or two
Out of Tom Trundle's burrow here, the coach?
This is the master of the carriages!
How is thy driving, Tom, good as't was?
Trundle. It serves my lady, and our officer Pru.   40
Twelve mile an hour! Tom has the old trundle still.
Tipto. I am taken with the family here, fine fellows,
Viewing the muster-roll.
Trundle.   They are brave men.
Ferret. And of the Fly-blown discipline all, the quartermaster!
Tipto. The Fly's a rare bird in his profession.   45
Let's sip a private pint with him: I would have him
Quit this light sign of the Light Heart, my bird,
And lighter house. It is not for his tall
And growing gravity, so cedar-like,
To be the second to an host *in cuerpo*   50
That knows no elegancies. Use his own
Dictamen and his genius: I would have him
Fly high and strike at all.

[*Enter* PIERCE.]
Here's young Anon too.

34.1 *Enter* . . . TRUNDLE.] *G.*   51. elegancies.] *This ed.; elegancies, O;*
elegancies – *H.& S.*   53.1. *Enter* PIERCE.] *G.*

---

quibble on *jowse*, juice, i.e. of the grape' (*H.& S.*).

35. *pioneers*] 'they are the Pioners of the Campe, that are imployed onely
(like Moles) in casting vp of earth and digging of trenches' (Dekker, *N.D.*, I,
110).

36. *bolt*] spring or ferret out (*O.E.D.*, v.2.4b).

cony] (1) rabbit; (2) dupe; (3) whore (*O.E.D.*, 5b).

37. *burrow*] punning on barrow; Tipto is mocking Trundle's coach.

43. *muster-roll*] list of men.

44. *Fly-blown . . . quartermaster*] the officer responsible for rations. A bad
one might provide fly-blown meat.

48. *lighter*] disreputable, unfashionable.

49. *cedar-like*] The cedar is the tallest of plants in 1 Kings iv.33.

52. Dictamen] dictate, pronouncement; cf. IV.iv.79.

53. *strike at*] dart at and seize like a falcon (*O.E.D.*, 39).

Pierce. What wine is't, gentlemen, white or claret?

Tipto.   White,

My brisk Anon.

Pierce.   I'll draw you Juno's milk   55

That dyed the lilies, colonel.

Tipto.   Do so, Pierce.

[*Exit* PIERCE.]

[*Enter* PECK.]

Peck. A plague of all jades, what a clap he has gi'en me!

Fly. Why, how now, cousin?

Tipto.   Who is that?

Ferret.   The ostler.

Fly. What ail'st thou, cousin Peck? [*Takes him aside.*]

Peck.   O me, o my haunches!

As sure as you live, sir, he knew perfectly   60

I meant to cozen him. He did leer so on me,

And then he sneered as who would say, 'Take heed,
    sirrah';

And when he saw our half-peck, which you know

Was but an old court-dish, lord, how he stamped!

I thought 't had been for joy. When suddenly   65

He cuts me a back caper with his heels,

And takes me just o' the crupper. Down come I

54–5. White,/ My . . . milk] *G;* claret?/ *Tip.* White . . . *Anone.*/ *Pei.* Ile . . .
milke. *O.*   56.1. *Exit* PIERCE] *G.*   *Enter* PECK.] *G.*   58. Who is] *H.& S.;*
Who's *O.*   *Ferret.* The ostler.] *A separate line in O.*   59. *Takes . . . aside.*]
G.

55–6. *Juno's . . . lilies*] 'Lilies were sacred to Juno, as being made white with
her milk that fell upon the earth when Jove took Hercules away, whom by
stealth he had laid to her breast' (Jonson's note to *Hym.*, l. 219).

57–168.] For Fletcher's adaptation of these lines in *Love's Pilgrimage*, see
Appendix II.

57. *jades*] (1) vicious or ill-tempered horse; (2) whore, hussy.

clap] (1) blow; (2) gonorrhea.

62. *as . . . say*] as if one said; Partridge, *Syntax*, § 58.

64. *court-dish*] apparently means short allowance; see Dekker, *1 Honest
Whore*: 'three court dishes . . . and not one good bit in them' (II.i).
Alternatively a court-dish may have been a collection of scraps; see G.
Goodman, *The Court of James I* (London, 1839): 'The King . . . caused his
carver to cut him a court-dish, that is something of every dish . . .' (I, 311),
cited *O.E.D.*, which dates the quotation 1655.

67. *crupper*] buttocks (originally of a horse); *O.E.D.*, 3.

And my whole ounce of oats! Then he neighed out,
As if he had a mare by the tail.

Fly.   Troth, cousin.
You are to blame to use the poor dumb Christians   70
So cruelly, defraud 'em o' their *dimensum*.
Yonder's the colonel's horse (there I looked in)
Keeping our Lady's eve! The divel a bit
He has got, sin' he came in yet! There he stands,
And looks and looks, but 'tis your pleasure, coz,   75
He should look lean enough.

Peck.   He has hay before him.

Fly. Yes, but as gross as hemp, and as soon will choke him
Unless he eat it buttered. H' had four shoes,
And good ones, when he came in: it is a wonder
With standing still he should cast three.

Peck.   Troth, quartermaster,   80
This trade is a kind of mystery that corrupts
Our standing manners quickly: once a week
I meet with such a brush to mollify me,
Sometimes a brace, to awake my conscience,
Yet still I sleep securely.

Fly.   Cousin Peck,   85
You must use better dealing, faith, you must.

Peck. Troth, to give good example to my successors,
I could be well content to steal but two girths,

74. sin'] *F3;* sin'e *O.*   76. He should . . . him.] *H.& S.;* He should . . .
enough./ *Pec.* . . . him. *O.*

---

70. *Christians*] The word was used at this time for a 'human being' (as
opposed to an animal or beast) *O.E.D.*, 3a.

71. dimensum] fixed allowance.

73. *our . . . eve*] the eve of the Annunciation (25 March) was, like all saints'
days, a day of fasting.

77. *choke*] like the hempen rope of the hangman.

78. *buttered*] Cf. Shakespeare, *Lr.*, II.iv.123–4: ''Twas her brother that, in
pure kindness to his horse, butter'd his hay.' Horses dislike grease and would
reject hay that had been 'buttered' so that the ostler could steal it.

81. *mystery*] (1) something inexplicable; (2) skilled trade.

82. *standing*] (1) customary, established (*O.E.D.*, 16 & 17); (2) of a horse in
its stall.

83. *brush*] setback (*O.E.D.*, 'brush' sb.3,2).

mollify] Cf. the phrase 'to mollify the fist' which *O.E.D.* records from 1698
meaning to 'grease the palm'.

And now and then a saddle-cloth, change a bridle
For exercise, and stay there.

Fly.   If you could,   90
There were some hope on you, coz. But the fate is
You are drunk so early you mistake whole saddles,
Sometimes a horse.

Peck.   Ay, there's –

                 [*Enter* PIERCE *with wine*.]

Fly.   The wine. Come, coz.
I'll talk with you anon.

                            [*They return to the others*.]

Peck.   Do, lose no time,
Good quartermaster.

Tipto.   There are the horse come, Fly.   95

Fly. Charge in, boys, in.

                 [*Enter* JORDAN.]
                 Lieutenant o' the ordnance,
Tobacco and pipes.

Tipto.   Who's that? Old Jordan! Good.
A comely vessel, and a necessary.
New-scoured he is. Here's to thee, marshal Fly;
In milk, my young Anon says.   [*Drinks*.]

Pierce.   Cream o' the grape,   100
That dropped from Juno's breasts and sprung the lily!
I can recite your fables, Fly. Here is too
The blood of Venus, mother o' the rose!   [*Music within*.]

92. You are] *G;* you 'are *O.*   93.1. *Enter . . . wine*.] *G.*   93–5.
Sometimes . . . coz,/ I'll . . . time,/ Good . . . Fly.] *W;* Sometimes . . .
there's – / *Fli.* The . . . anone./ *Pec.* Doe . . . Master./ *Tip.* . . . Flie.
O.   94. *They . . . others*.] *This ed.; They come forward. G.*   96.1. *Enter*
JORDAN] *G.*   96. ordnance] *This ed.;* ordinance *O.*   97. that? . . . Good.]
O; that? *Fly.* Old Jordan. *Tip.* Good. *conj. W.*   99. marshal] *G;* Martiall
O.   100. *Drinks*.] *G.*   103. *Music within*.] *G.*

89. *saddle-cloth*] placed on a horse's back beneath the saddle.
90. *stay there*] leave it at that.
92. *mistake*] purloin (*O.E.D.*, 1).
98. *vessel*] A jordan was a chamber pot.
100. *milk*] white wine (cf. *Liebfraumilch*); see l. 55 above.
101. *Juno . . lily*] See l. 55n. above.
103. *blood . . . rose*] red wine. *The Pervigilium Veneris*, l.20, says of the rose,
'facta Cypridis de cruore' (made from the blood of Venus), and the legend of

Jordan. The dinner is gone up.

Jug.   I hear the whistle.

Jordan. Ay, and the fiddlers. We must all go wait.   105

Pierce. Pox o' this waiting, quartermaster Fly.

Fly. When chambermaids are sovereigns, wait their ladies;

  Fly scorns to breathe –

Peck.   Or blow upon them, he.

Pierce. Old parcel Peck, art thou there? How now, lame?

Peck. Yes, faith: it is still halting afore cripples;   110

  I ha' got a dash of jade here, will stick by me.

Pierce. O you have had some phant'sie, fellow Peck,

  Some revelation –

Peck.   What?

Pierce.   To steal the hay

  Out o' the racks again.

Fly.   I told him so,

  When the guests' backs were turned.

Pierce.   Or bring his peck   115

  The bottom upwards, heaped with oats; and cry,

  'Here's the best measure upon all the road!' When,

  You know, the guest put in his hand to feel

  And smell to the oats, that grated all his fingers

---

114. again.] *This ed.;* againe: *O.*   118. know, the guest] *G;* know the ghest, *O.*

Adonis records that a white rose was stained by blood from Venus' foot as she ran to help her lover; see Spenser, *Daphnaida*, ll. 108–9.

  104. *gone up*] from the kitchens.

  whistle] to call the servants.

  105. *fiddlers*] 'musicke in *Tauerns* makes that wine go downe merily, till it confound vs, which (if the *Fidlers* were not there) would hardly be tasted' (Dekker, *N.D.*, III, 312). Tavern fiddlers were generally despised – see *B.F.*, I.iii.4.

  108. *blow*] lay eggs (obscene); cf. l. 44n. above.

  109. *parcel*] because he gave short measure (a parcel peck = a small amount); cf. *E.M.I.*, III.vii.93, 'parcell of a souldier'; and *Poet.*, III.iv.160n.

  110. *ill . . . cripples*] Tilley, H60; 'it is difficult to gull those who are as wily as yourself'; cf. Chaucer, *Troilus and Criseyde*, IV.1457–8: 'It is ful hard to halten unespyed / Bifore a crepil, for he can the craft' and *T.of T.*, II.vi.5.

  111. *dash*] blow, affliction, depression (*O.E.D.*, 1 & 3).

  112. *phant'sie*] See I.iv.17n., V.v.120–2n.

  115–16. *bring . . . upwards*] bring the container upside-down with oats piled on the bottom, contained by the rim.

  119. *smell to*] smell (*O.E.D.*, 6).

Upo' the wood –
Peck.   Mum!
Pierce.   And found out your cheat.   120
Peck. I ha' been in the cellar, Pierce.
Pierce.   You were then there,
 Upo' your knees, I do remember it,
 To ha' the fact concealed. I could tell more:
 Soaping of saddles, cutting of horse tails,
 And cropping – pranks of ale and hostelry –   125
Fly. Which he cannot forget, he says, young knight,
 No more than you can other deeds of darkness,
 Done i' the cellar.
Tipto.   Well said, bold professor.
Ferret. We shall ha' some truth explained.
Pierce.   We are all mortal,
 And have our visions.
Peck.   Truly, it seems to me,   130
 That every horse has his whole peck, and tumbles
 Up to the ears in litter.
Fly.   When, indeed,
 There's no such matter, not a smell of provender.
Ferret. Not so much straw as would tie up a horse-tail!
Fly. Nor anything i' the rack but two old cobwebs   135
 And so much rotten hay as had been a hen's nest.
Trundle. And yet he's ever apt to sweep the mangers!
Ferret. But puts in nothing.
Pierce.   These are fits and fancies
 Which you must leave, good Peck.
Fly.   And you must pray
 It may be revealed to you at some times   140

---

124. *horse*] an uninflected genitive; Partridge, *Accidence*, § 12.II.

127. *deeds of darkness*] skulduggery or carnal acts; cf. 'the act of darkness' of Shakespeare, *Lr.*, III.iv.84.

130. *visions*] See V.v.120–2n.; the moment anticipates and parodies Lovel's 'vision' of Lady Frampul's beauty in IV.iv.1ff.

132. *litter*] straw.

134. *straw . . . horse–tail*] Horses' tails were plaited up with straw either for fashion to keep them out of the harness. I am told that in Kent this sometimes indicated the horse was for sale.

138. *fits and fancies*] 'Cf. the title of A. Copley's *Wits Fittes and Fancies*, 1595 . . .' (H.& S.); and see I.iv.17n.

140. *at some times*] Partridge, *Accidence*, § 55.

Whose horse you ought to cozen; with what conscience;
The how, and when. A parson's horse may suffer –
Pierce. Whose master's double beneficed; put in that.
Fly. A little greasing i' the teeth; 'tis wholesome,
And keeps him in a sober shuffle.
Pierce.   His saddle too   145
May want a stirrup.
Fly.   And, it may be sworn,
His learning lay o' one side, and so broke it.
Peck. They have ever oats i' their cloak-bags to affront us.
Fly. And therefore 'tis an office meritorious
To tithe such soundly.
Pierce.   And a grazier's may –   150
Ferret. O they are pinching puckfists!
Trundle.   And suspicious –
Pierce. Suffer before the master's face, sometimes.
Fly. He shall think he sees his horse eat half a bushel –
Pierce. When the sleight is, rubbing his gums with salt
Till all the skin come off, he shall but mumble   155
Like an old woman that were chewing brawn,
And drop 'em out again.
Tipto.   Well argued, cavalier.
Fly. It may do well, and go for an example.
But, coz, have care of understanding horses,

142–3. *parson's . . . beneficed*] A way of evading the law which prohibited the
holding of more than one benefice was to pretend to buy something like a
horse from a patron; see Harington's *Epigrams* (1628), iv.39.

144. *greasing . . . teeth*] a common ostlers' trick to prevent the horses from
eating; see Dekker, *N.D.*, III, 297; Beaumont, *The Knight of the Burning
Pestle* (ed. Hattaway), II.370.

148. *cloak-bags*] portmanteaux, valises.

150. *grazier's*] those who graze or feed cattle for market, proverbial for their
greed; see Stubbes, *An Anatomy of Abuses* (1583), ch. ii; 'greedie grasiers . . .
who hauing raked togither infinite pasture, feed all themselves, and will not
sell for anie reasonable gaine' (cited *O.E.D.*). Fletcher inveighs against them
frequently: see *Wit at Several Weapons* (1609), I.ii; *The Woman's Prize*
(1611), IV.ii; *Wit Without Money* (1614), I.i; *The Pilgrim* (1621), I.ii
(collected by Baldwin Maxwell, *Studies in Beaumont, Fletcher, and Massinger*,
p. 115n.).

151. *puckfists*] properly windballs and so empty braggarts, as in *E.M.O.*,
I.ii.159; but here 'close-fisted', 'miserly'.

155. *mumble*] chew as with toothless gums.

156. *brawn*] pickled or potted flesh of a boar.

159. *understanding*] a quibble; cf. Ded. 12n.

Horses with angry heels, nobility horses,   160
Horses that know the world; let them have meat
Till their teeth ache, and rubbing till their ribs
Shine like a wench's forehead. They are divels else,
Will look into your dealings.
Peck.   For mine own port,
The next I cozen o' the pampered breed,   165
I wish he may be founder'd.
Fly.   Foun-der-ed:
Prolate it right.
Peck.   And of all four, I wish it;
I love no crupper compliments.
Pierce.   Whose horse was it?
Peck. Why, Master Burst's.
Pierce.   Is Bat Burst come?
Peck.   An hour
He has been here.
Tipto.   What Burst?
Pierce.   Mas. Bartholmew Burst,   170
One that hath been a citizen, since a courtier,
And now a gamester: hath had all his whirls
And bouts of fortune, as a man would say,
Once a bat and ever a bat! A reremouse
And bird o' twilight, he has broken thrice.   175
Tipto. Your better man, the Genoway proverb says:

166. Foun-der-ed] *H.& S.;* Foun-de-red *O;* Founder-ed *G.*   169–70.
Peck. . . . hour/ He . . . Burst,] *G; Pec.* Why . . . come?/ *Pec.* An . . . heere./
Tip. What . . . Burst. *O.*   170. Mas. Bartholmew] *This ed.;* Mas. Bar-
tolmew *O;* Bartolmew *conj. H.& S.*

---

161. *meat*] food.
166. *founder'd*] affected with founder, lame.
167. *prolate*] bring out, lengthen in utterance.
four] i.e. legs.
168. *crupper*] See l. 67 above.
compliments] here 'kicks' – see l. 59 above.
170. *Mas.*] 'a vulgar or jocular shortening of *master*' (*O.E.D.,*); see *T.of T.,*
II.ii.76n.
Bartholmew] accented on the first syllable.
174. *Once . . . ever a bat*] Cf. the proverb 'Once a knave and ever a knave'
(Tilley, K133).
reremouse] bat; cf. I.ii.42.
175. *broken*] become bankrupt (*O.E.D.,* 11b).
176–7. *Genoway . . . steel*] 'The Genoese had learned the value of a judicious
bankruptcy' (Sugden).

Men are not made of steel.
Pierce.   Nor are they bound
Always to hold.
Fly.   Thrice honourable colonel!
Hinges will crack –
Tipto.   Though they be Spanish iron.
Pierce. He is a merchant still, adventurer,   180
At in-and-in, and is our thoroughfare's friend.
Tipto. Who, Jug's?
Pierce.   The same; and a fine gentleman
Was with him!
Peck.   Master Huffle.
Pierce.   Who, Hodge Huffle?
Tipto. What's he?
Pierce.   A cheater, and another fine gentleman,
A friend o' the chamberlain's Jordan's. Master Huffle,   185
He is Burst's protection.
Fly.   Fights and vapours for him.
Pierce. He will be drunk so civilly –
Fly.   So discreetly –
Pierce. And punctually! Just at his hour.
Fly.   And then
Call for his jordan with that hum and state,
As if he pissed the *Politics.*
Pierce.   And sup   190
With his tuftaffeta night-gear here so silently!
Fly. Nothing but music.
Pierce.   A dozen of bawdy songs.
Tipto. And knows the general this?
Fly.   O no, sir; *dormit,*

183. Huffle?] *Huffle! Oc; Huffle.* Ou.

---

178. *hold*] keep their words.
179. *Spanish iron*] See I.i.32n.
181. *in-and-in*] See *Pers.* 64n.
186. *protection*] See IV.ii.59 and 84, IV.iii.38–9; 'an affectation like that of "countenance" and "resolution" in *E.M.O.*, IV.v.68' (*H.& S.*).
vapours] blusters; the word is used extensively in *B.F.*, for pointless hectoring, supposed to be caused by fumes arising from the stomach or other organs. See *B.F.*, II.iii.23n.
190. Politics] Aristotle's treatise.
191. *tuftaffeta*] See II.ii.42n.
night-gear] dressing gown, possibly here a light wench; cf. *L.R.*, l. 158n.

Dormit patronus still; the master sleeps,
They'll steal to bed.
Pierce.   In private, sir, and pay   195
The fiddlers with that modesty next morning.
Fly.   Take a disjune of muscadel and eggs.
Pierce.   And pack away i' their trundling cheats, like gipsies.
Trundle.   Mysteries, mysteries, Ferret.
Ferret.   Ay, we see, Trundle,
What the great officers in an inn may do;   200
I do not say the officers of the Crown,
But the Light Heart.
Tipto.   I'll see the Bat and Huffle.
Ferret.   I ha' some business, sir, I crave your pardon –
Tipto.   What?
Ferret   To be sober.   [*Exit.*]
Tipto.   Pox, go get you gone then.
Trundle shall stay.
Trundle.   No, I beseech you, colonel,   205
Your lordship has a mind to be drunk private
With these brave gallants. I will step aside
Into the stables and salute my mares.   [*Exit.*]
Pierce.   Yes, do, and sleep with 'em. – Let him go – base
whipstock –
He's as drunk as a fish now, almost as dead.   210
Tipto.   Come, I will see the flickermouse, my Fly.   [*Exeunt.*]
204.1. *Exit.*] G.   208.1. *Exit.*] G.   211.1. *Exeunt.*] G.

---

194. Dormit patronus] The master sleeps.

195. *They*] the company described in ll. 180ff. above.

196. *that*] such; Abbott, § 277.

197. *disjune*] breakfast.

muscadel and eggs] an aphrodisiac; see *Conv. Drum.*, ll. 527–31; Massinger,
A New Way to Pay Old Debts, IV.ii.85; Middleton, *Women Beware Women*,
I.ii.122ff.; and *A Trick to Catch the Old One*, III.i.91.

198. *pack away*] take themselves off with their possessions (*O.E.D.*, 10).

trundling cheats] coaches; cheats was thieves' cant for (stolen) things; see
Dekker, *N.D.*, III, 195–6; *G.M.*, l. 84.

199–202. *we . . . Heart*] an indication that the preceding passage was part of
the play's court-satire.

208. *salute*] pay a visit to (*O.E.D.*, 3).

209. *whipstock*] stick to which the lash is attached; hence, by transference,
one who drives horses.

210. *drunk . . . fish*] Tilley, F299.

dead] Cf. the phrase 'dead as a herring' (Tilley, H446).

211. *flickermouse*] bat (altered form of flittermouse; see *Alc.*, V.iv.88).

Act III Scene II

[Musicians *play while*] PRUDENCE, *ushered by the* HOST, *takes her seat of judicature;* NURSE, FRANK, *the two lords* BEAUFORT *and* LATIMER[, JUG, JORDAN, TRUNDLE, *and* FERRET] *assist of the bench.*

Pru. Here set the hour; but first produce the parties
    And clear the court: the time is now of price.
Host. Jug, get you down and, Trundle, get you up:
    You shall be crier. Ferret here, the clerk.
    Jordan, smell you without till the ladies call you.   5
    Take down the fiddlers too, silence that noise,
    Deep i' the cellar, safe.
                  [*Exeunt* JUG, JORDAN, *and* Musicians.]
Pru.   Who keeps the watch?
Host. Old Shelee-nien here is the Madam Tell-Clock.
Nurse. No, fait' and trot', sweet maister, I shall sleep,
    I' fait', I shall.
Beaufort.   I prithee do then, screech-owl.   10
    She brings to mind the fable o' the dragon

0.1.] *This ed.; Prudence* vsher'd by the *Host*, takes her seat of Iudicature, *Nurse, Franke*, the two Lords *Beaufort*, and *Latimer*, assist of the bench: The *Lady* and *Louel* are brought in, and sit on the two sides of the stage, confronting each the other. *Ferret. Trundle. O.*

0.1ff.] The setting is that of a court (Love's Court of Requests II.vi.191) or parliament, and suggests the medieval Courts of Love; Cf. *D.is A.*, I.vi.83.
    0.1. ushered . . . *HOST*] with the Host acting as usher (court attendant).
    0.4 assist of] 'The *of*, for which there seems to be no parallel, is partitive: assist as of, as being members of, the Bench' (*H.& S.*).
    the bench] on which the justices were seated, hence the justices collectively.
    1. *set*] determine the limits of (*O.E.D.*, 51).
    2. *of price*] valuable.
    3.] The Host instructs Jug to leave and Trundle to join the bench.
    4. *crier*] the court officer who makes the public announcements; see l. 15 below.
    5. *smell you*] (1) sniff about; (2) go and stink.
    6. *noise*] band of tavern musicians; cf. *T.of T.*, I.iv.50; *S.W.*, III.iii.86.
    8. *Tell-clock*] properly an idler (cf. *The Malcontent*, III.ii.10); here time-keeper.
    10. *screech-owl*] a bird of ill-omen; see Pliny, *Nat. Hist.*, X.xii; *Cat.*, IV.508.
    11–12. *dragon . . . fruit*] Hera set the dragon Ladon to protect her apple tree from the Hesperides, daughters of Atlas; see Hesiod, *Theog.*, ll. 333–5; cf. *E.M.I.*, III.ii.104. Variant versions of the myth may be pursued in U. von Wilamowitz-Moellendorff, *Der Glaube der Hellenen* (Berlin, 1931), I, 267ff.

That kept the Hesperian fruit. Would I could charm
   her.

Host. Trundle will do it with his hum. Come, Trundle;
   Precede him, Ferret, i' the form.

[*As* FERRET *proclaims,* TRUNDLE *repeats after him at the
breaks here and through the rest of this scene.*]

Ferret [*and*] *Trundle.* Oyez, oyez, oyez . . .   15
   Whereas there hath been awarded . . .
   by the queen regent of love . . .
   in this high court of sovereignty . . .
   two special hours of address . . .
   to Herbert Lovel, appellant . . .   20
   against the Lady Frampul, defendant . . .
   Herbert Lovel, come into the court . . .
   make challenge to thy first hour . . .
   and save thee and thy bail.

[*Enter* LOVEL, *and ranges himself on one side of the stage.*]

Host. Lo, louting, where he comes into the court!   25
   Clerk of the sovereignty, take his appearance,

7.1. *Exeunt* . . . Musicians.] *G.*   8. Shelee-nien] *This ed.; Sheelinin
O.*   10. screech-owl] *G; Schrich-Owle O.*   14.1–2. *As* . . . *scene.*]
G.   15–24, 30–33, 51–55.] *This ed.; O divides the page at these points with a
vertical rule, printing Trundle's s.p. to the left of it and the first words of the
repeated phrases to the right. So:* (15–24) *O yez, &c.*/ Whereas, &c./ By the Qu.
&c./ In this high, &c./ Two speciall, &c./ To *Herebert,* &c./ Against the, &c./
Herebert Lov. &c./ Make, &c./ And saue, &c. (30–33) *Francis,* &c./ Come into
the, &c./ Make answer, &c./ And saue thee &c. (51–55) I'the &c./ Notice is
&c./ To the Ap. &c./ That the &c./ And *Loue* &c.   15, 50. *Oyez* etc.] *H.&
S.;* O yez *O;* O yes *F3.*   20, 22. Herbert] *W, G;* Herebert *O.*

---

and dramatic references in Middleton, *The Changeling,* III.iii.173–5n.
(Revels).
   13. *hum*] See III.i.189 and punning on Trundle's echoing of Ferret's
proclamation below and 'hum' meaning strong or double ale (*D.is A.,* I.i.114);
O.E.D. quotes (sb.1.2c) the present usage as 'an indistinct murmur'.
   20. *Herbert*] See *Pers.* 7n.
   appellant] one who 'appeals' or accuses another of a crime.
   23. *challenge*] claim (*O.E.D.,* 5).
   24. *bail*] power, jurisdiction (*O.E.D.,* 1).
   24.1] Part of Jonson's opening stage direction has been transferred here; see
collation.
   25. *louting*] making obeisance; see *E.Welb.,* l. 216.
   26. *take*] note down (*O.E.D.,* 33a).

And how accoutred, how designed he comes!

Ferret. 'Tis done. Now, crier, call the Lady Frampul,
and by the name of:

[Ferret and] Trundle. Frances, Lady Frampul, defendant . . .
come into the court . . .   30
make answer to the award . . .
and save thee and thy bail.

> *Enter* LADY [FRAMPUL, *and ranges herself on the other side
> of the stage, confronting Lovel.*]

Host. She makes a noble and a just appearance.
Set it down likewise, and how armed she comes.

Pru. Usher of love's court, give 'em their oath   35
According to the form, upon love's missal.

Host. Arise, and lay your hands upon the book.
Herbert Lovel, appellant, and Lady Frances Frampul,
defendant, you shall swear upon the liturgy of love, Ovid
De Arte Amandi, that you neither have, ne will have, nor   40
in any wise bear about you, thing or things, pointed or
blunt, within these lists, other than what are natural and
allowed by the court: no enchanted arms or weapons,

28. 'Tis] *F3;* T's *O.*   36. 'em] *This ed.;* 'hem *O;* them both *G.*

---

27. *designed*] designated – a legal term (*O.E.D.,* 2).

32. 1–2.] See l. 24.1n. above.

35. *armed*] furnished, ready.

37ff.] For the religion of love, see Introduction, pp. 30ff.

38ff.] 'William Seegar, *Honor, Military, and Ciuill,* 1602, pp. 133–4, gives
the old legal formulae: "(1) Oiez, G.D. Defendant in this Combat, appeare
now, for in this day thou hast taken vpon thee to acquit thy pledges in
presence of the Lords, Constable, and Marshall, and also defend thy person
against A.B. who challenged thee to maintaine the cause of this Combat. (2)
The second Oath was also indifferently propounded to either of them, *viz.*
That they had not brought into the Lists other Armour or weapon then was
allowed, neither any engin, instrument, herbe, charme, or enchantment, and
that neither of them, should not affiance or trust in any thing other then God,
and their owne valors, as God and the holy Euangelists should helpe them.
This done they were both sent to their places of entrie' (*H.& S.*).

39–40. *Ovid . . . Amandi*] By invoking Ovid, the Host reveals that he is
expecting a 'banquet of sense', i.e. a celebration of fleshly love, rather than the
Platonic banquet described by Lovel. See the 'heavenly banquet' that Ovid
arranges for his friends in *Poet,* IV, and cf. 'The Banquet of Sense' in F.
Kermode, *Renaissance Essays* (London, 1971). Dramatic references to the
lurid reputation of Ovid's work may be pursued in Middleton, *The
Changeling,* III.iii.179n. (Revels).

stones of virtue, herb of grace, charm, character, spell,
philtre, or other power than Love's only, and the justness   45
of your cause. So help you Love, his mother, and the
contents of this book. Kiss it.

                        [*Lovel kisses the book.*]

Return unto your seats. Crier, bid silence.

Trundle. Oyez, oyez, oyez.

Ferret [and] Trundle. I' the name o' the sovereign of Love . . .   50
    notice is given by the court . . .
    to the appellant and defendant . . .
    that the first hour of address proceeds . . .
    and Love save the sovereign.

Trundle. Every man or woman keep silence, pain of   55
    imprisonment.

Pru. Do your endeavours, in the name of Love.

Lovel. To make my first approaches, then, in love.

Lady F. Tell us what love is, that we may be sure
    There's such a thing, and that it is in nature.

Lovel. Excellent lady, I did not expect   60
    To meet an infidel, much less an atheist
    Here in Love's list! Of so much unbelief
    To raise a question of his being –

Host.   Well charged!

Lovel. I rather thought, and with religion think,
    Had all the character of love been lost,   65
    His lines, dimensions, and whole signature
    Razed and defaced with dull humanity,

45. justness] *H.& S.;* iustneste *O.*   47. *Lovel . . . book.*] G.   63. Well
charged] *F3;* Well-charg'd *O.*   65. character] *O;* characters *W.*

---

44. *stones of virtue*] stones which had magical properties; see *Alc.*,
II.i.47–8n. (Revels).

   herb of grace] or herb-grace, rue; associated with its homonym
'rue' = sorrow, grief. It was associated with Saturn by H. C. Agrippa (see
I.ii.42n.).

   character] magic sign; cf. *D.is A.*, I.ii.9.

   45. *philtre*] aphrodisiac.

   45. *Love . . . mother*] Cupid and Venus.

   56. *Do . . . endeavours*] do all you can (*O.E.D.*, 'endeavour' sb.1b).

   59. *is in nature*] does exist (*O.E.D.*, 12e).

   61. *infidel*] unbeliever.

   64–71.] Cf. the style of compliment in *Ep.*, cv, cxxii, cxxv; *Und.*,
lxxix.32–4; *P.R.*, ll. 279–87.

   66. *signature*] particularity of form (*O.E.D.*, 4).

That both his nature and his essence might
Have found their mighty instauration here,
Here where the confluence of fair and good   70
Meets to make up all beauty. For what else
Is love, but the most noble, pure affection
Of what is truly beautiful and fair?
Desire of union with the thing beloved?

Beaufort. Have the assistants of the court their votes,   75
And writ of privilege to speak them freely?

Pru. Yes, to assist, but not to interrupt.

Beaufort. Then I have read somewhere, that man and
            woman
Were in the first creation both one piece,
And being cleft asunder, ever since   80
Love was an appetite to be rejoined.
As for example –   [*Kisses Frank.*]

Nurse.   *Cra-mo-cree!* What mean'sh 'tou?

75. *Beaufort.*] *This ed.; (Beau. O.*   82. *Kisses Frank.*] *G.*

---

69. *instauration*] restoration, renewal; possibly a reference to Bacon's great project, the *Instauratio Magna*, unfinished at his death in 1626.

70ff.] Lovel's speech is inspired by Plato's discourse on love, the *Symposium*, with a few points derived from the commentary by Marsilio Ficino who, at the behest of his patron Lorenzo de Medici, had, with other members of the Florentine Academy, met in a 'banquet' to discuss Plato's dialogue. (See his *Commentaria in Platonem*, in *Opera* (Basel, 1576), II, 1320–63.) Both authors were concerned to distinguish 'heavenly' love, lasting, virtuous and enobling, from 'earthly' love which is merely sensual and degrading. The discussion of Platonic theories of love was fashionable in court circles – see Introduction, pp. 31ff.

70. *confluence . . . good*] See Diotima's exposition of the way lovers desire the beautiful and the good in *Symposium*, § 206.

75. *votes*] Jonson seems to be using the word with a meaning recorded in *O.E.D.* only from Scottish sources, 'a formal expression of opinion by a member of a deliberative assembly' ('vote', sb.II.4).

76. *writ of privilege*] to protect members of parliament from arrest; see G. R. Elton, *The Tudor Constitution* (Cambridge, 1972), pp. 257–8.

77. *assist*] be present.

78–81. *man . . . rejoined*] Aristophanes' burlesque fable relates how there were originally three sexes, male, female and androgynous, and how the original being, round with two faces, four hands and feet, was cut in two after attacking Zeus. This explains 'the desire of one another which is implanted in us, reuniting our original nature, seeking to make one of two, and to heal the state of man'. See *Symposium*, §§ 189d–192 (tr. Jowett); cf. *L.T.*, ll. 54ff.

82. Cra-mo-cree] 'the Irish "Grádh mo chroidhe", love of my heart. Cf.

Beaufort. Only to kiss and part.
Host.   So much is lawful.
Latimer. And stands with the prerogative of Love's court.
Lovel. It is a fable of Plato's in his *Banquet*,   85
       And uttered there by Aristophanes.
Host. 'Twas well remembered here, and to good use.
       But on with your description what love is:
       'Desire of union with the thing beloved'.
Lovel. I meant a definition. For I make   90
       The efficient cause, what's beautiful and fair;
       The formal cause, the appetite of union;
       The final cause, the union itself.
       But larger, if you'll have it, by description:
       It is a flame and ardour of the mind,   95
       Dead in the proper corps, quick in another's:
       Transfers the lover into the loved.
       The he or she that loves, engraves or stamps

87. use.] *This ed.; vse.) O.*   97. loved] *O; beloved G.*

Shirley, *Poems*, 1646, "Vpon the Princes Birth": "The valiant Irish, *Cram-a-Cree* / It pledged hath / In *Vsquebagh*, / And being in this iovial vein, / They made a bogg even of their brain"' (*H.& S.*).
    84. *stands*] accords (*O.E.D.*, 79e).
    prerogative] right, privilege.
    91–3.] The four causes of Aristotle were the material cause, the matter of which something is composed, the formal cause, 'the archetype, i.e. the statement of the essence . . . (e.g. of the octave the relation of 2:1)', the efficient cause, 'the primary source of the change or coming to rest', and the final cause, 'the sense of end or "that for the sake of which" a thing is done' (*Physics*, § 194b).
    94. *larger*] more fully.
    95. *flame*] Cf. *Und.*, II.ii.23–6.
    96. *proper corps*] body of the subject or lover; cf. II.iv.240n.
    96–7. *Dead . . . loved*] 'Ille, inquit [Plato], amator animus est proprio in corpore mortuus: in alieno corpore uiuus . . . Moritur autem quisquis amat. Eius enim cogitatio, sui oblita semper in amato se uersat' (Ficino, *op.cit.*, oratio II.vii, cited *H.& S.*).
    98–101.] Jonson refers to the basic Aristotelian theory of sensory perception, that the brain perceives a picture of an object. See Aristotle, *De Anima*, II.xii.424a: 'Sensation is the reception of the form of sensible things without the matter, just as the wax receives the impression of the signet-ring without the iron or the gold'; and cf. Davies, *Nosce Teipsum*, ll. 957–60. For once *H.& S.* (III.ii.98n.) are misleading, as the passages from Sidney and Varchio they quote speak of one lover being *transformed* into another. Jonson uses the word 'transfer' (convey) rather than translating Ficino's 'in amato se uersat'

Th' idea of what they love, first in themselves;
Or, like to glasses, so their minds take in 100
The forms of their beloved, and them reflect.
It is the likeness of affections
Is both the parent and the nurse of love.
Love is a spiritual coupling of two souls,
So much more excellent as it least relates 105
Unto the body; circular, eternal,
Not feigned or made, but born; and then, so precious
As nought can value it but itself; so free
As nothing can command it but itself;
And in itself so round and liberal 110
As where it favours, it bestows itself.

Beaufort. And that do I: [*To Frank.*] here my whole self I
tender,
According to the practice o' the court.

Nurse. Ay, 'tish a naughty practish, a lewd practish;
Be quiet, man, dou shalt not leip her here. 115

Beaufort. Leap her! I lip her, foolish queen-at-arms;

---

101. them] *O;* then *G.*   107. feigned] *1716;* fain'd *O.*   born] *This ed.;*
borne *O.*   112. *Beaufort] This ed.; (Bea. O.   To Frank.] G.*

(ll. 96–7n.) 'turns itself into the lover'.

99. *idea*] Plato's *idéa* the archetype, or form.

100. *glasses*] 'Sed enim anima utique spiritui praesens imagines corporum in eo tanquam in speculo relucentes facile inspicit; perque illas corpora iudicat: atque haec cognitio sensus a Platonicis dicitur, dum eas inspicit, similes illis imagines multo etiam puriores sua ui concipit in se ipsa' (Ficino, oratio VI.vi); and cf. Davies, *Nosce Teipsum,* ll. 1157–60.

106. *circular*] 'Amor circulus est bonus a bono in bonum perpetuo reuolutus' (Ficino, oratio II.ii); cf. *L.T.*, ll. 136–7; *E. Bols.*, l. 14.

107. *Not . . . born*] Cf. the post-classical proverb of unknown origin: *Orator fit, poeta nascitur,* 'The orator is made, the poet is born' (Tilley, P451).

108–11. *so free . . . bestows it self*] 'Amor enim liber est . . . quam neque Deus etiam coget. . . . Huius tanta libertas est, ut caeterae animi affectiones vel artes, operationesque praemium aliquod, ut plurimum, a se diversum exoptent; Amor se ipso tamquam sui ipsius praemio sit contentus, quasi non sit praemium aliud praeter amorem quod amore sit dignum' (Ficino, *Commentarium in Convivium Platonis,* V.viii, ed. Jayne (Columbia Missouri, 1944), p. 74).

112–13.] See l. 154n. below.

114. *naughty*] bad, wicked.
lewd] wicked.

115. *leip*] indicates the Nurse's Irish pronunciation of 'leap', copulate with (*O.E.D.*, 9).

116. *lip*] kiss.

Thy blazon's false: wilt thou blaspheme thine office?

Lovel. But we must take and understand this love
Along still as a name of dignity,
Not pleasure.

Host. [*To Beaufort.*] Mark you that, my light young lord?   120

Lovel. True love hath no unworthy thought, no light,
Loose, unbecoming appetite or strain,
But fixèd, constant, pure, immutable.

Beaufort. [*Aside.*] I relish not these philosophical feasts;
Give me a banquet o' sense, like that of Ovid: 125
A form to take the eye; a voice, mine ear;
Pure aromatics, to my scent; a soft,
Smooth, dainty hand to touch; and for my taste,
Ambrosiac kisses to melt down the palate.

Lovel. They are the earthly, lower form of lovers   130
Are only taken with what strikes the senses,
And love by that loose scale. Although I grant
We like what's fair and graceful in an object,

---

117. office?] *This ed.;* office?) *O.*   120. *To Beaufort.*] *G.*   127. aromatics]
O; Aromatick *1716, W.*

---

117. *blazon*] description (*O.E.D.*, 4); cf. I.iii.46n.

119 *Along*] at length, in full (*O.E.D.*, 7).

125. *banquet . . . Ovid*] the anti-type of the philosophical banquet,
exemplified in Plato's *Symposium*, and the title of an erotic poem by
Chapman, *Ovid's Banquet of Sence* (1595); cf. *Poet.*, IV.v, and *E.Bols.* 'Lovel
speaks for Ourania, Beaufort for Pandemos, illustrating his case with kisses
stolen from Laetitia, which are qualitatively very different from that formal,
licensed, Platonic kiss, mixture of souls, which is to be Lovel's reward from
Lady Frampul' (Frank Kermode, 'The Banquet of Sense', *Renaissance Essays*
(London, 1973), pp. 84–115).

126–29. *A form . . . palate*] 'Aristotle (*De Anima*, II.vi–xii) establishes the
order Vision-Hearing-Smell-Taste-Touch; in the *De Sensu* (441a) he calls
taste a form of touch, which may explain why in literary treatment the order of
these two is sometimes reversed' (Kermode, p. 94n).

128–29. *taste . . . palate*] Cf. Catullus, xcix.2, 'Suaviolum dulci dulcius
ambrosia'; and Chapman, *Ovid's Banquet*, st. 97: 'Her moouing towards him,
made Ouids eye, / Beleeue the Firmanent was coming downe / To take him
quick to immortalitie, / And that th'Ambrosian kisse set on the Crowne: /
Shee spake in kissing, and her breath infusde / Restoring syrrop to his tast, in
swoune.'

129. *Ambrosiac*] divinely sweet; ambrosia was the fabled food of the gods in
Greek mythology.

132. *scale*] used in its Latinate sense = 'ladder'; the figure of the ladder by

And, true, would use it, in the all we tend to,
Both of our civil and domestic deeds: 135
In ordering of an army, in our style,
Apparel, gesture, building, or what not.
All arts and actions do affect their beauty.
But put the case: in travel I may meet
Some gorgeous structure, a brave frontispiece,   140
Shall I stay captive i' the outer court,
Surprised with that, and not advance to know
Who dwells there and inhabiteth the house?
There is my friendship to be made, within,
With what can love me again; not with the walls,   145
Doors, windows, architrabes, the frieze, and coronice.
My end is lost in loving of a face,
An eye, lip, nose, hand, foot, or other part,
Whose all is but a statue, if the mind
Move not, which only can make the return.   150
The end of love is to have two made one
In will and in affection, that the minds
Be first inoculated, not the bodies.

Beaufort. Gi' me the body, if it be a good one.[*Kisses Frank.*]

Frank. Nay, sweet my lord, I must appeal the sovereign   155

---

134. the] *O*: them *F3*.   137. not.] *This ed.*; not? *O*.   155. *Kisses Frank.*] *G*.

---

which a virtuous soul might ascend towards absolute beauty derives from the
Symposium, § 211c.

134. *all*] used substantively = perfection.

136. *ordering*] preparation.

style] manner, outward demeanour (*O.E.D.*, 19).

138. *affect*] aspire to (*O.E.D.*, 1).

139–50. *But . . . return*] It was presumably this passage (or ll. 65–71 above?)
that Hazlitt was remembering when he wrote: 'Two of the most poetical
passages in Ben Jonson, are the description of Echo in Cynthia's Revels, and
the fine comparison of the mind to a temple in the New Inn; a play which, on
the whole, however, I can read with no patience' (*Lectures on the Dramatic
Literature of the Age of Elizabeth*, in *The Collected Works of William Hazlitt*,
edd. A. R. Waller and A. Glover (London, 1902–6), V, 265).

140. *frontispiece*] the decorated entrance to a building.

146. *architrabes . . . coronice*] 'These latinised forms connected with *trabem*
[beam] and *corona* [crown] are also found in *2 Theobald*, 29, 30' (*H.& S.*).

150. *make the return*] return; i.e. towards the 'scale of perfection' (see. l.
132n. above).

153. *inoculated*] engrafted, joined; the metaphor is from horticulture.

154. *the body*] Cf. Morello's sardonic interruptions of Bembo's discourse on

For better quarter, if you hold your practice.
Trundle. Silence, pain of imprisonment! Hear the court.
Lovel. The body's love is frail, subject to change,
    And alters still with it; the mind's is firm,
    One and the same, proceedeth first from weighing   160
    And well examining what is fair and good;
    Then what is like in reason, fit in manners,
    That breeds good will, good will desire of union.
    So knowledge first begets benevolence,
    Benevolence breeds friendship, friendship love;   165
    And where it starts or steps aside from this,
    It is a mere degenerous appetite,
    A lost, oblique, depraved affection,
    And bears no mark or character of love.
Lady F. How am I changed! By what alchemy   170
    Of love or language am I thus translated!
    His tongue is tipped with the philosophers' stone,
    And that hath touched me thorough every vein.
    I feel that transmutation o' my blood,
    As I were quite become another creature,   175
    And all he speaks, it is projection!

---

156. practice] *This ed.;* practise *O.*   159. alters] *G;* alter *O.*   165. love] *Oc;*
loues *Ou, F3.*   173. thorough] *H.& S.;* through *O;* thro' my *W.*

---

love in *The Courtier* – Morello believes that 'the possessing of this beautie
which he prayseth so much, without the bodie, is a dreame' (tr. Hoby
(Everyman ed.), p. 307).
    156. *quarter*] treatment, terms (*O.E.D.*, 17b).
    hold] continue.
    practice] the method of procedure used in the law-courts (*O.E.D.*, 2b).
    164–5.] 'Jonson has elsewhere proceeded thus far; but the part most
difficult and delicate, yet, perhaps, not the least capable of being both morally
and poetically treated, is the union itself, and what, even in this life, it can be'
(Coleridge, p. 190).
    166. *starts*] moves suddenly from its course.
    167. *degenerous*] Lat. *degener*, degenerate; *Sej.*, III.387.
    170. *How . . . changed*] For further examples of sudden conversions to love
see L. Babb, *The Elizabethan Malady*, pp. 143–4.
    171. *translated*] changed in form.
    172. *philosophers' stone*] a reputed solid said to possess the quality of
transmuting base metal into gold or silver. The history of the term may be
pursued in *O.E.D.* ('philosophers' stone').
    173. *touched*] infected (*O.E.D.*, 7).
    vein] punning on veins of ore and veins of blood.
    175. *another creature*] 'The lady goes the way of all flesh in Jonson's

Pru. Well feigned, my lady: now her parts begin.
Latimer. And she will act 'em subtly.
Pru.   She fails me else.
Lovel. Nor do they trespass within bounds of pardon,
    That, giving way and licence to their love,   180
    Divest him of his noblest ornaments
    Which are his modesty and shamefacedness;
    And so they do that have unfit designs
    Upon the parties they pretend to love.
    For what's more monstrous, more a prodigy,   185
    Than to hear me protest truth of affection
    Unto a person that I would dishonour?
    And what's a more dishonour than defacing
    Another's good with forfeiting mine own,
    And drawing on a fellowship of sin?   190
    From note of which, though, for a while we may
    Be both kept safe by caution, yet the conscience
    Cannot be cleansed: for what was hitherto
    Called by the name of love becomes destroyed
    Then with the fact; the innocency lost,   195
    The bating of affection soon will follow;
    And love is never true that is not lasting:
    No more than any can be pure or perfect,
    That entertains more than one object. *Dixi.*
Lady F. O speak, and speak for ever! Let mine ear   200

---

177. feigned] *1716;* fain'd *O.*   182. shamefacedness] *G;* shamefac'tnesse *O;*
Shamfac'dness *F3.*   197. lasting:] *This ed.;* lasting. *O;* lasting, *H.&*
S.   200. mine ear] *G;* min'eare *O.*

---

comedies – to gold' (E. B. Partridge, *The Broken Compass* (New York, 1958),
p. 196, and see l. 259n. below).
    176. *projection*] the twelfth and last process in alchemy; see Ripley, *The
Compound of Alchymy* (1591); cf. *Alc.*, II.ii.5.
    178. *subtly*] artfully (*O.E.D.*, 1).
    179. *trespass . . . bounds*] come within the jurisdiction.
    182. *shamefacedness*] modesty.
    185. *prodigy*] monster, something unnatural.
    188. *more*] greated; Partridge, *Accidence*, § 38.
    191. *note*] stigma, reproach (*O.E.D.*, 'note' sb.2.II.8).
    192. *caution*] i.e. avoiding public notice.
    196. *bating*] abating.
    199. Dixi] 'There I rest my case' – the technical term at the end of a speech,
as in Cicero, *Verr.*, i fin.; and cf. Marston, *The Dutch Courtesan*, I.ii.53.

Be feasted still, and filled with this banquet;
No sense can ever surfeit on such truth!
It is the marrow of all lovers' tenents!
Who hath read Plato, Heliodore, or Tatius,
Sidney, d'Urfé, or all Love's fathers, like him?   205
He's there the Master of the Sentences,
Their school, their commentary, text, and gloss,
And breathes the true divinity of Love!

Pru. Excellent actor, how she hits this passion!

Lady F. Where have I lived in heresy so long   210
Out o' the congregation of Love,
And stood irregular, by all his canons?

Latimer. But do you think she plays?

Pru.   Upo' my sovereignty,
Mark her anon.

Latimer.   I shake and am half jealous.

---

206. He's] *W, G;* He, is *O, F3;* He'is *H.& S.*

201. *banquet*] See l. 125n. above.

202. *surfeit*] feast gluttonously.

203. *marrow*] Bone-marrow was a gastronomic delicacy. It was common in poetry of the period to speak of love 'burning' or 'melting' the marrow; see Shakespeare, *Ven.*, l. 142; and IV.iv.259.

tenents] tenets – used in the seventeenth century with plural subject (Lat. *tenent*, they hold).

204. *Plato*] on love in the *Symposium, Phaedrus* etc.; with this passage cf. *S.S.*, I.v.96ff.

Heliodore] a third-century writer born in Emesa in Syria, and author of *Aethiopica*, a romance translated into English in 1569; Jonson owned a copy (McPherson, 76).

Tatius] Achilles Tatius, an Alexandrian imitator of Heliodorus, and author of *The Loves of Leucippe and Cleitophon*, first published in Latin (Basel, 1554), then in Greek (Heidelberg, 1601).

206. *Sidney*] Lady Frampul refers to his *Arcadia*, first published in 1580. but constantly popular during the Stuart period – there were issues in 1621, 1622, 1623, 1627 and two in 1629, the year of this play.

d'Urfé] Honoré d'Urfé (1567–1625), author of a pastoral novel, *L'Astrée*, one of the favourite books of the Queen (Henrietta Maria) and the book which served as the prime text of the Platonic lovers of her reign.

206. *Master . . . Sentences*] Peter Lombard, whose *Sententiae* (1145–50) was still an important theological text in the Renaissance. Lady Frampul is complimenting Lovel on his 'sentences' or apt formulations.

207. *school*] doctrine (*O.E.D.*, 11).

209. *hits*] imitates exactly (*O.E.D.*, 14).

212. *irregular*] not in conformity with a religious order (*O.E.D.*, 5).

Lady F. What penance shall I do to be received   215
　　　And reconcilèd to the church of Love?
　　　Go on procession, barefoot, to his image,
　　　And say some hundred penitential verses
　　　There out of Chaucer's *Troilus and Cressid*?
　　　Or to his mother's shrine vow a wax candle   220
　　　As large as the town maypole, and pay it?
　　　Enjoin me anything this court thinks fit,
　　　For I have trespassed and blasphemèd Love:
　　　I have, indeed, despised his deity,
　　　Whom (till this miracle wrought on me) I knew not.   225
　　　Now I adore Love, and would kiss the rushes
　　　That bear this reverend gentleman, his priest,
　　　If that would expiate – but I fear it will not.
　　　For though he be somewhat struck in years and old
　　　Enough to be my father, he is wise,   230
　　　And only wise men love, the other covet.
　　　I could begin to be in love with him,
　　　But will not tell him yet because I hope
　　　T' enjoy the other hour with more delight,
　　　And prove him farther.
Pru.   Most Socratic lady,   235

---

216. reconcilèd] *H.& S.;* reconcil'd *O.*   219. *and*] *H.& S.;* and *O*,
F3.   229. struck] *F3;* strooke *O.*

---

214. *jealous*] ardently amorous (*O.E.D.*, 2).

215. *received*] admitted.

217. *on procession*] obs. constr. for 'in procession'.

218. *penitential*] Cf. the so-called seven 'penitential psalms' (nos. vi, xxxii, xxxviii, li, cii, cxxx, cxliii) often versified by Renaissance poets.

219–21.] Lady Frampul's protestations are a nice mixture of remorse and sarcasm. *Troilus and Cressid* could be either a celebration of love or a cautionary tale for lovers; her imagined ritual of penitence blasphemously identifies Venus with the Virgin Mary, and contains a suppressed *double entendre* as well as a parody of Mariolatry.

221. *large . . . maypole*] Tilley, M778.

223. *trespassed*] offended against (*O.E.D.*, 3b).

229. *struck*] For Jonson's use of the form 'strooke' see Partridge, *Accidence*, § 91.

231. *other*] others; Partridge, *Accidence*, § 25.

covet] lust (*O.E.D.*, 4a).

235. *prove*] test.

Socratic] 'This is to answer Socratically, and in answering not to answer', Smectymnuus, *Answ.* (1641), xiii.154, cited *O.E.D.* under 'Socratically'.

Or, if you will, ironic! Gi' you joy
O' your Platonic love here, Master Lovel.
But pay him his first kiss yet, i' the court,
Which is a debt and due: for the hour's run.

Lady F. How swift is time, and slyly steals away   240
From them would hug it, value it, embrace it!
I should have thought it scarce had run ten minutes,
When the whole hour is fled. Here, take your kiss, sir,
Which I most willing tender you in court. [*Kisses Lovel.*]

Beaufort. And we do imitate –   [*Kisses Frank.*]   245

Lady F.   And I could wish
It had been twenty – so the sovereign's
Poor narrow nature had decreed it so –
But that is past, irrevocable, now:
She did her kind according to her latitude –

Pru. Beware you do not conjure up a spirit   250
You cannot lay.

Lady F.   I dare you, do your worst,
Show me but such an injustice; I would thank you
To alter your award.

Latimer.   Sure she is serious!
I shall have another fit of jealousy,
I feel a grudging!

Host.   Cheer up, noble guest,   255
We cannot guess what this may come to yet;
The brain of man, or woman, is uncertain.

Lovel. Tut, she dissembles; all is personated,
And counterfeit comes from her! If it were not,

237. your] *F3;* you *O.*   244. *Kisses Lovel.*] G.   245. *Beaufort.*] *This ed.;*
(*Bea. O.*   imitate –] *This ed.;* imitate –) *O.*   *Kisses Frank.*] G.

---

236. *ironic*] the earliest recorded use in *O.E.D.*;=dissembling (*O.E.D.*,
'ironical' 3).
  247. *poor*] small, mean.
  narrow] strict, careful (*O.E.D.*, 5).
  249. *did her kind*] acted properly (*O.E.D.*, 'kind' 8).
  latitude] scope, power (*O.E.D.*, 2 & 3).
  250-1. *Beware . . . lay*] standard bawdy; cf. Shakespeare, *Rom.*, II.i.16ff.;
Middleton, *The Family of Love*, V.i.10ff and *Women Beware Women*, I.i.8off.
(Revels).
  255. *grudging*] sympton of an approaching illness.
  258. *personated*] feigned.

The Spanish monarchy with both the Indies   260
Could not buy off the treasure of this kiss
Or half give balance for my happiness.
Host. Why, as it is yet, it glads my Light Heart
To see you roused thus from a sleepy humour
Of drowsy, accidental melancholy;   265
And all those brave parts of your soul awake
That did before seem drowned and buried in you.
That you express yourself as you had backed
The Muses' horse, or got Bellerophon's arms –

[*Enter* FLY.]

What news with Fly?
Fly.   News of a newer lady,   270
A finer, fresher, braver, bonnier beauty,
A very *bona-roba*, and a bouncer
In yellow, glistering, golden satin!
Lady F.   Pru,
Adjourn the court.
Pru.   Cry, Trundle –

269.1. *Enter* FLY.] *G.*

---

259. *counterfeit*] refers to acting and to forged coin – the image runs through 'treasure' and 'balance' in the next three lines.

260. *both . . . Indies*] i.e. the East and West Indies from which adventurers could expect to return with fabulous wealth; cf. Shakespeare, *H8*, IV.i.45; *Alc.*, II.i.36n. (Revels).

265. *accidental*] casual, occasional.

266. *brave . . . soul*] According to Castiglione, the soul could be drawn from the body by a kiss that it might join with the soul of the loved one – see *The Book of the Courtier*, tr. Hoby (Everyman ed.), pp. 315–16; for the Platonic cult of kissing, see N. A. Robb, *Neaplatonism of the English Renaissance* (1955), p. 191.

268. *backed*] ridden.

269. *Muses' . . . arms*] Bellerophon, grandson of Sisyphus, captured the Muses' horse, Pegasus, in order to kill the chimaera (Hesiod, *Theog.*, ll. 319ff.). He later defeated the Amazons. At the height of his fortunes he attempted to fly to Olympus on Pegasus but Zeus sent a gadfly to sting Pegasus so that Bellerophon was flung down to earth. Jonson may be amusing himself by bringing Fly on at this moment.

272. bona-roba] 'a showy wanton' (*O.E.D.*); See *Pers.* 67n.; cf. *Alc.*, II.vi.30n. (Revels).

bouncer] No example of this word is recorded in *O.E.D.* before 1762. It presumably means 'high-spirited, lively' and refers to her likely sexual prowess. See IV.iii.22.

273. *yellow*] possibly produced by saffron starch, a fashion introduced by

Trundle. Oyez, any man or woman that hath any personal 275
attendance to give unto the court: keep the second hour,
and Love save the sovereign. [*Exeunt.*]

275–7. Oyez . . . sovereign.] *This ed.;* Oyez,/ Any . . . attendance/ To . . .
houre,/ And *O;* Oyez,/ Any . . . Sou'raigne. *H.& S.* 277.1 *Exeunt.*] *G.*

---

the notorious Mrs Turner who was an agent of Lady Essex in the Overbury
murder – see *D.is A.*, I.i.113n. It was also the colour of jealousy; cf.
Shakespeare, *Wint.*, II.iii.106.

Act IV

[*Enter*] JUG, BARNABY, [*and*] JORDAN.

[*Jug.*] O Barnaby!

Jordan. Welcome, Barnaby! Where hast thou been?

Barnaby. I' the foul weather.

Jug. Which has wet thee, Ban.

Barnaby. As dry as a chip! Good Jug, a cast o' thy name,
   As well as thy office: two jugs!

Jug. By and by. [*Exit* JUG.]

Jordan. What lady's this thou has brought here?

Barnaby. A great lady! 5
   I know no more; one that will try you, Jordan;
   She'll find your gauge, your circle, your capacity.
   How does old Staggers the smith, and Tree the saddler?
   Keep they their penny-club still?

Jordan. And th' old catch too
   Of 'Whoop Barnaby –'

0.1. BARNABY] *G;* Barnabe *O.*   2. Ban] *O; Bar 1716, W;* Barnaby *G.*   4.1. *Exit* JUG.] *G.*   7. gauge] *This ed.;* gage *O.*

---

3. *As . . . chip*] Tilley, C351.

   cast] a quibble on cast = couple (of hawks, *O.E.D.*, 14) and cast = quantity of ale made at one time (*O.E.D.*, 15).

   6. *try*] put to the test.

   7. *gauge . . . capacity*] of the jordan (chamberpot) – see *Pers.* 60; but perhaps Jordan has been boasting of his private endowments for Pinnacia is obviously huge – see IV.iii.23.

   circle] compass, measure (*O.E.D.*, 16).

   9. *penny-club*] at the inn; 'club' means a combination of contributions to defray the expenses of an entertainment in a sense recorded in *O.E.D.* (10) from 1660. *O.E.D.*, 11, is 'a meeting or assembly in a tavern' but this is recorded only from 1648. Presumably each of Jonson's drinkers contributed a penny to the occasion.

   10. *Whoop Barnaby*] a ballad; cf. V.i.30; *G.M.*, l. 948.

Barnaby.   Do they sing at me?   10
Jordan. They're reeling at it in the parlour now.

[*Enter* JUG *with wine.*]

Barnaby. I'll to 'em. Gi' me a drink first.
Jordan.   Where's thy hat?
Barnaby. I lost it by the way – Gi' me another.
Jug. A hat?
Barnaby.   A drink.
Jug.   Take heed of taking cold, Ban –
Barnaby. The wind blew't off at Highgate, and my lady   15
    Would not endure me 'light to take it up,
    But made me drive bare-headed i' the rain.
Jordan. That she might be mistaken for a countess?
Barnaby. Troth, like enough! She might be an o'er-grown
        duchess,
    For aught I know.
Jug.   What, with one man!
Barnaby.   At a time –   20
    They carry no more, the best of 'em.
Jordan.   Nor the bravest.
Barnaby. And she is very brave!
Jordan.   A stately gown,
    And petticoat she has on!
Barnaby.   Ha' you spied that, Jordan?
    You're a notable peerer, an old rabbi,
    At a smock's hem, boy.

11. They're] *This ed.;* They'are *O.*   11.1. *Enter . . . wine.*] *G.*   12. first.]
O; first. *Drinks. G.*   14. drink.] *O;* drink. *Drinks. G.*   Ban] *O; Bar 1716,*
W.   15. blew't off] *Oc;* blew toff *Ou.*   24. You're] *This ed.;* you'are *O.*

---

11. *reeling*] rioting (*O.E.D.*, 3).
16. *'light*] alight.
17. *drive bare-headed*] The coachmen of the great wore no hats; cf. *T.of T.*,
V.vii.39–40; *D.is A.*, II.iii.36–7.
18–21] A vein of bawdy runs through these lines. For the obscene sense of
'mistaken' cf. Shakespeare, *Wint.*, II.iii.81.
19. *duchess*] lady; i.e. the wife of a lord, not necessarily of a duke (*O.E.D.*, 2).
20. *man*] servant.
21. *bravest*] most finely arrayed.
24. *peerer*] nonce-word, not in *O.E.D.*
rabbi] here, well versed in the knowledge of women (see *O.E.D.*, 26).
25. *smock's hem*] Cf. Cotgrave, '*Brigaille*, a noteable smel-smocke, or

Jug.   As he is chamberlain,   25
 He may do that by his place.
Jordan.   What's her squire?
Barnaby. A toy, that she allows eight-pence a day,
 A slight mannet, to port her up and down.
 Come, show me to my playfellows, old Staggers,
 And Father Tree.
Jordan.   Here, this way, Barnaby.   [*Exeunt.*]   30

ACT IV SCENE ii

[*Enter*] TIPTO, BURST, HUFFLE, [*and*] FLY.

[*Tipto.*] Come, let's take in fresco here one quart.
Burst. Two quarts, my man-of-war, let's not be stinted.
Huffle. Advance three jordans, varlet o' the house.
Tipto. I do not like your Burst, bird; he is saucy:
 Some shopkeeper he was?
Fly.   Yes, sir.
Tipto.   I knew it.   5
 A broke-winged shopkeeper? I nose 'em straight.
 He had no father, I warrant him, that durst own him;
 Some foundling in a stall or the church-porch;
 Brought up i' the Hospital; and so bound prentice;
 Then master of a shop; then one o' the Inquest;   10
 Then breaks out bankrupt or starts alderman:
 The original of both is a church-porch –

---

25. smock's hem] *This ed.;* smocks-hem *O.*   28. mannet] *This ed.;* Man-net
O.
1. let's] *This ed.;* let'vs *O;* let vs *H.& S.*   2. let's] *W;* let'vs *O.*

---

muttonmungar, a cunning solicitor of a wench' (cited *H.& S.*).
 27. *toy*] plaything (*O.E.D.*, 8).
 28. *mannet*] little man (nonce word).
 port] bear.

 1. *in fresco*] in the fresh air (first recorded in *O.E.D.* in 1620).
 2. *man-of-war*] warrior (*O.E.D.*, 1).
 3. *Advance*] continuing the military metaphor.
 6. *broke-winged*] bankrupt; see II.i.10n.
 8. *stall*] stable.
 9. *Hospital*] Christ's Hospital, founded in 1552 for poor children.
 10. *o' the Inquest*] the Court of Inquest at the Guildhall that dealt with
complaints for debts under forty shillings; cf. *E.H.*, IV.ii.39–40.

Fly. Of some, my colonel.

Tipto.   Good faith, of most
O' your shop citizens: they're rude animals!
And let 'em get but ten mile out o' town,   15
Th'out-swagger all the wapentake.

Fly.   What's that?

Tipto. A Saxon word to signify the hundred.

Burst. Come, let us drink, Sir Glorious, some brave health
Upon our tiptoes.

Tipto.   To the health o' the Bursts.

Burst. Why Bursts?

Tipto.   Why Tiptos?

Burst.   O, I cry you mercy!   20

Tipto. It is sufficient.

Huffle.   What is so sufficient?

Tipto. To drink to you is sufficient.

Huffle.   On what terms?

Tipto. That you shall give security to pledge me.

Huffle. So you will name no Spaniard, I will pledge you.

Tipto. I rather choose to thirst and will thirst ever   25
Than leave that cream of nations uncried up.
Perish all wine and gust of wine!

                    [*Throws the wine at Huffle.*]

Huffle.   How, spill it?

13. most] *H.& S.;* most! *O.*   15. o' town] *This ed.;* a towne *O.*   27.
Throws . . . Huffle.] *G.*

---

16. *wapentake*] 'a subdivision of certain English shires, corresponding to
the "hundred" of other counties' (*O.E.D.*).

23. *security . . . me*] 'The old manner of pledging each other when they
drank, was thus: the person who was going to drink, asked any one of the
company who sat next him, whether he would pledge him, on which he
answering that he would, held up his knife or sword, to guard him whilst he
drank; for while a man is drinking he necessarily is in an unguarded posture,
exposed to the treacherous stroke of some hidden or secret enemy' (Strutt,
quoted in Brand, 'Drinking Usages'). The topic may be pursued in Peter
Clark, 'The Alehouse and the Alternative Society' in D. Pennington and K.
Thomas edd., *Puritans and Revolutionaries* (Oxford, 1978), 47–72.

24. *Spaniard*] unpopular since the Armada; see Sugden, p. 478, for
analogous references.

26. *uncried up*] unextolled (*O.E.D.*, cry 22).

27. *gust of*] liking for (*O.E.D.*, sb.2,2).

27–8. *spill . . . spilt it*] the vapouring of a drunkard; cf. the thumb-biting
sequence in Shakespeare, *Rom.*, I.i.

Spill it at me?
Tipto.   I reck not, but I spilt it.
Fly. Nay, pray you be quiet, noble bloods.
Burst.   No Spaniards
  I cry, with my cousin Huffle.
Huffle.   Spaniards! Pilchers!   30
Tipto. Do not provoke my patient blade; it sleeps
  And would not hear thee: Huffle, thou art rude
  And dost not know the Spanish composition.
Burst. What is the recipe? Name the ingredients.
Tipto. Valour.
Burst.   Two ounces!
Tipto.   Prudence.
Burst.   Half a dram!   35
Tipto. Justice.
Burst.   A pennyweight!
Tipto.   Religion.
Burst. Three scruples!
Tipto.   And of *gravedàd*.
Burst.   A face-full!
Tipto. He carries such a dose of it in his looks,
  Actions, and gestures, as it breeds respect
  To him from savages, and reputation   40
  With all the sons of men.
Burst.   Will it give him credit
  With gamesters, courtiers, citizens, or tradesmen?

28. reck] *W;* wrek *O;* wreck *F3.*   split] *O;* spill *W.*   35–7.] *Tip.* . . .
Ounces!/ *Tip.* . . . Dram!/ *Tip.* . . . weight!/ *Tip.* . . . Scruples!/ *Tip.* . . . -
full! *F3.*   37. *gravedàd*] *This ed.; grauida'd O; Gravidâd F3.*

---

28. *reck*] care.
30. *Pilchers*] 'A term of abuse, frequent at the beginning of the seventeenth
century. It has been conjecturally explained as meaning "One who wears a
pilch or leather jerkin or doublet", or "One who pilches, a thief"' (*O.E.D.*); cf.
Poet., III.iv.4n.
33. *composition*] constitution (*O.E.D.*, 16).
35. *dram*] one sixteenth of an ounce.
36. *pennyweight*] one twentieth of an ounce Troy.
37. *scruples*] weights of one twenty-fourth of an ounce.
 gravedàd] (Sp.) gravity, dignity; cf. *Witt's Recreations* (1641), no. 579: 'He
weare[s] a hoope ring on his Thumbe; he has / Of Gravidud a dose full in his
face' (cited *H. & S.*); and Nashe's description of Spanish pride in *Works*, I,
176.
 face-full] a nonce word.

Tipto. He'll borrow money on the stroke of his beard,
     Or turn of his *mustaccio*! His mere *cuello*,
     Or ruff about his neck, is a bill of exchange   45
     In any bank in Europe! Not a merchant
     That sees his gait but straight will furnish him
     Upon his pace!
Huffle.   I have heard the Spanish name
     Is terrible to children in some countries,
     And used to make them eat – their bread and butter,   50
     Or take their wormseed.
Tipto.   Huffle, you do shuffle.

       [*Enter*] to them STUFF [*and*] PINNACIA [*richly dressed.*]

Burst. 'Slid, here's a lady!
Huffle.   And a lady gay!
Tipto. A well-trimmed lady!
Huffle.   Let's lay her aboard.
Burst. Let's hail her first.
Tipto.   By your sweet favour, lady.
Stuff. Good gentlemen, be civil; we are strangers.   55

---

44. of] *This ed.;* off *O.*   51.1. *Enter . . . dressed.*] *This ed.;* ——————— to
them: *Stuff, Pinnacia. O.*   53. aboard] *F3;* a boord *O.*

---

44. *turn of*] If the *O* reading 'off' stands, 'turn off' means 'peel off' (*O.E.D.*, 73).

cuello] ruff (Sp. *cuello*, neck). Ruffs were the object of puritan vituperation and attempts were periodically made to regulate their size by law. They went out of fashion at the end of James's reign; see *Sh.Eng.*, I, 25–7 and II, 92–4.

50. *eat*—] The dash indicates that Huffle's wit momentarily deserts him.

51. *wormseed*] swine's fennel, sulphurwort, cameline etc. were used; see Gerard's *Herbal*, II.xxii.

shuffle] (1) use shifty arguments (*O.E.D.*, 7); (2) continues the 'gait' metaphor.

51.1 to them] For Jonson's use of this phrase in entrances, see *E.M.I.*, II.iii.margin (*H.& S.*'s note). See also Introduction n.45.

52. *lady gay*] a ballad refrain; see ll. 65–6 below and *M.L.*, IV.viii.72. Variants of 'The Wife of Usher's Well' contain this refrain: see B. H. Bronson, *The Traditional Tunes of the Child Ballads* (Princeton, 1962), II, 246ff.

53–4. *well-trimmed . . . first*] Nautical bawdy, connected here with Pinnacia's name (*Pers.* 67n.), was common: see Shakespeare, *Wiv.*, II.i.78ff.; Donne, Satire IV, l. 190; Middleton, *The Changeling*, I.i.91–2n. (Revels).

55–7. *civil . . . Seville*] a common pun: see Shakespeare, *Ado*, II.i.263, and Sugden, p. 463.

55. *strangers*] foreigners.

Burst. And you were Flemings, sir!

Huffle.   Or Spaniards!

Tipto. There are here have been at Seville i' their days,
    And at Madrid too!

Pinnacia.   He is a foolish fellow,
    I pray you mind him not, he is my Protection.

Tipto. In your Protection he is safe, sweet lady;   60
    So shall you be in mine.

Huffle.   A share, good coronel.

Tipto. Of what?

Huffle.   Of your fine lady! [*To Pinnacia.*] I am Hodge,
    My name is Huffle.

Tipto.   Huffling Hodge, be quiet.

Burst. And I pray you, be you so, glorious coronel;
    Hodge Huffle shall be quiet.

Huffle [*Singing.*]   'A lady gay, gay;   65
    For she is a lady gay, gay, gay. For she's a lady gay.'

Tipto. Bird o' the vespers, *vespertilio* Burst,
    You are a gentleman o' the first head,
    But that head may be broke as all the body is,
    Burst, if you tie not up your Huffle quickly.   70

Huffle. Tie dogs, not man.

Burst.   Nay, pray thee, Hodge, be still.

Tipto. This steel here rides not on this thigh in vain.

Huffle. Show'st thou thy steel and thigh, thou glorious dirt,

---

57. There are] *This ed.;* The'are *O.*   65. *Singing.*] G.   71. man] *O;* men
W.

---

56. *Flemings*] There were large numbers of Dutch refugees in London and
they were often unpopular for their drunkenness; see Nashe, *Works*, I, 204–7
etc.; Dekker, *N.D., passim.*

  59. *Protection*] See III.i.186n.

  61. *coronel*] See I.v.10n.

  65–6. *lady . . . gay*] the ballad alluded to at l. 52 above; cf. Beaumont, *The
Knight of the Burning Pestle* (ed. Hattaway), III.546; and Shakespeare, *Pilgr.,*
xv.15.

  67. vespertilio] Lat. 'bat' – Tipto's bombast for Bat (Bartholomew).

  68. *o' the first head*] the first gentleman of his family. The term is derived
from venery. Cf. Cotgrave, 'gentilhomme de ville, a gentleman of the first
head, an upstart gentleman'; and *E.M.O.*, III.iii.48n.

  73. *glorious*] vain-glorious.

  dirt] excrement.

Then Hodge sings 'Sampson', and no ties shall hold.

[*They fight.*]

[*Enter*] PIERCE, JUG, JORDAN.

Pierce. Keep the peace, gentlemen: what do you mean?   75
Tipto. I will not discompose myself for Huffle.

[*Exeunt all but Stuff and Pinnacia, fighting.*]

Pinnacia. You see what your entreaty and pressure still
    Of gentlemen to be civil doth bring on?
    A quarrel and perhaps manslaughter! You
    Will carry your goose about you still, your planing-iron!   80
    Your tongue to smooth all! Is not here fine stuff?
Stuff. Why, wife?
Pinnacia.   Your wife! Ha' not I forbidden you that?
    Do you think I'll call you husband i' this gown,
    Or anything, in that jacket, but Protection!
    Here, tie my shoe and show my vellute petticoat   85
    And my silk stocking! Why do you make me a lady,
    If I may not do like a lady in fine clothes?
Stuff. Sweet heart, you may do what you will with me.
Pinnacia. Aye, I knew that at home, what to do with you.
    But why was I brought hither? To see fashions?   90
Stuff. And wear them too, sweet heart. But this wild
        company –
Pinnacia. Why do you bring me in wild company?
    You'd ha' me tame and civil in wild company?
    I hope I know wild company are fine company,

---

74. *They fight.*] G.   74.1. *Enter . . .* JORDAN.] *This ed.;* ———— *Peirce.*
Iug. Iorden. {*To them. Oc.; Peirce. Iug. Iorden.* {*To them Ou.*   76.1.
Exeunt . . . fighting.] G.   85. *vellute*] *O; Velvet F3.*

---

74. '*Sampson*'] the ballad of Sampson; see Simpson, p. 680; parodied in
E.H., II.ii.39.

no . . . hold] See Sampson's mockery of Delilah in Judges xvi.6–14. He has
her bind him in withes and ropes which he promptly breaks.

76. *discompose*] a fustian word of Tipto; see l. 33 above and IV.iii. 5–6.

80. *goose*] smoothing-iron (from the shape of its handle); also a swelling
caused by venereal disease (*O.E.D.*, 3); cf. Shakespeare, *Mac.*, II.iii.16.

82. *wife*] a dirty word for a resolute libertine.

84. *in that jacket*] Stuff wears a footman's velvet jacket (IV.iii.57–71) while
his wife wears a gentlewoman's costume.

85. *vellute*] obs. form of velvet: velvet had sexual connotations – see
Massinger, *P.& P.*, *The Unnatural Combat*, I.i.118n.

And in fine company, where I am fine myself,   95
A lady may do anything, deny nothing
To a fine party, I have heard you say't.

[Enter] to them PIERCE.

Pierce. There are a company of ladies above
  Desire your ladyship's company, and to take
  The surety of their lodgings from the affront   100
  Of these half-beasts were here e'en now, the centaurs.
Pinnacia. Are they fine ladies?
Pierce.   Some very fine ladies.
Pinnacia. As fine as I?
Pierce.   I dare use no comparisons,
  Being a servant, sent –
Pinnacia.   Spoke like a fine fellow!
  I would thou wert one: I'd not then deny thee.   105
  But thank thy lady.   *[Exit* PIERCE.]

[Enter] to them HOST.

Host.   Madam, I must crave you
  To afford a lady a visit, would excuse
  Some harshness o' the house you have received
  From the brute guests.
Pinnacia.   This's a fine old man!
  I'd go with him an' he were a little finer.   110
Stuff. You may, sweet heart, it is mine host.
Pinnacia.   Mine host!
Host. Yes, madam, I must bid you welcome.
Pinnacia.   Do, then.
Stuff. But do not stay.
Pinnacia.   I'll be advised by you, yes!
                                    [Exeunt.]

106. thy] *O; my F3.*   106. *Exit* PIERCE.] *G.*   106.1 *Enter . . .* HOST.] *This
ed.;* ———— To them Host. *O.*   113.1. *Exeunt.] G.*

100. *surety*] safety.
  affront] attack.
  101. *centaurs*] When their neighbours the Lapithae were holding a wedding
feast for their king Pirithous, drunken Centaurs tried to carry off his bride
Hippodamia; see Ovid, *Met.,* xii.210ff; cf. *S.W.,* IV.v.46.
  104. *servant*] punning on the sense 'lover'.
  107. *visit, would*] for the omitted relative pronoun see Abbott, §§ 244–6.

ACT IV SCENE iii

[*Enter*] *to them* LATIMER, BEAUFORT, LADY [FRAMPUL],
PRUDENCE, FRANK[, *and* NURSE.]

Latimer. What more than Thracian barbarism was this?
Beaufort. The battle o' the centaurs with the Lapithes!
Lady F. There is no taming o' the monster drink.
Latimer. But what a glorious beast our Tipto showed!
 He would not discompose himself, the don!   5
 Your Spaniard n'er doth discompose himself.
Beaufort. Yet how he talked and roared i' the beginning!
Pru. And ran as fast as a knocked marrowbone.
Beaufort. So they all did at last when Lovel went down
 And chased 'em 'bout the court.
Latimer.   For all's Don Lewis, 10
 Or fencing after Euclid!
Lady F.   I ne'er saw
 A lightning shoot so as my servant did;
 His rapier was a meteor, and he waved it
 Over 'em like a comet as they fled him.
 I marked his manhood; every stoop he made   15
 Was like an eagle's at a flight of cranes
 (As I have read somewhere).
Beaufort.   Bravely expressed.
Latimer. And like a lover!
Lady F.   Of his valour, I am.

0.1.] *This ed.;* ————— To them *Latimer. Beaufort. Lady. Pru. Frank.
Host. Pinnacia. Stuffe. O.*

---

1. *Thracian*] Thracians cultivated Mars and Dionysus and were reputed
great warriors and drinkers; see Sugden, pp. 513–4; and cf. Horace, *Odes*,
I.xxvii. 1–3.

2. *Lapithes*] See IV.ii.101n.

8. *knocked marrowbone*] The marrow was caused to run out by knocking the
bone.

10. *court*] See Arg. 82n.

10–11. *Don . . . Euclid*] See II.v.88–90.

13–14. *rapier . . . comet*] Lovel drives Tipto out with Spanish swordsmanship which favoured the cut rather than the thrust. See A. L. Soens, 'Tybalt's
Spanish Fencing in Romeo and Juliet', *S.Q.*, XX (1969), 121–7.

17. *As . . . somewhere*] 'Perhaps Sophocles, *Ajax*, 167–71 . . . Jonson
underlined the Latin version of these lines in his copy of the *Poetae Graeci
Veteres, Tragici, Lyrici &c* [McPherson, 95] now at Cambridge . . .: "Sed

He seemed a body rarefied to air,
Or that his sword and arm were of a piece,   20
They went together so!

                   [*Enter* HOST *with* PINNACIA.]
                      Here comes the lady.
Beaufort. A bouncing *bona-roba* as the Fly said!
Frank. She is some giantess: I'll stand off
   For fear she swallow me.
Lady F.   Is not this our gown, Pru,
   That I bespoke of Stuff?
Pru.   It is the fashion.   25
Lady F. Ay, and the silk; feel, sure it is the same!
Pru. And the same petticoat, lace, and all!
Lady F.   I'll swear it.
   How came it hither? Make a bill of enquiry.
Pru. You've a fine suit on, madam, and a rich one!
Lady F. And of a curious making.
Pru.   And a new.   30
Pinnacia. As new as day.
Latimer.   She answers like a fishwife.
Pinnacia. I put it on since noon, I do assure you.
Pru. Who is your tailor?
Lady F.   Pray you, your fashioner's name?
Pinnacia. My fashioner is a certain man o' mine own;
   He's i' the house: no matter for his name.   35
Host. O, but to satisfy this bevy of ladies

21.1. *Enter . . .* PINNACIA] *G.*   29. You've] *This ed.;* Yo'haue *O.*   33.
Pray] *This ed.;* 'Pray *O.*   35. He's] *This ed.;* He'is *O.*

---

quando illi . . . faciem tuam vident, / Trepidant, velut avium greges, /
Magnam aquilam vel vulturem metuentes"' (*H.& S.*). *T.* quotes *Iliad,*
xv.690–2.

   19. *rarefied to air*] Cf. *Und.,* lix.10.

   22. bona-roba] See *Pers.* 67.

   28. *bill of enquiry*] more properly a writ of enquiry (Tennant); see *O.E.D.,*
'writ' 3c.

   30. *curious*] skilful.

   31. *As . . . fishwife*] See *F.I.,* l. 470n.; *S.of N.,* I.v.81, 'and a London song in
the *Shirburn* Ballads, ed. Clarke, p. 338, from MS Rawlinson poet. 185: "New
place, new, as new as the daye; / New whitings, new, here haue yow maye"'
(*H.& S.*). Billingsgate fishwives were proverbial scolds – see Nashe, *Works,*
III, 387.

   33. *fashioner*] a modish appellation for a tailor, first recorded in *O.E.D.* in
S.N., V.i.16.

Of which a brace here longed to bid you welcome.

Pinnacia. He's one, in truth, I title my Protection:
Bid him come up.

Host [*Calls.*]   Our new lady's Protection! –
What is your ladyship's style?

Pinnacia.   Countess Pinnacia.   40

Host. Countess Pinnacia's man, come to your lady.

[*Enter* STUFF.]

Pru. Your ladyship's tailor! Master Stuff!

Lady F.   How, Stuff!
He the Protection?

Host.   Stuff looks like a remnant.

Stuff. I am undone, discovered.   [*Falls on his knees.*]

Pru.   'Tis the suit, madam,
Now without scruple; and this some device   45
To bring it home with.

Pinnacia.   Why upon your knees?
Is this your lady godmother?

Stuff.   Mum, Pinnacia;
It is the Lady Frampul, my best customer.

Lady F. What show is this that you present us with?

Stuff. I do beseech your ladyship, forgive me;   50
She did but say the suit on.

Lady F.   Who? Which she?

Stuff. My wife, forsooth.

Lady F.   How? Mistress Stuff? Your wife?
Is that the riddle?

Pru.   We all looked for a lady,
A duchess or a countess at the least.

Stuff. She is my own lawfully begotten wife,   55
In wedlock: we ha' been coupled now seven years.

---

38. He's] *This ed.;* He'is *O.*   39. *Calls.*] *G.*   41.1. *Enter* STUFF.] *G.*   42.
Master] *G;* mas, *O;* Mass, *F3.*   44. *Falls . . . knees.*] *G.*   47. your lady] *O;*
lady your *W.*

40. *style*] title (*O.E.D.*, 18).
45. *scruple*] doubt.
49. *show*] dramatic spectacle.
51. *say . . . on*] try on; Partridge, *Accidence*, § 111g.
55. *my . . . wife*] 'So Lancelot Gobbo in Shakespeare, *Mer.V.*, II.ii.30, "my
true-begotten father"' (*H.& S.*).

Lady F. And why thus masked? You look like a footman,
      ha!
      And she your countess!
Pinnacia.   To make a fool of himself,
      And of me too.
Stuff.   I pray thee, Pinnace, peace.
Pinnacia. Nay, it shall out since you have called me wife,   60
      And openly dis-ladied me: though I am dis-countessed,
      I am not yet dis-countenanced. These shall see.
Host.   Silence!
Pinnacia. It is a foolish trick, madam, he has;
      For though he be your tailor, he is my beast.
      I may be bold with him and tell his story.   65
      When he makes any fine garment will fit me,
      Or any rich thing that he thinks of price,
      Then I must put it on and be his countess
      Before he carry it home unto the owners.
      A coach is hired and four horse; he runs   70
      In his velvet jacket thus to Rumford, Croydon,
      Hounslow, or Barnet, the next bawdy road;
      And takes me out, carries me up, and throws me
      Upon a bed –
Lady F.   Peace, thou immodest woman!

70. horse] *O;* Horses *F3.*

---

57. *masked*] dressed.
   footman] ran by the coach – see l. 70 and cf. *E.H.*, III.ii.43.
   64. *beast*] Cf. *Ep.*, xxv, 'On Sir Voluptuous Beast', who, like Stuff, takes his
wife in various disguises.
   66–74.] With these lines cf. *Und.*, xliii.37–42; *Volp.*, III.vii.225ff.
   67. *price*] worth.
   70. *coach is hired*] Coach riding was frequently satirised as a kind of
conspicuous extravagance often indulged in by whores; see *Poet.*, IV.ii.17n.;
B.F., IV.v.96ff. (Revels); Massinger, *The Picture*, IV.iii.109–11n.
   71–2. *Rumford . . . Barnet*] favourite places of resort for Londoners:
Romford is in Essex, twelve miles north-east of London; Croydon is in
Surrey, nine miles south; Hounslow in Middlesex eleven miles west. (cf.
E.M.O., III.vi.148); and Barnet is in Herts., eleven miles north-north-west.
H.& S. cite John Taylor, *The World runnes on wheeles* (*Workes*, 1630, p. 238):
'euery *Gill Turnetripe*, Mistris *Fumkins*, Madame *Polecat*, and my Lady
Trash, *Froth* the tapster, *Bill* the Taylor, . . . with their companion Trugs,
must be coach'd to . . . *Croydon*, *Windsor*, *Vxbridge*, and many other places,
like wilde Haggards prancing vp and downe'. Cf. *B.F.*, I.iii.60n. and
IV.v.38n. (Revels).

She glories in the bravery o' the vice.   75
Latimer. 'Tis a quaint one!
Beaufort.   A fine species
Of fornicating with a man's own wife,
Found out by – what's his name!
Latimer.   Master Nick Stuff!
Host. The very figure of preoccupation
In all his customers' best clothes.
Latimer.   He lies   80
With his own succuba in all your names.
Beaufort. And all your credits.
Host.   Ay, and at all their costs.
Latimer. This gown was then bespoken for the sovereign?
Beaufort. Ay, marry, was it.
Lady F.   And a main offence
Committed 'gainst the sovereignty, being not brought   85
Home i' the time; beside, the profanation,
Which may call on the censure of the court.
Host. Let him be blanketed. Call up the quartermaster.
Deliver him o'er to Fly.

[*Enter* FLY.]

Stuff.   O good my lord!
Host. Pillage the pinnace.
Lady F.   Let his wife be stripped.   90
Beaufort. Blow off her upper deck.
Latimer.   Tear all her tackle.
Lady F. Pluck the polluted robes over her ears;
Or cut them all to pieces, make a fire o' them.
Pru. To rags and cinders, burn th' idolatrous vestures.

84. *Lady F.*] *O; Lat. F3.*   89.1. *Enter* FLY.] *G.*

76. *quaint*] finely dressed (*O.E.D.*, 5) with a pun on quaint, 'a woman's priuities' (Florio, '*Becchina*'); cf. *Alc.*, II.iii.303n. (Revels).

species] Jonson prints the word in italics; *O.E.D.* records its first use in the sense 'class composed of individuals having some common qualities' in 1630, the year after the play; the word may therefore have its Latin meaning of 'spectacle'.

79. *preoccupation*] bawdy; Arg. 102n.

81. *succuba*] female demon supposed to have intercourse with men in their sleep; cf. *Alc.*, II.ii.48n. (Revels).

87. *censure*] sentence.

88. *blanketed*] the fate of Horace (Jonson) in Dekker's *Satiromastix*, IV.iii.

Host. Fly and your followers, see that the whole censure   95
     Be thoroughly executed.
Fly.   We'll toss him bravely
     Till the stuff stink again.
Host.   And send her home
     Divested to her flannel in a cart.
Latimer. And let her foorman beat the basin afore her.
Fly. The court shall be obeyed.
Host.   Fly and his officers   100
     Will do it fiercely.
Stuff.   Merciful Queen Pru!
Pru. I cannot help you.

                    [*Exit* FLY, *with* STUFF *and* PINNACIA.]
Beaufort.   Go thy ways, Nick Stuff,
     Thou hast nicked it for a fashioner of venery.
Latimer. For his own hell, though he run ten mile for't!
Pru. O here comes Lovel for his second hour.   105
Beaufort. And after him the type of Spanish valour.

ACT IV SCENE iv

  [*Enter to them*] LOVEL [*with a paper, followed by*] TIPTO.

[*Lady F.*] Servant, what have you there?
Lovel.   A meditation
     Or rather a vision, madam, and of beauty,
     Our former subject.
Lady F.   Pray you let us hear it.

102.1. *Exit . . .* PINNACIA.] G.
0.1.] *This ed.;* Lady. Lovel. Tipto. Latimer. Beaufort. Pru. Franke. Nurse.
Host. O.

   98–9. *Divested . . . afore her*] Whores were stripped and whipped at a cart's
tail with a basin beaten before; see the woodcut to the title-page of Harman's
Caveat for Common Cursetors (1567); cf. *S.W.*, III.v.87–8; Dekker, *2 Honest
Whore*, V.ii. See Arg. 105n.
   103. *nicked it*] hit the mark; *M.L.*, II.iv.34.
   104. *hell*] has a secondary bawdy meaning, vagina; cf. Shakespeare. *Sonn.*,
cxliv.12.
   106. *type*] image (*O.E.D.*, 2).

   2. *vision*] a revelation as opposed to a fantasy; see *U.V.*, xxx.11ff.
   3. *hear it*] It may have been a social custom to read a poem aloud before
singing it; for other examples in seventeenth-century drama see W. J.
Lawrence, 'The Wedding of Poetry and Song', in his *Those Nut-Cracking*

Lovel.   It was a beauty that I saw,
                           So pure, so perfect, as the frame   5
                           Of all the universe was lame
                           To that one figure, could I draw
                           Or give least line of it a law!

                           A skein of silk without a knot,
                           A fair march made without a halt,   10
                           A curious form without a fault,
                           A printed book without a blot:
                           All beauty, and without a spot.

Lady F. They are gentle words, and would deserve a note
      Set to 'em as gentle.

Lovel.   I have tried my skill   15
      To close the second hour, if you will hear them;
      My boy by that time will have got it perfect.

Lady F. Yes, gentle servant. [*Aside.*] In what calm he speaks
      After this noise and tumult, so unmoved,
      With that serenity of countenance   20
      As if his thoughts did acquiesce in that
      Which is the object of the second hour
      And nothing else.

Pru.   Well then, summon the court.

Lady F. I have a suit to the sovereign of Love,
      If it may stand with the honour of the court,   25
      To change the question but from love to valour,
      To hear it said but what true valour is,
      Which oft begets true love.

Latimer.   It is a question
      Fit for the court to take true knowledge of
      And hath my just assent.

Pru.   Content.

Elizabethans (London, 1935), pp. 144–52.

   4–13.] The poem is discussed by Barbara Everett, *C.Q.*, I (1959), 238–44.
   6. *lame*] defective.
   11. *curious*] artful.
   14. *gentle*] noble.
   note] tune.
   17. *by . . . time*] See the end of the play (V.v.149).
   21. *acquiesce*] rest (*O.E.D.*, 1).
   25. *stand with*] be consistent with.
   29. *knowledge*] cognizance.

Beaufort.   Content.   30
Frank. Content. I am content, give him his oath.
Host. Herbert Lovel, thou shalt swear upon *The Testament*
    of Love to make answer to this question propounded
    to thee by the court, what true valour is; and therein
    to tell the truth, the whole truth, and nothing but   35
    the truth. So help thee Love, and thy bright sword at
    need.
Lovel. So help me Love, and my good sword at need.
    It is the greatest virtue, and the safety
    Of all mankind; the object of it is danger.   40
    A certain mean 'twixt fear and confidence:
    No inconsiderate rashness, or vain appetite
    Of false encount'ring formidable things;

---

32. Herbert.] *This ed.; Herebert* O.

---

32. The . . . Love] the title of a work by Thomas Usk (died in 1388) which in
Jonson's day was attributed to Chaucer.

36. *thy . . . sword*] a sexual innuendo.

39ff.] As W. D. Briggs pointed out, Jonson's principal source for this scene
is Seneca: see 'Ben Jonson: Notes on *Underwood*, xxx and *The New Inn*',
M.P., X (1913), 573–85. And as Jonson tells us in *The Magnetic Lady*,
III.vi.87–97, by valour he means fortitude: '*Com.* I should be glad to heare of
any valours, / Differing in kind; who have knowne hitherto, / Only one vertue,
they call *Fortitude*, / Worthy the name of valour.   *Iro.* Which, who hath not, /
Is justly thought a Coward . . . / *Dia.* O, you ha'read the Play there, the *New
Inne*, / Of *Ionson*, that decries all other valour / But what is for the
publicke.   *Iro.* I doe that too, / But did not learn it there; I thinke no valour /
Lies for a private cause.' / For analogous passages in contemporary plays see
Clifford Leech, 'Pacificism in Caroline Drama', *Durham University Journal*,
XXXI (1939), 126–36.

39. *safety*] protection (*O.E.D.*, 3).

41–8.] The source is Seneca, *Epistulae*, lxxxv.28: 'Non dubitarent quid
conveniret forti viro si scirent quid esset fortitudo. Non est enim inconsulta
temeritas nec periculorum amor nec formidabilium appetit~ ꞏscientia est
distinguendi, quid sit malum et quid non sit.' Jonson also   itated this
passage in *Und.*, xiii.105–112: 'I thought that Fortitude had been a meane /
'Twixt feare and rashnesse: not a lust obscene, / Or appetite of offending, but
a skill, / Or Science of discerning Good and Ill. / And you Sir know it well to
whom I write, / That with these mixtures we put out her light. / Her ends are
honestie, and publike good! / And where they want, she is not understood.' /
Cf. Montaigne, 'Cowardize, the Mother of Crueltie' (II.xxvii, (Macpherson,
128, 129)) and Bacon, *Charge Concerning Duels* (1614): 'For fortitude
distinguisheth of the grounds of quarrels whether they be just; and not only
so, but whether they be worthy.'

43. *false*] wrongly.

But a true science of distinguishing
What's good or evil. It springs out of reason   45
And tends to perfect honesty; the scope
Is always honour and the public good:
It is no valour for a private cause.
Beaufort. No, not for reputation?
Lovel.   That's man's idol
Set up 'gainst God, the maker of all laws,   50
Who hath commanded us we should not kill;
And yet we say we must for reputation.
What honest man can either fear his own
Or else will hurt another's reputation?
Fear to do base, unworthy things is valour;   55
If they be done to us, to suffer them
Is valour too. The office of a man
That's truly valiant is considerable
Three ways: the first is in respect of matter,
Which still is danger; in respect of form,   60
Wherein he must preserve his dignity;
And in the end, which must be ever lawful.
Latimer. But men when they are heated and in passion,
Cannot consider.
Lovel.   Then it is not valour.
I never thought an angry person valiant: 65
Virtue is never aided by a vice.
What need is there of anger and of tumult,
When reason can do the same things, or more?
Beaufort. O yes, 'tis profitable, and of use:
It makes us fierce and fit to undertake.   70

50. 'gainst] *O;* against *F3.*

---

46. *scope*] mark (for shooting at) (*O.E.D.*, sb.2.1).
56–9. *If they . . . ways*] *Und.*, lix.14–19, are very similar.
58. *considerable*] capable of being considered.
59–62.] Cf. the parallel analysis at III.ii.91–3.
66.] Seneca, *De Ira*, I.ix.1: 'Numquam enim virtus vitio adiuvanda est se contenta.'
67–8.] *Ibid.*, xi.2: 'Deinde quid opus est ira, cum idem proficiat ratio?'
67. *tumult*] violent emotion (*O.E.D.*, 3).
69–70.] *Ibid.*, vii.1: 'Numquid, quamvis non sit naturalis ira, adsumenda est, quia utilis saepe fuit? Extollit animos et incitat . . .'.
70. *undertake*] commit oneself to an enterprise (*O.E.D.*, 8).
71–7. *Why . . . it*] *Ibid.*, xiii.3–5: '"Utilis," inquit, "ira est, quia pugnaciores

Lovel. Why, so will drink make us both bold and rash,
  Or frenzy if you will: do these make valiant?
  They are poor helps and virtue needs them not.
  No man is valianter by being angry
  But he that could not valiant be without: 75
  So that it comes not in the aid of virtue,
  But in the stead of it.
Latimer.   He holds the right.
Lovel. And 'tis an odious kind of remedy
  To owe our health to a disease.
Tipto.   If man
  Should follow the *dictamen* of his passion,   80
  He could not 'scape –
Beaufort.   To discompose himself.
Latimer. According to Don Lewis!
Host.   Or Carranza!
Lovel. Good Colonel Glorious, whilst we treat of valour,
  Dismiss yourself.
Latimer.   You are not concerned.
Lovel.   Go drink,
  And congregate the ostlers and the tapsters,   85
  The under-officers o' your regiment;
  Compose with them, and be not angry valiant.
                                        TIPTO *goes out.*
Beaufort. How does that differ from true valour?

---

facit." Isto modo et ebrietas; facit enim protervos et audaces . . . isto modo
dic et phrenesin atque insaniam viribus necessarium, quia saepe validiores
furor reddit, . . . Sed ira, ebrietas, metus . . . foeda et caduca irritamenta sunt
nec virtutem instruunt, quae nihil vitiis eget . . . Nemo irascendo fit fortior,
nisi qui fortis sine ira non fuisset. Ita non in adiutorium virtutis venit, sed in
vicem.'

74. *valianter*] Partridge, *Accidence*, § 31.

78–9.] *Ibid.*, xii.6: 'Abominandum remedi genus est sanitatem debere
morbo.'

80. dictamen] dictation; cf. III.i.52n.; possibly 'a play on "dictamen" /
"dictamnum" / "dittany", a herb eaten – according to Pliny – by wounded
deer to make their arrows drop out; Renaissance commentators contrasted the
plight of lovers irretrievably wounded by Cupid.' Ian Donaldson's note to
Und., ii.9, *Ben Jonson: Poems* (Oxford, 1975).

81. *discompose*] See IV.ii.77n.

82. *Don Lewis . . . Carranza*] See II.v.87n.

85. *congregate*] gather together.

87. *Compose*] make your peace; cf. IV.ii.77n.

Lovel.   Thus:
    In the efficient, or that which makes it:
    For it proceeds from passion not from judgment;   90
    Then brute beasts have it, wicked persons: there
    It differs in the subject; in the form,
    'Tis carried rashly and with violence;
    Then i' the end, where it respects not truth
    Or public honesty, but mere revenge.   95
    Now confident and undertaking valour
    Sways from the true two other ways as being
    A trust in our own faculties, skill, or strength,
    And not the right, or conscience o' the cause
    That works it; then i' the end, which is the victory   100
    And not the honour.
Beaufort.   But the ignorant valour
    That knows not why it undertakes, but doth it
    T' escape the infamy merely –
Lovel.   Is worst of all:
    That valour lies i' the eyes o' the lookers on,
    And is called valour with a witness.
Beaufort.   Right.   105
Lovel. The things true valous is exercised about
    Are poverty, restraint, captivity,

---

103. T' escape] *O;* T[o]'escape *H.& S.*

89–101. *In . . . the honour*] See III.ii.91–3n.

95. *mere*] sheer, pure.

96. *confident*] over-bold, presumptuous.
under-taking] bold; cf. l. 69 above.

97–100. *as being . . . works it*] Cf. Montaigne, 'Constancie is valour, not of armes and legs, but of mind and courage: it consisteth not in the spirit and courage of our horse, nor of our armes, but of ours' ('Of the Canniballes', I.xxx, p. 226).

99. *conscience*] equity.

104–5.] 'Bacon, *Considerations touching a War with Spaine* (*Letters*, ed. Spedding, VII, 499): "Of valour I speak not, take it from the witnesses that have been produced before; yet the old observation is not untrue, that the Spaniard's valour lieth in the eye of the looker-on; but the English valour lieth about the soldier's heart"' (*H.& S.*).

105. *with a witness*] with a vengeance; cf. Tilley, L238, 'That is a lie with a witness' and Shakespeare, *Shr.*, V.i.105.

106–8.] Seneca, *De Constantia*, x.4: 'Alia sunt quae sapientem feriunt, etiam si non pervertunt, ut dolor corporis et debilitas aut amicorum liberorumque amissio et patriae bello flagrantis calamitas.'

107. *restraint*] confinement.

> Banishment, loss of children, long disease:
> The least is death. Here valour is beheld,
> Properly seen: about these it is present;   110
> Not trivial things which but require our confidence.
> And yet to those we must object ourselves
> Only for honesty: if any other
> Respect be mixed, we quite put our her light.
> And as all knowledge when it is removed   115
> Or separate from justice is called craft
> Rather than wisdom: so a mind affecting
> Or undertaking dangers for ambition
> Or any self pretext, not for the public,
> Deserves the name of daring not of valour,   120
> And over-daring is as great a vice
> As over-fearing.

Latimer.   Yes, and often greater.

Lovel. But as it is not the mere punishment
> But cause that makes a martyr, so it is not
> Fighting or dying but the manner of it   125
> Renders a man himself. A valiant man
> Ought not to undergo or tempt a danger
> But worthily and by selected ways:
> He undertakes with reason not by chance.
> His valour is the salt to his other virtues,   130
> They are all unseasoned without it. The waiting-maids
> Or the concomitants of it, are his patience,
> His magnanimity, his confidence,
> His constancy, security, and quiet;

123. as it] *F3;* as *O.*

---

112. *object*] expose (Lat. *obicio*).

113–4.] Cf. *Und.*, xv.24–5.

114. *Respect*] consideration (*O.E.D.*, 14).

115–20.] 'Cicero, *De Officiis*, I.xix.1: "Praeclarum igitur illud Platonis: Non, inquit, solum scientia quae est remota ab iustitia calliditas potius quam sapientia est appellanda, verum etiam animus paratus ad periculum, si sua cupiditate, non utilitate communi impillitur, audaciae potius nomen habet quam fortitudinis." The reference is to Plato, *Menexenus*, § 246E' (*H.& S.*).

119. *self*] personal.

public] See IV.iv.39n.

127. *tempt*] try, test (*O.E.D.*, 1).

131. *waiting-maids*] Cf. Lat. *ancillae*, often used figuratively in this sense.

134. *quiet*] peace of mind.

He can assure himself against all rumour,   135
Despairs of nothing, laughs at contumelies,
As knowing himself advancèd in a height
Where injury cannot reach him, nor aspersion
Touch him with soil!
Lady F.   Most manly uttered all!
As if Achilles had the chair in valour   140
And Hercules were but a lecturer.
Who would not hang upon these lips for ever
That strike such music? I could run on them;
But modesty is such a schoolmistress
To keep our sex in awe.
Pru.   Or you can feign,   145
My subtle and dissembling lady mistress!
Latimer. I fear she means it, Pru, in too good earnest!
Lovel. The purpose of an injury 'tis to vex
And trouble me: now nothing can do that
To him that's valiant. He that is affected   150
With the least injury is less than it.
It is but reasonable to conclude
That should be stronger still which hurts than that
Which is hurt. Now no wickedness is stronger

145.6. feign,/ My . . . mistress!] *G;* faine! my/ Subtill . . . mistresse. *O, F3.*

---

136. *contumelies*] insults.

141. *lecturer*] The term was first used at Gresham College, London. (see *O.E.D.*).

143. *run on*] discourse on (*O.E.D.*, 'run' 65).

148ff.] The sentiments in these lines take their place in the contemporary debates about the morality of duelling. See particularly Bacon's *Charge Concerning Duels* (1614) and the account in *Sh.Eng.*, II, 401–7; and see *D.is A.*, III.iii.66n; for a connection with Massinger's *The City Madam*, see *P.& P.*, IV, 10.

148. *injury*] insult, calumny, taunt (*O.E.D.*, 2); at l. 162, however, Jonson uses the word to mean a physical action.

148–50. *The purpose . . . valiant*] Seneca, *De Constantia*, v.3: 'Iniuria propositum hoc habet aliquem malo adficere . . . nulla ad sapientem iniuria pertinet.'

152–5. *It is . . . opposeth it*] *Ibid.*, vii.2: 'Denique validius debet esse quod laedit eo quod laeditur; non est autem fortior nequitia virtute.'

155–7. *not . . . less*] from Cato's speech in Lucan, ix.569–70: 'An noceat vis ulla bono, fortunaque perdat opposita virtute minas?' Jonson had used these lines in *Sej.*, III.324–5. Cf also Seneca, *De Constantia*, viii.3: 'non habet [sapiens] ubi accipiat iniuriam – ab homine me tantum dicere putas? Ne a

Than what opposeth it: not Fortune's self,   155
When she encounters virtue but comes off
Both lame and less! Why should a wise man, then,
Confess himself the weaker by the feeling
Of a fool's wrong? There may an injury
Be meant me. I may choose if I will take it.   160
But we are now come to that delicacy
And tenderness of sense, we think an insolence
Worse than an injury, bear words worse than deeds;
We are not so much troubled with the wrong
As with the opinion of the wrong; like children   165
We are made afraid with visors! Such poor sounds
As is the lie or common words of spite,
Wise laws thought never worthy a revenge;
And 'tis the narrowness of human nature,
Our poverty and beggary of spirit,   170

---

fortuna quidem, quae quotiens cum virtute congressa est, numquam par recessit.'

156. *comes off*] leaves the field of combat.

159–60. *There may . . . take it*] *Ibid.*, vii.3: 'Hoc loco intellegere nos oportet posse evenire, ut faciat aliquis iniuriam mihi et non accipiam.'

160. *take*] accept.

163. *injury*] See l. 147n. above.

164–5. *We are . . . the wrong*] 'Cf. Epictetus, *Enchiridion*, v . . . . For 'opinion' cf. *Disc.*, 43–9,' (*H.& S.*).

164–6. *We are . . . visors*] Seneca, *De Constantia*, v.2: 'Ad tantas ineptias perventum est, ut non dolore tantum sed doloris opinione vexemur more puerorum, quibus metum incutit umbra et personarum deformitas.'

166. *visors*] Cf. Stubbes, *Anatomy of Abuses* (1583), ch.vi, ed. Furnivall (London, 1877–9), p. 80: 'When [women] vse to ride abrod, they haue . . . visors made of veluet . . . So that if a man, that knew not their guise before, should chaunce to meet one of them, hee would think hee met a monster or a deuil' (cited *T.*).

166–76. *Such . . . taking it*] Seneca, *De Constantia*, x.1–3: '[Contumelia] est minor iniuria, quam queri magis quam exsequi possumus, quam leges quoque nulla dignam vindicta putaverunt. Hunc affectum movet humilitas animi contrahentis se ob dictum factumve inhonorificum: "Ille me hodie non admisit, cum alios admitteret," et "sermonem meum aut superbe aversatus est aut palam risit," et "non in medio me lecto sed in imo collocavit," et alia huius notae, quae quid vocem nisi querellas nausiantis animi? . . . his [iniuriis] commoventur, quorum pars maior constat vitio interpretantis.'

167. *the lie*] 'In his copy of Clement Edmondes's *Observations upon Caesars Commentaries* (1609?; McPherson, 56), pp. 198–9, Jonson marked a passage against the folly of duelling which centres on the sentence 'the word lye is of as great consequence, as any stabbe or villanie whatsoeuer . . .' (*H.& S.*).

To take exception at these things. He laughed at me!
He broke a jest! A third took place of me!
How most ridiculous quarrels are all these!
Notes of a queasy and sick stomach labouring
With want of a true injury: the main part   175
Of the wrong is our vice of taking it.

Latimer. Or our interpreting it to be such.

Lovel. You take it rightly. If a woman or child
Give me the lie, would I be angry? No,
Not if I were i' my wits, sure I should think it   180
No spice of a disgrace. No more is theirs,
If I think it, who are to be held
In as contemptible a rank or worse.
I am kept out a masque, sometime thrust out,
Made wait a day, two, three, for a great word   185
Which (when it comes forth) is all frown and forehead:
What laughter should this breed rather than anger!
Out of the tumult of so many errors,
To feel with contemplation mine own quiet!
If a great person do me an affront,   190
A giant of the time, sure I will bear it
Or out of the time, sure I will bear it
Or cut of patience or necessity.
Shall I do more for fear than for my judgment?
For me now to be angry with Hodge Huffle   195
Or Burst, his broken charge, if he be saucy,
Or our own type of Spanish valour, Tipto,
(Who, were he now necessited to beg,

197. necessited] *O;* necessitated *F3.*

---

174. *Notes*] signs.
178. *a woman . . . child*] *De Constantia*, xii.1: 'Quem animum nos adversus pueros habemus, hunc sapiens adversus omnes, quibus etiam post iuventam canosque puerilitas est'; xiv.1: 'Tanta quosdam dementia tenet, ut sibi contumeliam fieri putent posse a muliere.'
181. *spice*] kind (*O.E.D.*, 3b).
184.] There are many examples of people being turned out of performances at court: see *C.R.*, V.iii.16n.; *Conv.Drum.*, ll. 155–9; *Ep.*, xxxiin.
186. *forehead*] impudence (*O.E.D.*, 2b).
188. *errors*] vexations, extravagances of passion (*O.E.D.*,2).
192. *Or . . . or*] either . . . or.
197. *necessited*] necessitated (see *O.E.D.*,'necessite').

Would ask an alms like Conde Olivares,)
Were just to make myself such a vain animal
As one of them. If light wrongs touch me not,   200
No more shall great; if not a few, not many.
There's nought so sacred with us but may find
A sacrilegious person, yet the thing is
No less divine 'cause the profane can reach it.
He is shot-free in battle is not hurt,   205
Not he that is not hit. So he is valiant
That yields not unto wrongs, not he that scapes 'em.
They that do pull down churches and deface
The holiest altars, cannot hurt the godhead.
A calm wise man may show as much true valour   210
Amidst these popular provocations
As can an able captain show security
By his brave conduct through an enemy's country.
A wise man never goes the people's way,
But as the planets still move contrary   215

---

198. *Conde Olivares*] Gaspar de Guzman y Pimental, Conde-Duque de
Olivares (1587–1645), court favorite of Philip IV and from 1623 until 1643
prime minister of Spain. He appears as the Black Duke in Middleton's *A
Game at Chess* (1623). He is here a figure of Spanish pride – England was at
war with Spain from 1624 to 1636.

200. *If . . . many*] Seneca, *De Constantia*, xv.2: 'In quantumcumque
ista [molesta] vel numero vel magnitudine creverint, eiusdem naturae erunt.
Si non tangent illum parva, ne maiora quidem; se non tangent pauca, ne plura
quidem.'

202. *find*] attract.

202–6. *There's . . . hit*] *Ibid.*, iii.3: 'Nihil in rerum natura tam sacrum est,
quod sacrilegium non inveniat, sed non ideo divina minus in sublimi sunt, si
exsistunt qui magnitudinem multum ultra se positam non tacturi appetant;
invulnerabile est non quod non feritur, sed quod non laeditur.' Cf. *Poet.*,
Apol.Dial. 38–9; *Und.*, xxv.48–9.

205.] The sense is plainer when 'who' is supplied after 'battle'.

208–13.] Seneca, *De Constantia*, iv.2–3: 'Ut caelestia humanas manus
effugiunt et ab his qui templa diruunt ac simulacra conflant nihil divinitati
nocetur, ita quicquid fit in sapientem proterve, petulanter, superbe, frustra
temptatur . . . Immo nescio an magis vires sapientiae ostendat tranquillitas
inter lacessentia, sicut maximum argumentum est imperatoris armis virisque
pollentis tuta securitas in hostium terra.'

212. *security*] confidence.

214–16.] Seneca, *De Constantia*, xiv.4: 'Non it qua populus, sed ut sidera
contrarium mundo iter intendunt, ita hic adversus opinionem omnium vadit.'
Cf. *Beauty*, ll. 258–62; '"Spondanus"' commentary on the *Iliad*, xii.237–40,
discusses the question fully' (*H.& S.*). For a contrary dictum based on
Seneca, *Epist.*, v.3, see *Ep.*, cxix. 11–12. See also 2 Epil. o.3n.

To the world's motion, so doth he to opinion.
He will examine if those accidents
(Which common fame calls injuries) happen to him
Deservedly or no: come they deservedly,
They are no wrongs, then, but his punishments;   220
If undeservedly, and he not guilty,
The doer of them first should blush, not he.

Latimer. Excellent!

Beaufort.   Truth, and right!

Frank.   An oracle
Could not have spoken more!

Lady F.   Been more believed!

Pru. The whole court runs into your sentence, sir;   225
And see your second hour is almost ended.

Lady F. It cannot be! O clip the wings of Time,
Good Pru, or make him stand still with a charm.
Distill the gout into it, cramps, all diseases
T'arrest him in the foot and fix him here: 230
O for an engine to keep back all clocks,
Or make the sun forget his motion!
If I but knew what drink the time now loved,
To set my Trundle at him, mine own Barnaby!

Pru. Why, I'll consult our Shelee-nien Thomas.   235
                                        [*Shakes her.*]

Nurse. Er grae Chreest.

Beaufort.   Wake her not.

Nurse.   *Tower een cuppan*

230. T' arrest] *O;* T[o]'arrest *H.& S.*   235. Thomas] *This ed.;* To-mas
O.   Shakes her.] *G.*   236. cuppan] *O;* Cuppaw *G.*

217–22.] *De Constantia,* xvi.3: 'Utrum meriot mihi ista accidunt an
inmerito? Si merito, non est contumelia, iudicium est; si inmerito, illi qui
iniusta facit erubescendum est.'

225. *sentence*] meaning (*O.E.D.*, 7).

227. *wings of Time*] For Time (or Opportunity) as a winged figure see E.
Panofsky, *Studies in Iconology* (New York, 1939), pp.71ff.

231. *engine*] contrivance.

233.] Cf. the similar conceit in *D.is A.,* V.vi.10, derived perhaps from
Plautus, *Amphitruo,* l. 282.

234. *Trundle*] a heavy drinker who might be able to get Time intoxicated.
    Barnaby] also a toper (IV.ix); 'but Lady Frampul means no more than "my
coachman"' (*H.& S.*).

235. *Shelee-nien*] See II.vi.263n.

236–7. Er . . . usque bagh] 'When Jonson wrote *The Irish Masque* in 1613 he

G

    D'usque bagh doone.

Pru.   *Usque bagh*'s her drink,
    But 'twi' not make the time drunk.

Host.   As't hath her.
    Away with her, my lord, but marry her first.

              [*Exeunt* LORD BEAUFORT *and* FRANK.]

Pru. Ay, that'll be sport anon too for my lady,   240
    But she hath other game to fly at yet:
    The hour is come, your kiss.

Lady F.   My servant's song first.

Pru. I say the kiss first; and I so enjoined it:
    At your own peril do, make the contempt.

Lady F. Well, sir, you must be paid and legally. [*Kisses Lovel.*] 245

Pru. Nay nothing, sir, beyond.

Lovel.   One more – I except:
    This was but half a kiss, and I would change
    it.

Pru. The court's dissolved, removed, and the play ended;
    No sound or air of love more, I decree it.

Lovel. From what a happiness hath that one word   250
    Thrown me, into the gulf of misery!
    To what a bottomless despair! How like
    A court removing or an ended play
    Shows my abrupt precipitate estate;
    By how much more my vain hopes were increased   255
    By these false hours of conversation!

---

239. first.] *G;* first. *Pru, O, H.& S.;* first, *Pru. F3.*   240. Ay, that'll] *O;* Ay,/
That will *G.*   245. *Kisses Lovel.*] *G.*

---

contented himself with a sort of Anglo-Irish jargon. He picked up a few
genuine Irish phrases for this play. *Er grae Chreest = ar ghrádh Chríest,* "for
the love of Christ". *Tower een Cuppan D'vsque bagh doone = tabhair aon
chupán d'uisage beathadh duinn,* "give us a cup of whiskey" . . . (Note by
Professor John Frazer.)' (*H.& S.*).

    usque bagh] whisky (Gaelic *uisgebeatha,* water of life).

    244. *contempt*] disregard for the authority of the court.

    246. *except*] take exception, object.

    249. *air*] breath (*O.E.D.,* 9).

    253.] taken from Donne's 'The Calme', l. 14, a poem Jonson quoted to
Drummond (*Conv. Drum.,* l. 119).

    254. *abrupt*] unrestrained (*O.E.D.,* 1).

    precipitate] precipitous.

    estate] condition.

Did I not prophesy this of myself,
And gave the true prognostics? O my brain,
How art thou turned and my blood congealed,
My sinews slackened, and my marrow melted,   260
That I remember not where I have been
Or what I am! Only my tongue's on fire
And burning downward, hurls forth coals and cinders
To tell this temple of Love will soon be ashes!
Come, Indignation, now and be my mistress.   265
No more of Love's ingrateful tyranny,
His wheel of torture and his pits of bird-lime,
His nets of nooses, whirlpools of vexation,
His mills to grind his servants into powder –
I will go catch the wind first in a sieve,   270
Weigh smoke and measure shadows, plough the water
And sow my hopes there, ere I stay in love.
Latimer. [*Aside*.] My jealousy is off, I am now secure.

                    [*Exit* LORD LATIMER.]

Lovel. Farewell the craft of crocodiles, women's piety
And practice of it, in this art of flattering   275
And fooling men. I ha' not lost my reason
Though I have lent myself out for two hours
Thus to be baffled by a chambermaid

258. O] *H.& S.; o O; o' F3*.

---

258. *prognostics*] prediction (first recorded use in *O.E.D.* is 1634).

260. *marrow melted*] See III.ii.203n.

265. *Indignation*] disdain (for Love), *O.E.D.*, 1.

266. *ingrateful*] unpleasing, harsh.

267. *wheel of torture*] Malefactors were tied to a large wheel on which they would be 'broken'.

bird-lime] 'Bird lime is the sweat of the Oake tree; the dung of the Blackbird falling on that tree, turnes into that slimie snare, and in that snare is the Bird herselfe taken', Dekker, *N.D.*, II, 138 (cited *T.*).

270.] Tilley, W416, 'He catches the wind in a net,' cites Erasmus, *Adagia*, 1720: 'Reti ventos venaris'; cf. *D.is A.*, V.ii.7.

271.–2. *Weigh . . . hopes*] Cf. Tilley, W417, 'He that weighs the wind must have a steady hand'; W451, 'To plow the winds'; and Geron's lament: 'He water ploughs and soweth in the sand, / And hopes the flickering wind with net to hold, / Who hath his hopes laid up in woman's hand' / (Sidney, *Arcadia*, ed. M. Evans (Harmondsworth, 1977), p. 421).

274. *craft of crocodiles*] See Tilley, C831, 'Crocodile tears'; *Volp.*, III.vii.199–200n.; and Middleton, *The Changeling*, V.iii.112n. (Revels).

278. *baffled*] disgraced.

And the good actor, her lady, afore mine host
Of the Light Heart here that hath laughed at all –   280
Host. Who, I?
Lovel.   Laugh on, sir. I'll to bed and sleep
And dream away the vapour of love, if th' house
And your leer drunkards let me.
          [*Exeunt all but Lady Frampul, Prudence, and Nurse.*]
Lady F.   Pru.
Pru.   Sweet madam.
Lady F. Why should you let him go thus?
Pru.   In whose power
Was it to stay him, prop'rer than my lady's?   285
Lady F. Why in your lady's? Art not you the sovereign?
Pru. Would you, in conscience, madame, ha' me vex
His patience more?
Lady F.   No, but apply the cure
Now it is vexed.
Pru.   That's but one body's work:
Two cannot do the same thing handsomely.   290
Lady F. But had not you the authority absolute?
Pru. And were not you i' rebellion, Lady Frampul,
From the beginning?
Lady F.   I was somewhat froward
I must confess, but frowardness sometime
Becomes a beauty, being but a visor   295
Put on. You'll let a lady wear her mask, Pru!
Pru. But how do I know when her ladyship is pleased
To leave it off except she tell me so?
Lady F. You might ha' known that by my looks and
          language
Had you been or regardant or observant.   300

283.1. *Exeunt . . . Nurse.*] G.   286. your] *G;* her *O.*   288. No,] *H.& S.;*
Not *O,* F3.

---

282. *vapour*] whim, fantasy; originally a fume from one of the vital organs;
cf. *B.F.,* II.iii.23.

283. *leer*] 'looking askance; oblique, indirect, sly, underhand' (*O.E.D.,*); cf.
B.F., Ind. 119.

289. *body's*] person's.

290. *handsomely*] fitly, readily (*O.E.D.,* 1 & 2).

296. *mask*] Masks had been fashionable since the mid-sixteenth century;
see Linthicum, pp. 271–2; *Poet.,* IV.i.13n.; *D.is A.,* II.i.162n.

300. *regardant*] watchful.

One woman reads another's character
Without the tedious trouble of deciphering
If she but give her mind to't; you knew well
It could not sort with any reputation
Of mine to come in first, having stood out	305
So long without conditions for mine honour.

Pru. I thought you did expect none, you so jeered him
And put him off with scorn –

Lady F.	Who, I, with scorn?
I did express my love to idolatry rather,
And so am justly plagued, not understood.	310

Pru. I swear I thought you had dissembled, madam,
And doubt you do so yet.

Lady F.	Dull, stupid, wench!
Stay i' thy state of ignorance still, be damned,
An idiot chambermaid! Hath all my care,
My breeding thee in fashion, thy rich clothes,	315
Honours, and titles wrought no brighter effects
On thy dark soul than thus? Well! Go thy ways:
Were not the tailor's wife to be demolished,
Ruined, uncased, thou should'st be she, I vow.

Pru. Why, take your spangled properties, your gown,	320
And scarfs.	[*Tearing off her gown.*]

Lady F.	Pru, Pru, what dost thou mean?

Pru. I will not buy this play-boy's bravery
At such a price, to be upbraided for it
Thus every minute.

Lady F.	Take it not to heart so.

Pru. The tailor's wife! There was a word of scorn!	325

Lady F. It was a word fell from me, Pru, by chance.

Pru. Good madam, please to undeceive yourself:
I know when words do slip and when they are darted
With all their bitterness: 'Uncased, demolished,

302–3. deciphering ... to't:] *W;* deciphering: ... to't, *O, F3.*	321.
Tearing ... gown.] *G.*

---

305. *come in*] submit (*O.E.D.*, 'come' 59f.).
312. *doubt*] suspect.
319. *uncased*] stripped, undressed.
320. *properties*] costumes.
321. *scarfs*] The plural in 'v' was not universal until the eighteenth century;
Partridge, *Accidence,* § 10.

An idiot chambermaid, stupid and dull,   330
Be damned for ignorance'! I will be so.
And think I do deserve it, that, and more,
Much more I do.

                        [Enter HOST.]

Lady F.   Here comes mine host: no crying,
Good Pru! Where is my servant Lovel, host?
Host. You ha' sent him up to bed; would you follow him   335
And make my house amends!
Lady F.   Would you advise it?
Host. I would I could command it. My Light Heart
Should leap till midnight.
Lady F.   Pray thee be not sullen,
I yet must ha' thy counsel. Thou shalt wear, Pru,
The new gown yet.
Pru.   After the tailor's wife?   340
Lady F. Come, be not angry or grieved: I have a project.

              [Exeunt LADY FRAMPUL *and* PRUDENCE.]

Host. Wake, Shelee-nien Thomas! Is this your heraldry
And keeping of records, to lose the main?
Where is your charge?
Nurse.   *Gra Chreest!*
Host.   Go ask th' oracle
O' the bottle at your girdle, there you lost it: 345
You are a sober setter of the watch.

                  [Exeunt HOST *and* NURSE.]

330. idiot-] *H.& S.;* idiot——— *O.*   345. You ha'] *This ed.;* Yo ha *O;*
Yo'ha' *F3.*   342.1. *Exeunt . . .* PRUDENCE.] *G.*   343. lose] *F3;* loose
O.   346.1. *Exeunt . . .* NURSE.] *G.*

---

338. *sullen*] melancholy.

343. *lose the main*] a term from the game of hazard. 'The caster, before
throwing the dice, called a main, which was a number from five to nine
inclusive. The player then threw with two dice, and if he threw a nick . . . a
throw . . . the same as the main . . . he won; but if he "threw out", i.e. threw
two aces, or a deuce and an ace, he lost' (*Sh.Eng.*, II, 470); cf. *S.W.*, III.iii.34;
there may be a pun on 'main' the heraldic term for hand.

344. *charge*] punning on the heraldic verb 'charge' = to place a bearing on an
escutcheon etc.

344–5. *th' oracle . . . bottle*] Cf. '*N.T.*, 77 where Jonson has a marginal note
"*Vid. Rabl. lib 5.*" See Rabelais's *Pantagruel*, V. ch.xxxiv, the Temple of the
Holy Bottle, approached through a large vineyard with a portal inscribed . . .
"In wine is truth" (*H.& S.*'s note to *S.N.*, IV.ii.8).

346. *setter*] poster.

Act V

[Enter] HOST *[and]* FLY.

[Host.] Come, Fly, and legacy, the bird o' the Heart:
    Prime insect of the inn, professor, quartermaster,
    As ever thou deservedst thy daily drink,
    Paddling in sack and licking i' the same,
    Now show thyself an instrument of price   5
    And help to raise a nap to us out of nothing.
    Thou sawst 'em married?
Fly.   I do think I did,
    And heard the words, 'I Philip, take thee Laetice'.
    I gave her too, was then the father Fly,
    And heard the priest do his part far as five nobles   10
    Would lead him i' the lines of matrimony.
Host. Where were they married?
Fly.   I' th' new stable.
Host.   Ominous!
    I ha' known many a church been made a stable,
    But not a stable made a church till now:
    I wish 'em joy. Fly, was he a full priest?   15
Fly. He bellied for it, had his velvet sleeves

8. I Philip] *G; Philip,* I *O.*   12. Where . . . Ominous!] *O;* Where . . . married?/ *Fly.* . . . Ominous! *F3.*

0.1 *[Enter* HOST*]* The Host re-entered after the music played between the acts at the Blackfriars playhouse – see Introduction, p. 7, Cf. *Alc*, IV. i.n. (Revels).
    1. *legacy*] See II.iv.16n.
    6. *raise . . . nothing*] equivalent to 'weave the threads of the story together for us'.
    10. *nobles*] gold coins having a value of 6*s* 8*d* (*c.* 33p) or 10*s* (50p).
    12. *new stable*] See Arg. 79–80n.
    15. *full*] punning on full = fat (*O.E.D.*, 10).
    16. *bellied*] had a good paunch.
    velvet sleeves] 'such as are worn by a doctor of divinity' (*H.& S.*).

And his branched cassock, a side sweeping gown,
All his formalities, a good crammed divine!
I went not far to fetch him, the next inn
Where he was lodged, for the action.

Host.   Had they a licence?   20

Fly. Licence of love; I saw no other; and purse
To pay the duties both of church and house,
The angels flew about.

Host.   Those birds send luck;
And mirth will follow. I had thought to ha' sacrificed
To merriment tonight i' my Light Heart, Fly,   25
And like a noble poet to have had
My last act best; but all fails i' the plot.
Lovel is gone to bed; the Lady Frampul
And sovereign Pru fall'n out; Tipto and his regiment
Of mine-men all drunk dumb; from his whoop Barnaby,   30
To his hoop Trundle: they are his two tropics.
No project to rear laughter on but this,
The marriage of Lord Beaufort with Laetitia.
Stay, what's here? The satin gown redeemed
And Pru restored in't to her lady's grace!   35

Fly. She is set forth in't, rigged for some employment!

Host. An embassy at least!

---

30. whoop] *F3;* whop *O.*

---

17. *branched*] embroidered with a figured pattern; cf. *M.L.,* I.v.22.
side] long (O.E. *síd*).
18. *formalities*] insignia of office (*O.E.D.,* 10).
20. *licence*] A licence for marriage had to be obtained if the banns had not been called in the weeks preceding.
21–3. *purse . . . luck*] The quibble on angels (coins bearing the figure of St Michael worth 10*s* (50p) or less, and incorporeal beings) means that in fact the purse was empty; cf. *Alc,* I.ii.37n. (Revels).
22. *duties*] dues.
27. *plot*] punning on plot = scheme and = story.
30. *mine-men*] miners; cf. III.i.35 where they are 'pioneers'.
whoop] See IV.i.10n.
31. *hoop*] the quantity of liquor between the bands of a quart pot (*O.E.D.,* 4).
tropics] limits of Tipto's influence; a quibble on the two circles of the celestial sphere (Cancer and Capricorn) suggested by 'whoop' and 'hoop'.
36–8. *rigged . . . about*] the nautical metaphors continue; see IV.ii.53n.

Fly.   Some treaty of state!

Host. 'Tis a fine tack about, and worth the observing!

                                     [They stand aside.]

Act V Scene ii

[*Enter*] LADY [FRAMPUL *and*] PRUDENCE [*magnificently dressed*].

[*Lady F.*] Sweet Pru, aye, now thou art a queen indeed!
    These robes do royally and thou becom'st 'em,
    So they do thee! Rich garments only fit
    The parties they are made for; they shame others.
    How did they show on Goody Tailor's back?   5
    Like a caparison for a sow, God save us!
    Thy putting 'em on hath purged and hallowed 'em
    From all pollution meant by the mechanics.

Pru. Hang him, poor snip, a secular shop-wit!
    H'hath nought but his shears to claim by, and his
        measures: 10
    His prentice may as well put in for his needle
    And plead a stitch.

Lady F.   They have no taint in 'em
    Now o' the tailor.

Pru.   Yes, of his wife's haunches.
    Thus thick of fat; I smell 'em, o' the say.

Lady F. It is restorative, Pru: with thy but chafing it,   15
    A barren hind's grease may work miracles.

38.1. *They . . . aside.*] G.
0.1.] *G; Lady. Prudence. Host. Fly.* O.

---

   37. *treaty*] conference (*O.E.D.*, 2).
   6. *caparison*] the cloth spread over a horse's back, often ornamented.
   8. *meant*] intended.
   9. *snip*] Cf. *E.M.O.*, IV.vii.27, where the tailor is Master Snip.
   secular] 'of or belonging to the "common" or "unlearned" people' (*O.E.D.*, 2b).
   10. *claim by*] assert himself with (*O.E.D.*, 5).
   11–12. *His prentice . . . stitch*] The sense is 'He has no more dignity than his apprentice whose rank comes only from plying his needle'. 'Plead a stitch' may mean 'bear a grudge against' – see *O.E.D.*, 'stitch' 1.i.4, and Tilley, S865.
   14. *say*] (1) from venery, the trial of grease: Chapman's *Iliad*, xix.246: 'There, hauing brought the Bore, Atrides with his knife took sey' (*O.E.D.*, 'say' 2.5) and see *Sir Gawain and the Green Knight*, ll. 1325ff.; (2) a cloth of fine texture (*O.E.D.*, 'say' 1.1).
   16–23. *A barren . . . to that*] According to E. B. Partridge, 'A Crux in

Find but his chamber door, and he will rise
To thee! Or if thou pleasest, feign to be
The wretched party herself, and com'st unto him
In forma pauperis to crave the aid   20
Of his knight-errant valour to the rescue
Of thy distressed robes. Name but thy gown,
And he will rise to that!

Pru.   I'll fire the charm first;
I had rather die in a ditch with Mistress Shore,
Without a smock as the pitiful matter has it,   25
Than owe my wit to clothes, or ha' it beholden.

Host. Still spirit of Pru!

Fly.   And smelling o' the sovereign!

Pru. No, I will tell him as it is indeed:
I come from the fine, froward, frampul lady,
One was run mad with pride, wild with self-love,   30
But late encount'ring a wise man who scorned her
And knew the way to his own bed, without
Borrowing her warming-pan, she hath recovered
Part of her wits: so much as to consider

Jonson's *The New Inne'*, *M.L.N*, LXXI (1956), 168–70, there is no reference
here to a lost popular superstition but a wilder product of Jonson's
imagination. The overt meaning is that Lady Fampul 'joyfully . . . seizes on
the tainting of her gown by the sweat and the smell of Pinnacia's haunches as a
means of restoring the love which Lovel had scornfully cast off at the end of
Act IV'. But the passage also contains a vein of *double entendres*: 'but' = 'just'
and 'buttocks'; hind = female deer, servant, and hind end or buttocks;
grease = sweat and the fat of the deer (see Turberville, *The Noble Art of
Venerie*) – 'greasing' was also used in contemporary anti-Catholic literature
for 'anointing' which connects it blasphemously with 'miracles' (cf. Lady
Frampul's description of the act as 'profanation' at IV.iii.86); barren =
'infertile' and 'naked' (bare); rise = rouse himself physically and sexually.
'The gown is so powerful that by itself it can call forth heroic service. Here, as
elsewhere in the play, clothes are spoken of as nearly having religious value
and independent existence.'

20. In forma pauperis] 'One allowed [by Act II Henry VII c.12] on account
of poverty, to sue or defend in a court of law without paying costs' (*O.E.D.*).

23. *fire the charm*] burn the custome.

24. *ditch . . . Shore*] a popular but false etymology deriving from the story
that Jane Shore, mistress of Edward IV, had died in this unsavoury north-east
London parish which in fact had been called Shoreditch or Soerditch since
the twelfth century.

25. *matter*] story (*O.E.D.*, 10).

29. *frampul*] See *Pers.* 1n.

33. *warming-pan*] See I.iii.13n.

How far she hath trespassed, upon whom, and how.   35
And now sits penitent and solitary,
Like the forsaken turtle, in the volary
Of the Light Heart, the cage she hath abused,
Mourning her folly, weeping at the height
She measures with her eye from whence she is fallen   40
Since she did branch it on the top o' the wood.
Lady F. I prithee, Pru, abuse me enough, that's use me
As thou think'st fit, any coarse way, to humble me,
Or bring me home again or Lovel on:
Thou dost not know my suff'rings, what I feel,   45
My fires and fears are met; I burn and freeze,
My liver's one great coal, my heart shrunk up
With all the fibres, and the mass of blood
Within me is a standing lake of fire
Curled with the cold wind of my gelid sighs   50
That drive a drift of sleet through all my body
And shoot a February through my veins.
Until I see him, I am drunk with thirst
And surfeited with hunger of his presence.
I know not whe'r I am, or no, or speak,   55
Or whether thou dost hear me.
Pru.   Spare expressions.
I'll once more venture for your ladyship

---

43. think'st] *H. & S.;* thinkest *O.*   coarse] *This ed.;* course *O.*   48. fibres]
W; fiuers *O.*   55. whe'r] *This ed.;* whêr *O.*

---

37. *turtle*] The turtle which pairs for life is a symbol of constancy (Tilley, T
624). Cf. Shakespeare, *Wint.*, V.ii.132–5n. (New Arden).

volary] a large bird-cage.

41. *branch it*] flourish like the topmost limb of a tree (?).

44. *bring . . . on*] force me to return or advance the cause of love.

46. *burn and freeze*] conventional symptoms of love; see *S.S.*, II.iv. 19–44,
and Babb, *The Elizabethan Malady*, pp. 145 and 149.

47. *liver*] according to the ancients the seat of love and violent passion
generally; cf. *Und.*, lxxxvi.12; *Volp.*, II.iv.9.

48. *fibres*] For Jonson's 'fiuers' cf. *Und.*, xxxviii.111.

mass] 'The whole quantity of blood or fluid dispersed through an animal
body' (*O.E.D.*, 'mass' 2.2c; the first recorded use is 1693).

49. *standing*] still.

52. *February*] Cf. *T. of T.*, I.i.2.

55. *whe'r*] obsolete form of whether; cf. *Ep.*, xcvi.1; Partridge *Accidence*, §
69.

So you will use your fortunes reverently.

Lady F. Religiously, dear Pru: Love and his mother,
  I'll build them several churches, shrines, and altars,   60
  And overhead I'll have, in the glass windows,
  The story of this day be painted, round,
  For the poor laity of love to read;
  I'll make myself their book, nay their example,
  To bid them take occasion by the forelock,   65
  And play no after-games of love hereafter.

Host. [*Coming forward with Fly.*] And here your host and's
      Fly witness your vows.
  And like two lucky birds bring the presage
  Of a loud jest: Lord Beaufort married is.

Lady F.   Ha!

Fly. All-to-be married.

Pru.   To whom? Not your son?   70

Host. The same, Pru. If her ladyship could take truce
  A little with her passion, and give way
  To their mirth now running.

Lady F.   Runs it mirth, let't come;
  It shall be well received, and much made of it.

Pru. We must of this, it was our own conception.   75

---

67. *Coming . . . Fly.*] *G.*   69. *Lord . . . is.*] *O;* Lord Beaufort's married.
G.   73. *let't*] *O;* let's *F3.*

---

58. *use . . . reverently*] 'Ausonius, *Ep.*, viii.7,8: "Fortunam reverenter habe
quicumque repente dives ab exili progrediere loco" Jonson affected the
phrase: *Volp.*, III.vii.88–9 . . .' (*H.& S.*'s note to *Sej.*, II.137).

60. *several*] individual.

65. *take . . . forelock*] Tilley, T311, 'Take Time (Occasion) by the forelock,
for she is bald behind'. The idea is ancient – see E. Panofsky, *Studies in
Iconology*, pp. 71–2; cf. *C.R.*, IV.v.101.

66. *after-games*] Cf. *B.F.*, II.iii.41; 'A second game played in order to
reverse or improve the issues of the first' (*O.E.D.*).

68. *lucky*] of good omen.

70. *All-to-be*] wholly, completely. The 'to' derives from the O.E. prefix
'to-' expressing separation. 'From an early time to-verbs were often
strengthened by the qualifying *adv. all* [see *O.E.D.*, 'all' C.14 & 15] in sense
"wholly". . . . Consequently the prefix began to be viewed as *all-to* . . .[and]
treated as itself an adverb' (*O.E.D.*); cf. *C.R.*, IV.iii.16; *B.F.*, V.iv.41; *M.L.*,
Chorus I. 24.

73. *mirth*] sport, jest.

75. *We . . . this*] i.e. 'We must make much of this'.

ACT V SCENE iii

[*Enter* LORD] LATIMER *to them.*

[*Latimer.*] Room for green rushes, raise the fiddlers,
    chamberlain,
  Call up the house in arms.
Host.   This will rouse Lovel.
Fly. And bring him on too.
Latimer.   Shelee-nien Thomas
  Runs like a heifer bitten with the breeze
  About the court, crying on Fly and cursing.   5
Fly. For what, my lord?
Latimer.   Yo' were best hear that from her;
  It is no office, Fly, fits my relation.
  Here come the happy couple! Joy, Lord Beaufort!
Fly. And my young lady too!
Host.   Much joy, my lord!

ACT V SCENE iv

[*Enter* LORD] BEAUFORT, FRANK, [FERRET, JORDAN, PIERCE,
JUG, Fiddlers, *and*] Servant[s] *to them.*

[*Beaufort.*] I thank you all, I thank thee, father Fly.
  Madam, my cousin, you look discomposed,
  I have been bold with a salad after supper,
  O' your own Laetice here.
Lady F.   You have, my lord.

0.1.] *This ed.;* ————— *Latimer. To them. O.*   3. Shelee-nien Thomas]
G; Sheelee-neen *O, F3*.
4. Laetice] *This ed.;* lettice *O*.

---

   1. *green rushes*] Fresh rushes were strewn on the floor for special festivities –
see *T.of T.*, I.iii.21–2. They were also strewn on the stage: 'let our Gallant . . .
presently aduance himselfe . . . on the very Rushes where the Comedy is to
daunce' (Dekker, *N.D.*, II, 247–8).
   2–3. *rouse . . . bring*] See V.ii.16–23n.
   4. *breeze*] gadfly which annoys horses and cattle; cf. *E.M.I.*, V.iii.309n.
   7. *relation*] narration.
   8–9. *Joy . . . joy*] 'God give you joy' was the usual greeting for a newly
married couple'; see *E.M.I.*, V.iv.12n.; the phrase resonates through the
scene as 'Joy' is the name of Beaufort's bride – see *Pers.* 21n.
   2. *discomposed*] See IV.ii.77n.
   4. *Laetice*] a pun on *Laetitia* (*Pers.* 6); see III.ii.125n.

But laws of hospitality and fair rites 5
Would have made me acquainted.

Beaufort. I' your own house,
I do acknowledge: else I much had trespassed.
But in an inn, and public, where there is licence
Of all community, a pardon o' course
May be sued out.

Lady F. It will, my lord, and carry it. 10
I do not see how any storm or tempest
Can help it now.

Pru. The thing being done and past,
You bear it wisely and like a lady of judgment.

Beaufort. She is that, secretary Pru.

Pru. Why secretary?
My wise lord? Is your brain lately married? 15

Beaufort. Your reign is ended, Pru, no sovereign now;
Your date is out and dignity expired.

Pru. I am annulled; how can I treat with Lovel
Without a new commission?

Lady F. Thy gown's commission.

Host. Have patience, Pru, expect; bid the lord joy.

Pru. And this grave lady too. I wish them joy. 20

Pierce. Joy!

Jordan. Joy!

Jug. All joy!

Host. Ay, the house full of joy.

Fly. Play the bells; fiddlers, crack your strings with joy.

[*Music.*]

Pru. But, Lady Laetice, you showed a neglect
Un-to-be-pardoned to'ards my lady, your kinswoman, 25

10. *Lady F.*] *Tennant; Lat. O, F3.* 15. brain] *O;* brain too *conj. G.* 23.
Music.] *G.*

---

5. *laws of hospitality*] 'The party were Lady Frampul's guests' (Argument 28, Persons 36)' (*H.& S.*).

9. *community*] social intercourse, fellowship.
o' course] by regular process.

10. *sued out*] applied for before a court (*O.E.D.*, 12).

14. *secretary*] minister, official.

17. *date*] term.

19. *expect*] wait (*O.E.D.*, 1).

25. *Un-to-be-pardoned*] Cf. *E.M.I.*, I.v.121: 'un-in-one-breath-vtterable'; and *D.is A.*, III.iii.51.

Not to advise with her.

Beaufort.   Good politic Pru,
Urge not your state-advice, your after-wit;
'Tis near upbraiding. Get our bed ready, chamberlain,
And, host, a bride-cup; you have rare conceits
And good ingredients; ever an old host   30
Upo' the road has his provocative drinks.

Latimer. He is either a good bawd or a physician.

Beaufort. 'Twas well he heard you not, his back was turned.
A bed, the genial bed! A brace of boys
Tonight I play for.

Pru.   Give us points, my lord.   35

Beaufort. Here take 'em, Pru, my cod-piece point and all.
I ha' clasps, my Laetice' arms; here take 'em, boys.
                         [*Throws off his doublet, etc.*]
What, is the chamber ready? Speak! Why stare you
On one another?

Jordan.   No, sir.

Beaufort.   And why no?

Jordan. My master has forbid it. He yet doubts   40
That you are married.

Beaufort.   Ask his vicar-general,
His Fly here.

Fly.   I must make that good: they are married.

Host. But I must make it bad, my hot young lord.
Gi' him his doublet again, the air is piercing.

27. state-] *O;* stale *conj. W.*   37. *Throws . . . etc.*] *G.*

---

26. *advise*] consult.

27. *after-wit*] wisdom after the event; cf. Fr. *l'esprit de l'escalier.*

29. *bride-cup*] See Arg. 110n.
conceits] fancy trifles for the table.

31. *provocative*] aphrodisiac.

34. *genial bed*] marriage bed. Cf. *Hym.*, l. 168, where Jonson notes:
'Properly that which was made ready for the new-married bride, and was
called *Genialis, à generandis liberis, Serv*[*ius*], in vi *Aen*[*eid*]'.

35. *points*] 'the tagged laces which fastened the breeches to the doublet. "To
show the impatience of the bridegroom, it was the custom . . . to tear them
off, instead of untying them, and throw them, to be scrambled for, among the
guests"' (*G.*, cited *H.& S.*). Cf. *T.of T.*, I.iv.21; and C. Brooke, 'An
Epithalamion' in *England's Helicon*: 'Youths, take his Poynts; your wonted
right; / And Maydens; take your due, her Garters.'

41. *vicar-general*] the office of the pope, but also the title of a lay official
serving as deputy to a Church of England bishop; cf. *Alc.*, I.ii.50.

You may take cold, my lord. See whom you ha'
    married: 45
Your host's son, and a boy.   *[Pulls off Frank's head-dress.]*
Fly.   You are abused.
Lady F. Much joy, my lord.
Pru.   If this be your Laetitia,
    She'll prove a counterfeit mirth and a clipped lady.
Servant. A boy, a boy; my lord has married a boy!
Latimer. Raise all the house in shout and laughter, a boy!   50
Host. Stay, what is here? Peace, rascals, stop your throats.

ACT V SCENE v

[Enter] NURSE *to them.*

[*Nurse.*] That maggot, worm, that insect! O my child,
    My daughter! Where's that Fly? I'll fly in his face,
    The vermin, let me come to him.
Fly.   Why, Nurse Shelee?
Nurse. Hang thee, thou parasite, thou son of crumbs
    And orts; thou hast undone me and my child,   5
    My daughter, my dear daughter.
Host.   What means this?
Nurse. O sir, my daughter, my dear child, is ruined
    By this your Fly here, married in a stable
    And sold unto a husband.
Host.   Stint thy cry,
    Harlot, if that be all; didst thou not sell him   10
    To me for a boy, and broughtst him in boy's rags
    Here to my door to beg an alms of me?
Nurse. I did, good master, and I crave your pardon:
    But 'tis my daughter and a girl.
Host.   Why saidst thou
    It was a boy, and soldst him then to me   15
    With such entreaty for ten shillings, carline?

46. *Pulls . . . head-dress.*] G.
0.1.] *This ed.;* ————— *Nurse.* {*To them.* O.

---

48. *clipped*] like a bad coin, continuing the conceit of 'counterfeit'.
5. *orts*] scraps left after a meal.
9. *sold*] given (*O.E.D.*, 1).
10. *Harlot*] a general term of abuse (*O.E.D.*, 5a); cf. *C.R.*, V.iv.416.
16. *carline*] old witch; cf. *M.L.*, I.v.23.

Nurse. Because you were a charitable man,
    I heard, good master, and would breed him well.
    I would ha' giv'n him you for nothing gladly.
    Forgive the lie o' my mouth, it was to save   20
    The fruit o' my womb. A parent's needs are urgent,
    And few do know that tyrant o'er good natures.
    But you relieved her and me too, the mother,
    And took me into your house to be the nurse,
    For which heaven heap all blessings on your head   25
    Whilst there can be one added.
Host.   Sure thou speakst
    Quite like another creature than th' hast lived
    Here i' the house, a Shelee-nien Thomas,
    An Irish beggar.
Nurse.   So I am, God help me.
Host. What art thou? Tell: the match is a good match   30
    For aught I see. Ring the bells once again.   *[Music.]*
Beaufort. Stint, I say, fiddlers.
Lady F.   No going off, my lord.
Beaufort. Nor coming on, sweet lady, things thus standing!
Fly. But what's the heinousness of my offence
    Or the degrees of wrong you suffered by it?   35
    In having your daughter matched thus happily
    Into a noble house, a brave young blood,
    And a prime peer o' the realm?
Beaufort.   Was that your plot, Fly?
    Gi' me a cloak, take her again among you.
    I'll none of your Light Heart fosterlings, no inmates,   40
    Supposititious fruits of an host's brain
    And his Fly's hatching, to be put upon me.
    There is a royal court o' the Star Chamber

31. *Music.*] G.

---

    33. *coming . . . standing*] bawdy.
    40. *fosterlings*] foster children.
    inmates] lodgers; cf. *Cat.*, II.116. 'In the 16th and 17th centuries there were stringent statutes and by-laws against the harbouring of poor persons as "inmates" . . . a practice which tended to increase the number of paupers locally chargeable' (*O.E.D.*).
    41. *Supposititious*] refers to a child 'set up to displace the real heir or successor; sometimes used for "illegitimate"' (*O.E.D.*).
    43. *Star-Chamber*] This much-feared court had jurisdiction over slanders and libels. It was abolished by the Long Parliament in 1641.

Will scatter all these mists, disperse these vapours,
And clear the truth. Let beggars match with beggars.   45
That shall decide it; I will try it there.
Nurse. Nay then, my lord, it's not enough, I see,
You are licentious but you will be wicked.
You're not alone content to take my daughter
Against the law, but having taken her,   50
You would repudiate and cast her off
Now at your pleasure, like a beast of power,
Without all cause or colour of a cause,
That or a noble or an honest man
Should dare t'except against: her poverty.   55
Is poverty a vice?
Beaufort.   Th' age counts it so.
Nurse. God help your lordship and your peers that think so,
If any be; if not, God bless them all,
And help the number o' the virtuous,
If poverty be a crime. You may object   60
Our beggary to us as an accident,
But never deeper, no inherent baseness.
And I must tell you now, young lord of dirt,
As an incensèd mother, she hath more
And better blood, running i' those small veins,   65
Than all the race of Beauforts have in mass,
Though they distil their drops from the left rib
Of John o' Gaunt.
Host.   Old mother of records,
Thou knowst her pedigree, then: whose daughter is she?
Nurse. The daughter and co-heir to the Lord Frampul,   70
This lady's sister!
Lady F.   Mine? What is her name?
Nurse. Laetitia.
Lady F.   That was lost?

55. against: her] *This ed.;* against, her *O;* against her: *conj. H.& S.*

---

44. *vapours*] See IV.iv.282n.
53. *colour*] semblance.
60. *object*] urge.
66. *mass*] See V.ii.48n.
67. *left rib*] The Beauforts were descended from John of Gaunt and his
mistress Catherine Swynford. Their issue was legitimised by Richard II in
1397; cf. *Pers.* 10.

Nurse.　　　　　　　　The true Laetitia.

Lady F. Sister, O gladness! Then you are our mother?

Nurse. I am, dear daughter.

Lady F.　　　　　　On my knees I bless

　　The light I see you by.

Nurse.　　　　　　And to the author　　　　　75

　　Of that blest light, I ope my other eye

　　Which hath almost now seven year been shut

　　Dark, as my vow was, never to see light

　　Till such a light restored it as my children

　　Or your dear father who, I hear, is not.　　　　　80

Beaufort. Give me my wife; I own her now and will

　　have her.

Host. But you must ask my leave first, my young lord,

　　Leave is but light. Ferret, go bolt your master,

　　Here's gear will startle him.　　　　　*[Exit* FERRET.*]*

　　　　　　　　　　I cannot keep

　　The passion in me, I am e'en turned child　　　　　85

　　And I must weep. Fly, take away mine host,

　　　　　　　　[Pulls off his disguise.]

　　My beard and cap here from me, and fetch my lord.

　　　　　　　　　　[Exit FLY.*]*

　　I am her father, sir, and you shall now

　　Ask my consent before you have her. Wife!

　　My dear and loving wife, my honoured wife!　　　　　90

　　Who here hath gained but I? I am Lord Frampul,

　　The cause of all this trouble; I am he

　　Have measured all the shires of England over,

84.1. *Exit* FERRET.] *G.*　　86. *Pulls . . . disguise.*] *G.*　　87.1. *Exit* FLY.]
G.　　92. trouble;] *H.& S.;* trouble? *O.*

---

72. *That . . . lost*] perhaps an echo of Perdita in Shakespeare, *Wint.*

83. *Leave . . . light*] Tilley, L170; cf. *E.Welb.*, ll. 64–6.

bolt] used specifically of a ferret springing a rabbit (*O.E.D.*, vb. 2.4b); cf
Alc., II.iii.80, 88.

84. *gear*] goings on (*O.E.D.*, 11b).

startle] rouse (*O.E.D.*, 7).

86–7. *Fly . . . lord*] 'Cf. Fuller, *The Holy State*, IV.vi. p. 269, of Lord
Burleigh: "At night when he put off his gown, he used to say, *Lie there, Lord
Treasurer*, and bidding adieu to all State-affairs, disposed himself to his quiet
rest' (*H.& S.*).

93–100.] These lines have an autobiographical ring. Jonson had visited the
Peak District (see *H.& S.*, XI, 377–9), had described those wandering trades

Wales and her mountains, seen those wilder nations
Of people in the Peak and Lancashire;   95
Their pipers, fiddlers, rushers, puppet-masters,
Jugglers, and gipsies, all the sorts of canters
And colonies of beggars, tumblers, ape-carriers,
For to these savages I was addicted,
To search their natures, and make odd discoveries;   100
And here my wife, like a she-Mandeville,
Ventured in disquisition after me.
             [*Enter* FLY *with Lord Frampul's robes.*]
Nurse. I may look up, admire, I cannot speak
    Yet to my lord.
Host.   Take heart and breathe, recover;
Thou hast recovered me who here had coffined   105
Myself alive in a poor hostelry
In penance of my wrongs done unto thee,
Whom I long since gave lost.
Nurse.   So did I you,
Till stealing mine own daughter from her sister,
I lighted on this error hath cured all.   110
Beaufort. And in that cure include my trespass, mother
    And father, for my wife –
Host.   No, the Star Chamber.
Beaufort. Away with that, you sour the sweetest lettuce
    Was ever tasted.
Host.   Gi' you joy, my son,
Cast her not off again.

             [*Enter* LOVEL.]

             O call me father,   115

102.1. *Enter . . . robes.*] G.   104. breathe] *W;* breath *O.*   113. lettuce]
This ed.; lettice *O.*   115.1. *Enter* LOVEL.] G.

---

in *B.F.*, the 'canters' in *S.N.*, and generally 'searched their natures and made
discoveries'.
    96. *rushers*] strewers of rushes.
    97. *gipsies*] See Arg. 118n.
    canters] one who uses the 'cant' of thieves, a rogue or vagabond; see I.v.39n.
    101. *she-Mandeville*] There was an edition of Mandeville's *Travels* in 1625.
    102. *disquisition*] search (*O.E.D.*, 1).
    103. *admire*] wonder.
    108. *gave*] accounted (*O.E.D.*, VIII,31b).
    113. *lettuce*] See III.ii.125n.

Lovel, and this your mother, if you like.
But take your mistress first, my child; I have power
To give her now with her consent; her sister
Is given already to your brother Beaufort.
Lovel. Is this a dream now, after my first sleep?   120
Or are these phant'sies made i' the Light Heart,
And sold i' the New Inn?
Host.   Best go to bed
And dream it over all. Let's all go sleep,
Each with his turtle. Fly, provide us lodgings,
Get beds prepared: you're master now o' the inn,   125
The lord o' the Light Heart, I give it you.
Fly was my fellow gipsy. All my family
Indeed, were gipsies, tapsters, ostlers, chamberlains,
Reducèd vessels of civility.
But here stands Pru neglected, best deserving   130
Of all that are i' the house, or i' my Heart,
Whom though I cannot help to a fit husband,
I'll help to that will bring one, a just portion:
I have two thousand pound in bank for Pru,
Call for it when she will.
Beaufort.   And I as much.   135
Host. There's somewhat yet, four thousand pound! That's
    better
Than sounds the proverb, 'four bare legs in a bed'.
Lovel. Me and her mistress, she hath power to coin

---

117. *But . . . child*] Lovel presumably takes Lady Frampul by the hand, thus
enacting a 'handfast' or marriage contract; cf. Ford, *'Tis Pity She's a Whore*,
III.vii.51n. (Revels).

120–1. *dream . . . phantsies*] 'Throughout the play [Jonson] distinguishes
between "phantasms", which have no relation to reality, and "visions",
which can be of high import' (Harriet Hawkins, 'The Idea of a Theater in
Jonson's *The New Inn*,' *Ren.Dr.*, (1966), 217).

124. *Each . . . turtle*] It would be dramatically inexpedient to celebrate
formal nuptials at this stage in the play, and too late to summon the divine
'from the next inn' (V.i.18).

128. *gipsies*] See Arg. 118n.

129. *vessels*] The metaphor is biblical; see Gen. xlix. 5 etc.
civility] citizenship.

130. *best*] most.

137. *four . . . bed*] Tilley, M1146: 'More belongs to marriage than four bare
legs in a bed'.

138–9. *coin Up*] fashion.

    Up into what she will.

Lady F.   Indefinite Pru!

Latimer. But I must do the crowning act of bounty!   140

Host. What's that, my lord?

Latimer.   Give her my self, which here
    By all the holy vows of love I do.
    Spare all your promised portions: she is a dowry
    So all-sufficient in her virtue and manners
    That fortune cannot add to her.

Pru.   My lord,   145
    Your praises are instructions to mine ears,
    Whence you have made your wife to live your servant.

Host. Lights, get us several lights!

Lovel.   Stay, let my mistress
    But hear my vision sung, my dream of beauty,
    Which I have brought, prepared to bid us joy   150
    And light us all to bed; 'twill be instead
    Of airing of the sheets with a sweet odour.

Host. 'Twill be an incense to our sacrifice
    Of love tonight, where I will woo afresh,
    And like Maecenas, having but one wife,   155
    I'll marry her every hour of life hereafter.

                     They go out with a song.

155. Maecenas] *W; Mecaenas O.*

---

   139. *Indefinite*] infinitely powerful (*O.E.D.*, 16, records this sense only from 1664).

   146. *instructions*] lessons.

   148. *several*] individual.

   155. *Maecenas*] 'A reference to Maecenas' frequent quarrels with his wife Terentia: "hunc esse qui uxorem miliens duxit cum unam habuerit" (Seneca, *Epist.*, cxiv. 6)' (*H.& S.*).

The Epilogue

Plays in themselves have neither hopes nor fears,
    Their fate is only in their hearers' ears;
If you expect more than you had tonight
    The maker is sick and sad. But do him right:
He meant to please you, for he sent things fit   5
    In all the numbers, both of sense and wit,
If they ha' not miscarried! If they have,
    All that his faint and falt'ring tongue doth crave
Is that you not impute it to his brain.
    That's yet unhurt, although set round with pain;   10
It cannot long hold out. All strength must yield.
    Yet judgment would the last be i' the field
With a true poet. He could have haled in
    The drunkards and the noises of the inn
In his last act, if he had thought it fit   15
    To vent you vapours in the place of wit.
But better 'twas that they should sleep or spew
    Than in the scene to offend or him or you.
This he did think (and this do you forgive):
    Whene'er the carcass dies, this art will live.   20
And had he lived the care of King and Queen,
    His art in something more yet had been seen;
But mayors and shrieves may yearly fill the stage,

---

2. *fate . . . ears*] Cf. Shakespeare, *L.L.L.*, V.ii.861–3.

4. *maker*] poet; cf. *S.W.*, Prol. 11.8; *Disc.*, 2347.

6. *numbers*] lines.

14. *noises*] tavern bands.

16. *vapours*] See III.i. 186n.

21. *care . . . Queen*] Jonson had suffered strokes in 1626 and 1628. Apparently this plea was successful – see *Und.*, lxii, 'An Epigram to King Charles for a Hundred Pounds He Sent Me in My Sickness, 1629'. He seems to be apologising for the reproach in *M.L.*, Chorus I.52.

23–4. *mayors . . . age*] '. . . adapted from the lines of Florus: "Consules fiunt

A king's or poet's birth do ask an age.

> *Another Epilogue there was, made for*
> *the Play in the Poet's Defence, but the*
> *Play lived not in Opinion to*
> *Have it Spoken.*

A jovial host and lord of the New Inn
    Clept the Light Heart, with all that passed therein,
Hath been the subject of our play tonight,
    To give the King and Queen and Court delight:
But then we mean the Court above the stairs   5
    And past the guard; men that have more of ears
Than eyes to judge us: such as will not hiss
    Because the chambermaid was namèd Cis.
We think it would have served our scene as true,
    If, as it is, at first we'd called her Pru;   10
For any mystery we there have found,
    Or magic in the letters or the sound.
She only meant was for a girl of wit
    To whom her lady did a province fit;
Which she would have discharged and done as well,   15
    Had she been christened Joyce, Grace, Doll, or Nell.

> *The just indignation the author*
> *took at the vulgar censure of his*
> *play by some malicious spectators*
> *begat this following Ode to*
> *Himself.*

Come, leave the loathèd stage,

0.1–4. *The just . . . following*] O; om. Q, D, A, H, Fo1–3.

---

quotannis et novi proconsules, / solus aut rex aut poeta non quotannis
nascitur." This was a favourite maxim of Jonson's, who quotes it in . . . *Disc.*
2433, and *Panegyre*, 163, and refers to it in *Epig.*, iv.3' (*H.& S.*'s note to
E.M.I., V.v.38–40).

    24. *do*] See Prol. 15n.

    0.3 Opinion] opposed to judgment; a Stoic technical term, see IV.iv.215,
Disc., 43–9, and cf. Marston, *Antonio and Mellida*, IV.i. 53–8 'He's a king . . .
who stands unmov'd/Despite the justling of opinion', and *The Fawn*, I.ii.59n.
(Revels).

    8. *Cis*] See *Pers.* 37n., *Und.*, viii. 25, and Introduction, pp. 9–10.
    14. *province*] office (see II.i.40n.).
With this cf. 'Ode to Himself', *Und.*, xxiii; and *Und.*, lxx.53–9.

And the more loathsome age,
Where pride and impudence, in faction knit,
   Usurp the chair of wit:
Indicting and arraigning every day   5
   Something they call a play.
Let their fastidious, vain
   Commission of the brain
Run on and rage, sweat, censure, and condemn:
They were not made for thee, less thou for them.   10

Say that thou pourst them wheat,
   And they will acorns eat:
'Twere simple fury still thyself to waste
   On such as have no taste:
To offer them a surfeit of pure bread   15
   Whose appetites are dead.
No, give them grains their fill,
   Husks, draff to drink, and swill;
If they love lees, and leave the lusty wine,
Envy them not, their palate's with the swine.   20

---

2. loathsome] *O;* loathed *Fo1.*   3. in . . . knit] *O;* together knit *H,*
Fo1–3.   8. the] *O;* their *Fo1.*   10. made] *O;* born *H.*   11. thou] *O; om.*
Q, D.   them] *O;* out *Fo2.*   12. will] *O;* would *Q, D, Fo2, 3.*   14. such as]
O; them that *H.*   18. and] *O;* their *Fo1.*   19. leave] *O;* loath *Fo1–3.*   20.
not,] *G;* not; *A;* not *O, Q, D, Fo1–3.*   palate's] *Q;* palate's, *O.*

---

4. *chair of wit*] Cf. the portraits of 'The Commission of Wit' in *B.F.*, Ind.
100–5, and 'the new Office of Wit' in *U.V.*, xlii. 19–30, and *S.N.*, Intermean
IV.45. Shirley echoed the phrase in his Prologue to *The Coronation* (1635),
and Denham, in his prefatory poem attached to the Beaumont and Fletcher
Folio, invokes the true 'Triumvirate of Wit' – Shakespeare, Jonson, and
Beaumont and Fletcher. Dramatists' hatred of the self-appointed critics at
Blackfriars can be traced at least as far back as Gay's *Isle of Gulls* and
Webster's Induction to *The Malcontent* (1604), even to the portrait of the
Parliament of theatre poets in Joseph Hall's *Virgidemiarum* (1598), I.iii.45ff.

   7. *fastidious*] proud (*O.E.D.*, 26).

   12. *acorns*] echoed by Ralph Brideoake in his elegiac poem in *Jonsonus*
Virbius, 1638, p. 53: 'Though the fine *Plush* and *Velvets* of the age / Did oft for
sixepence damne *thee* from the Stage, / And with their *Mast* and *Ackorne-*
stomacks, ran / To th'nastie sweepings of *thy* Servingman, / Before *thy* Cates'
(*H.& S.*, XI, 467).

   18. *draff*] dregs, hog's-wash.

   19. *lusty*] strong (*O.E.D.*, 7).

   20. *Envy . . . swine*] The apostrophe in *O*'s 'palate's' implies the insertion of
a comma after 'not'.

No doubt some mouldy tale
Like *Pericles*, and stale
As the shrieve's crusts, and nasty as his fish-
    Scraps out of every dish,
Thrown forth, and raked into the common tub,   25
    May keep up the play-club:
    There sweepings do as well
    As the best ordered meal.
For who the relish of these guests will fit
Needs set them but the alms-basket of wit.   30

    And much good do't you then:
    Brave plush and velvet men
Can feed on orts; and safe in your stage-clothes

21. some] *Q;* a *Q, D, H, A, Fo1–3.*   22. and] *O;* or *H.*   23. shrieve's] *O;*
Sheriffs *Fo2.*   fish-] *O;* fish, *Q, D, A.*   24. of] *Q; not in O.*   27. There,]
O; Brooms *Q, D, A;* Broome and his *H, Fo1–3.*   28. As . . . meal] *O;*
There, as his Masters meale *Q, D, H, A, Fo1–3.*   29. these] *O;* those
Fo2–3.   will] *O;* can *Fo1, 3;* would *Fo2.*   31. you] *O;* ye *Q, D.*
33. your] *O;* their *Fo2.*   stage-] *O;* scoene *Q, D, Fo1–3;* braue *A.*

21–2. *mouldy* . . . Pericles] *Pericles* had been first printed in 1609 and four
times reprinted by 1631. It was well received (see Arden Introduction pp. lxv–
lxvi). It had been revived at the Globe at least once between 1625 and 1631.
'Mouldy' therefore refers not only to its use of romance traditions but to its
being old-fashioned. Cf. *E.M.I.*, Prol. 7–9; *Volp.*, II.ii.50; and the sneering
allusion to *The Winter's Tale* and *The Tempest* in *B.F.*, Ind. 130.

23. *shrieve's*] Protests against prodigious feasts were common in the period;
see Stone, ch. x, 'Conspicuous Expenditure'.

25. *common tub*] Scraps collected from court and city feasts were put into an
alms-basket and given to the poor and to prisoners – see *E.H.*, V.iii.54.

26. *play-club*] Cf. the 'rhyming club' of *U.V.*, xxx.8.

27. *There sweepings*] originally 'Broome's sweepings'. Jonson excised his
earlier gibe at his old servant Richard Brome. (Cf. Randolph's 'Answer', l.
34). His jealousy may have been aroused by the success of Brome's non-extant
The Love-sick Maid performed within a couple of weeks of *The New Inn*
(Bentley, I.105) in 1629, but he repented and prefixed complimentary verses
to Brome's *The Northern Lass* in 1630 (*U.V.*, xxxviii). See R. J. Kaufmann,
Richard Brome (New York, 1961), pp. 23ff.

29. *relish*] taste, liking (*O.E.D.*, 2).

30. *alms-basket of wit*] Cf. Shakespeare, *L.L.L.*, V.i.39–40: 'the alms-basket
of words' and Day, *Isle of Dogs*, I.i, 'alm's basket scraps'.

32. *plush* . . . *men*] Plush was very expensive and Jonson associates the
phrase with debauched aristocrats – see *Und.*, xv.58; cf. *M.L.*, Chorus I.36;
D.is A., I.iv.40.

33. *orts*] See V.v.5n.

    Dare quit, upon your oaths,
The stagers and the stage-wrights too (your peers)   35
      Of larding your large ears
    With their foul comic socks,
    Wrought upon twenty blocks:
Which, if they are torn and turned and patched enough,
The gamesters share your guilt, and you their stuff.   40

    Leave things so prostitute,
    And take the Alcaic lute,
Or thine own Horace, or Anacreon's lyre;
    Warm thee by Pindar's fire:

---

35. -wrights . . . peers)] *O;* -wrights, to your peyces *A.*   your] *O:* theyr
Fo2.   36. larding] *O;* stuffing *Q, D, A, H, Fo1–3.*   your] *O;* their
Fo2.   37. their foul] *O;* rage of *Q, D;* raggs of *A, H, Fo1–3.*   39. are . . .
turned] *O;* 're torne, and foule *Q, D, A, Fo2, 3;* are but torne, and foule *H;*
returne, and fowl *Fo1.*   40. guilt] *O;* gilt *Q, D.*   42. the] *O;* th' *Q, D.*

---

stage-clothes] Cf. Fitzdottrell's theatre-going finery in *D.is A.*, I.iv; and
Und., xv.108–10.

34. *quit*] acquit, absolve.

35. *stagers*] players.

stage-wrights] probably a coinage referring to the new noble breed of
Caroline amateur authors (Introduction, p. 2); Jonson may also have coined
'playwright' – see *Ep.*, xlix, lxviii, c. See 'Playwriting for Love', ch. xii of W. J.
Lawrence, *Speeding up Shakespeare* (London, 1937).

36. *larding*] covering. The sense is that the audience is too obtuse to realise
that they are applauding foul drama.

37. *comic socks*] the light shoes (*socci*) worn by comic actors in ancient Rome.

39.] Jonson accuses his rivals of patching their plays together out of old
materials.

40. *gamesters*] players.

guilt] punning on 'gilt'.

stuff] 'a gilder's composition of size and whiting, used to form a surface over
wood to be gilded' (*Century Dictionary*, 1891), cited *O.E.D.*, 6d.

42. *Alcaic*] Alcaeus of Lesbos, a lyric poet and contemporary of Sappho. He
invented or adopted the Alcaic stanza which was imitated by Horace.

43. *Horace*] generally invoked by Jonson as a satirist (see *Poet.* etc.) but here
as a lyricist.

Anacreon] a lyric poet of the sixth century BC, born in Ionia. He wrote
graceful songs, generally about love and wine. Cf. 'Light Anacreon' of *F.I.*,
l. 522.

44. *Pindar*] the greatest of the Greek lyricists. Jonson's elegy on Cary and
Morison (*Und.*, lxx) is the first sustained attempt in English to imitate the
Pindaric ode.

And though thy nerves be shrunk and blood be cold   45
    Ere years have made thee old,
  Strike that disdainful heat
  Throughout, to their defeat:
As curious fools, and envious of thy strain,
May, blushing, swear no palsy's in thy brain.   50

  But when they hear thee sing
  The glories of thy king,
His zeal to God, and his just awe o'er men:
    They may, blood-shaken, then
Feel such a flesh-quake to possess their powers,   55
    As they shall cry: Like ours
  In sound of peace or wars
  No harp e'er hit the stars,
In tuning forth the acts of his sweet reign:
And raising Charles his chariot 'bove his wain.   60

The Ode is printed at the end of the Octavo edition of the play, 1632, (*O*), and also appears on an inserted sheet (f) in Benson's Quarto edition of the *Execration against Vulcan*, 1640, (*Q*) and the Duodecimo edition of Jonson's translation of Horace's *Art of Poetry* (1640) pp. 135–8 (*D*). These contain the snide reference to Brome (see l. 27n.) which Jonson had evidently suppressed by the time *The New Inn* was printed. There are also versions of the ode in several manuscripts, e.g., Bodleian Ashmole 38, pp. 80–1, (*A*, reprinted in Tennant), a Haslewood manuscript collated in the Dyce copy in the Victoria and Albert (*H*), Folger V.a.152, pp. 77ff., (*Fo1*), V.a.170, pp. 184ff., (*Fo2*),

---

46. have] *O;* hath *A*.   49. strain] *O;* veine *Fo1;* trayne *Fo2*.   53. o'er] *O;* of *Q, D, A, Fo1–3*.   55. such a] *O;* a chill *Fo1*.   56. As . . . ours] *O;* That no tun'd Harpe like ours *Q, D;* As noe . . . *A, Fo2, 3;* Cause no . . . *H;* cause noe lute tun'd like ours *Fo1*.   57. and] *O;* or *Fo2*.   58. No . . . stars] *O;* Shall truly hit the stars *Q, D, A, H, Fo2, 3;* can truly . . . *Fo1*.   59] *In . . . acts*] *O;* When they shall read the Acts *Q, D, H, Fo2, 3;* see the acts *Fo1*.   his sweet] *O;* Charles his *Q, D, A, Fo1–3*.   60. And . . . chariot] *O;* And see his Chariot triumph *Q, D, H, Fo1–3*.   'bove] *O;* O'er *H, Fo1–3*.

---

45. *nerves*] sinews (Lat. *nervi*), referring to Jonson's strokes.
48. *curious*] fastidious.
    strain] melody.
53. *awe*] power to inspire reverence (*O.E.D.*, 5).
58. *hit the stars*] 'echoes Horace, *Odes*, I.i.35–6: "Quodsi me lyricis vatibus inseres, / sublimi feriam sidera vertice"' (*H.& S.*)
60. *wain*] the wain of Charles the Great, the seven bright stars in the Great Bear; cf. Shakespeare, *1H4*, II.i.1–3.

and V.a.322, pp. 170ff., (*Fo3*). It was translated into Latin by John Earles (B.L. Add. MS 15227, Fols. 44–5), William Strode (Bodleian MS Montagu d.I., fol. 30–1), and Thomas Randolph. This last was first printed in *A Crew of Kind London Gossips . . . Written and newly enlarged by S[amuel] R[owlands]*, 1663. Strode and Randolph's translations also appear in *Fo1* and in Bodleian MSS. Rawlinson poetry 62, fols. 71–2, and 209, fol.22. These translations are printed in *H.& S.*, X, 333–8.

APPENDIX I

Repostes and Replies to Jonson's 'Ode to Himself'

1. THOMAS RANDOLPH'S REPLY TO JONSON'S 'ODE TO HIMSELF'

An Answer to Mr Ben Jonson's Ode to Persuade Him not to Leave the Stage

Ben, do not leave the stage
    'Cause 'tis a loathsome age;
For pride and impudence will grow too bold
    When they shall hear it told
They frighted thee: stand high as is thy cause,   5
    Their hiss is thy applause.
    More just were thy disdain
    Had they approved thy vein.
So thou for them, and they for thee were born,
They to incense, and thou as much to scorn.   10

    Wilt thou engross thy store
    Of wheat, and pour no more,
Because their bacon-brains have such a taste
    As more delights in mast?
No: set 'em forth a board of dainties, full   15
    As thy best muse can cull;
    While they the while do pine

7. thy] *Poems;* this *Fo3, Ha.*   8. vein] *Poems;* strayne *Fo2.*   10. as much to] *Poems;* again to *Fo1–3, Ha.*   13. their] *Poems;* these *Ha.*   14. delights] *Fo1–3;* delight *Poems.*   17. While ... the] *Poems;* whilst they that *Fo1.*

0.1. *Randolph*] The poet and dramatist Thomas Randolph (1602–35) the adopted 'son' of Ben Jonson – see his 'Gratulatory to Ben Jonson' (*H.& S.,* XI, 390–1).

  11. *engross*] collect together.

  13. *bacon-brains*] echoes Jonson's Ode, l. 20.

  14. *mast*] fruit of the beech, oak, or chestnut, fed to swine.

And thirst, 'midst all their wine.
What greater plague can hell itself devise,
Than to be willing thus to tantalise?   20

    Thou canst not find them stuff
    That will be bad enough
To please their palates; let 'em thine refuse
    For some Pie Corner muse;
She is too fair an hostess; 'twere a sin   25
    For them to like thine *Inn*:
  'Twas made to entertain
  Guests of a nobler strain;
Yet if they will have any of thy store,
Give 'em some scraps, and send them from thy door.   30

    And let those things in plush,
    Till they be taught to blush
Like what they will, and more contented be
    With what Brome swept from thee.
I know thy worth, and that thy lofty strains   35
    Write not to clothes but brains;
  But thy great spleen doth rise
  'Cause moles will have no eyes:
This only in my Ben I faulty find,
He's angry they'll not see him that are blind.   40

    Why should the scene be mute

21. not] *Poems;* om. *Ha.*   29. they] *Poems;* these *Fo1, 2.*   31. in] *Poems;* of
Fo2.   32. Till . . . to] *Poems;* Till they are taught to *Fo1, 2;* Whose follie
cannot *Fo3, Ha.*   33. more] *Poems;* well *Fo2.*   34. swept] *Poems;* forc'd
Fo2.   35. lofty] *Poems;* loftyer *Fo2, 3, Ha.*   36. Write . . . clothes] *Poems;*
Weight not to cloakes *Ha.*

---

24. *Pie Corner*] the corner of Giltspur Street and Cock Lane in West
Smithfield, London. The cooks' shops there were haunted by the needy; cf.
Alc., I.i.25.

31. *plush*] See Jonson's Ode, l. 32.

34. *Brome*] The original version of Jonson's ode contained a derogatory
reference to his fellow dramatist, Brome; see l. 27n.

37. *spleen*] the seat not only of melancholy and moroseness, but of
impetuous ill-temper.

38. *moles*] considered to be blind by classical and Renaissance writers
although they do in fact have limited vision.

'Cause thou canst touch a lute
And string thy Horace? Let each muse of nine
   Claim thee, and say, 'Thou art mine'.
'Twere fond to let all other flames expire   45
   To sit by Pindar's fire:
  For by so strange neglect,
  I should myself suspect
The palsy were as well thy brain's disease,
If they could shake thy muse which way they please.   50

   And though thou well canst sing
   The glories of thy King,
And on the wings of verse his chariot bear
   To heaven and fix it there,
Yet let thy muse as well some raptures raise   55
   To please him, as to praise.
  I would not have thee choose
  Only a treble muse;
But have this envious, ignorant age to know,
Thou that canst sing so high, canst reach as low.   60

Printed in *Poems with the Muses Looking-glasse and Amyntas*, Oxford, 1638 (*Poems*). The poem also appears in certain MSS: Folger V.a.152, pp. 83–4 (*Fo1*); V.a.170, pp. 187–90 (*Fo2*); V.a.322, pp. 170–80 (*Fo3*); Harvard fMS. 626 (*Ha*); Bodleian Ashmole 47, ff. 110–11; Eng. Poet. c.50, fol. 101; Rawl. poet, 62, fols. 38ff.; Firth e. 4, pp. 31–5.

45. fond] *Poems;* shame *Fo3.*   47. so] *Poems;* such *Fo3.*   54. fix it there] *Poems;* mak't a star *Fo1, 2.*   57. would . . . thee] *Poems;* know thou wouldst not *Fo1–3, Ha.*   60. reach] *Poems;* sing *Fo1.*

---

  43. *string thy Horace*] write odes worthy to be accompanied by Horace's lyre.

  45–6. *'Twere . . . fire*] write only poetry in imitation of Pindar; see Jonson's Ode, l. 44.

  53–4. *And . . . there*] referring to the assumption of Elijah in a chariot, 2 Kings II.11, and to 'Charles's wain' (Jonson's Ode, l. 60, and I.C.'s Ode, ll. 62–4).

  58. *treble muse*] presumably Erato, Muse of the lyre.

2. 'I.C.'S' REPLY TO JONSON'S 'ODE TO HIMSELF'

Ode: to Ben Jonson
Upon his Ode to Himself

Proceed in thy brave rage,
  Which hath raised up our stage
Unto that height as Rome in all her state
  Or Greece might emulate,
Whose greatest senators did silent sit,   5
  Hear and applaud the wit
  Which those more temperate times
  Used when it taxed their crimes:
Socrates stood, and heard with true delight
All that the sharp Athenian muse could write   10

  Against his supposed fault;
  And did digest the salt
That from that full vein did so freely flow.
  And though that we do know
The graces jointly strove to make that breast   15
  A temple for their rest,
  We must not make thee less
  Than Aristophanes:
He got the start of thee in time and place,
But thou hast gained the goal in art and grace.   20

  But if thou make thy feasts
  For the high-relished guests,
And that a cloud of shadows shall break in,
  It were almost a sin
To think that thou shouldst equally delight   25
  Each several appetite;
  Though art and nature strive

0.1 'I.C.'] I.C. has not been identified but he may be the James Clayton to
whom is attributed in a manuscript list in the Malone copy of *Jonsonus
Virbius*, the fifteenth poem in that collection; see *H.& S.*, XI, 429 and 450–1.
Gifford's attribution of the poem to John Cleveland is unlikely.

12. *salt*] stinging wit.

22. *high-relished*] expecting sharply flavoured dishes.

23. *that*] connected to the 'if' in l. 21 ('if that').

shadows] parasites, toadies (*O.E.D.*, 8a); cf. *S.W.*, II.ii, 'Laughed at by the
Lady of the Colledge, and her shadowes'.

H

Thy banquets to contrive,
Thou art our whole Menander, and dost look
Like the old Greek: think then but on his cook.   30

  If thou thy full cups bring
  Out of the muses' spring,
And there are some foul mouths had rather drink
  Out of the common sink
There, let 'em seek to quench th' hydroptic thirst   35
  Till the swollen humour burst.
 Let him who daily steals
 From thy most precious meals,
(Since thy strange plenty finds no loss by it)
Feed himself with the fragments of thy wit.   40

  And let those silken men
  (That know not how, or when
To spend their money or their time) maintain
  With their consumed no-brain,
Their barbarous feeding on such gross base stuff   45
  As only serves to puff
  Up the weak empty mind,

---

29. *whole Menander*] 'Caesar called Terence Menander halved [Caes. ap. Suetonius, *Vita Ter.*, fin.], because he wanted so much of his grace and sharpness. Ben Jonson may well be called our Manander whole, or more, exceeding him as much in sharpness and grace as Terence wanted of him' (I.C.'s note).

29–30. *look . . . Greek*] 'Ben Jonson is said to be very like the picture we have of Menander, taken from an ancient medal' (I.C.'s note).

30. *cook*] 'Menander in a fragrant of one of his comedies makes his cook speak after this manner of the diversity of tastes, viz.: "What is his usual fare, / What country man is he: / These things 'tis meet the cook should scan, / For such nice guests as in the Isles are bred, / With various sorts of fresh fish nourished, / In salt meat take little or no delight, / But taste them with fastidious appetite"' (I.C.'s note). These lines occur in the *Trophonius*, 462K. I.C. may also be remembering Jonson's culinary figures in his Prologue, ll. 3ff.

32. *muses' spring*] the Hippocrene on Mount Helicon.

34. *sink*] cesspool.

35. *hydroptic*] characteristic of a sufferer from dropsy.

36. *humour*] deviant character trait; a metonym in that the accumulation of watery fluids in bodily cavities is the chief symptom of dropsy.

39. *strange*] rare, wondrous.

41. *silken*] See Jonson's Ode, ll. 31–40.

Like bubbles, full with wind,
And strive t'engage the scene with their damned oaths,
As they do with the privilege of their clothes,   50

    Whilst thou tak'st that high spirit,
    Well purchased by thy merit.
Great prince of poets, though thy head be grey,
    Crown it with Delphic bay,
And from the chief pin in Apollo's choir   55
    Take down thy best tuned lyre,
    Whose sound shall pierce so far
    It shall strike out the star
Which fabulous Greece durst fix in heaven, whilst thine
With all due glory here on earth shall shine.   60

    Sing, English Horace, sing
    The wonder of thy king,
Whilst his triumphant chariot runs his whole
    Bright course about each pole;
Sing down the Roman harper; he shall rain   65
    His bounties on thy vein,
    And with his golden rays,
    So gild thy glorious bays
That fame shall bear on her unwearied wing
What the best poet sung of the best king.   70

Printed in Jonson's *Quintus Horatius Flaccus: His Art of Poetry* (London, 1640), Sig. A1ov–A12v.

---

49. *engage*] hold the attention of (*O.E.D.*'s first instance in this sense is 1642 – see 'engage' 14).
51–2. *Whilst . . . merit*] while you enjoy the divine inspiration which you have deserved.
54. *bay*] Poets' crowns were made from laurel.
58–59. *star . . . heaven*] Pindar.
65. *Roman harper*] Horace.

3. OWEN FELLTHAM'S RIPOSTE TO JONSON'S 'ODE TO HIMSELF'

An Answer to the Ode of
Come Leave the Loathed Stage, &c.

Come leave this saucy way
    Of baiting those that pay
Dear for the sight of your declining wit:
    'Tis known it is not fit
That a sale poet, just contempt once thrown,   5
    Should cry up thus his own.
    I wonder by what dower
    Or patent you had power
From all to rape a judgment. Let't suffice,
Had you been modest, y' had been granted wise.   10

    'Tis known you can do well,
    And that you do excel
As a translator; but when things require
    A genius and a fire
Not kindled heretofore by others' pains,   15
    As oft y' have wanted brains
    And art to strike the white,
    As you have levelled right;
Yet if men vouch not things apocryphal,
You bellow, rave, and spatter round your gall.   20

    Jug, Pierce, Peck, Fly, and all
    Your jests so nominal

1. this] *R;* that *PB.*   3. your] *R;* thy *PB.*   4. 'Tis known] *R;* I know *PB;* I
tell you *H.*   5. sale] *R;* stale *Sl.*   9. rape a] *PB, H, Sl;* rap't *R.*   Let't] *R;*
Let it *PB, Sl.*   12. do] *R;* can *PB.*   14. and a] *PB, H;* and *R.*   15. by] *R;*
from *H.*   16. y' have] *R;* you have *PB.*   21. Pierce, Peck] *R;* Peg, Pierce
PB.

0.1 *Felltham*] Owen Felltham (1602?–1668) author of the *Resolves*, a series
of moral essays.
    5. *sale*] venal, inferior (*O.E.D.*, sb.2.4).
    6. *cry up*] extol.
    7. *dower*] endowment.
    8. *patent*] privilege.
    9. *rape*] seize.
    17. *strike the white*] hit the iron when it is at its hottest; cf. Jonson's anvil
figure in his poem to the memory of Shakespeare, *U.V.*, ll. 58–61.

Are things so far beneath an able brain
    As they do throw a stain
Through all th' unlikely plot, and do displease   25
     As deep as *Pericles,*
   Where yet there is not laid
   Before a chambermaid
Discourse so weighed as might have served of old
For schools, when they of love and valour told.   30

    Why rage then? when the show
    Should judgment be and know-
ledge, that there are in plush who scorn to drudge
    For stages, yet can judge
Not only poets' looser lines but wits,   35
    And all their perquisites.
   A gift as rich as high
   Is noble poesy:
Yet though in sport it be for kings a play,
'Tis next mechanic when it works for pay.   40

    Alcaeus' lute had none,
    Nor loose Anacreon
E'er taught so bold assuming of the bays
    When they deserved no praise.
To rail men into approbation   45
    Is new; 'Tis yours alone
   And prospers not. For know
   Fame is as coy as you
Can be disdainful: and who dares to prove

---

23. beneath] *R;* below *PB, H.*   24. throw] *R;* cast *Sl.*   30. schools] *R;*
schoolboys *PB.*   32–3. judgment . . . ledge] *R;* temper be and knowe Ben
that *H, Sl.*   33. in . . . who] *R;* those in Plush that *PB.*   35. lines] *R;* laws
PB.   36. And] *R;* with *PB, H.*   37. as high] *R;* and high *PB.*   38. Is] *R;*
As *PB.*   39. Yet] *R;* Which *PB.*   43. E'er taught] *R;* That taught *PB;*
E'er thought *H.*   44. they] *R;* hee *H, Sl.*   46. 'Tis] *PB, Sl;* in *R.*

---

26. Pericles] Cf. Jonson's Ode, l. 22.
40.] See Introduction, p. 2.
41. *Alcaeus*] See Jonson's Ode, l. 42n.
none] no pay (see l. 40).
 42. *loose Anacreon*] a 6th century BC lyric poet whose poems celebrate the
wanton joys of love and wine.
49. *prove*] attempt.

A rape on her shall gather scorn, not love. 50

> Leave then this humour vain
> And this more pettish strain
Where self-conceit and choler of the blood
> Eclipse what else is good.
Then if you please those raptures high to touch, 55
> Whereof you boast so much,
> And but forbear your crown
> Till the world puts it on,
No doubt from all you may amazement draw,
Since braver theme no Phoebus ever saw. 60

Printed in 'Lusoria: or Occasional Pieces', no. xx, appended to *Resolves: Divine, Moral, Political. The eighth Impression* (London, 1661), (*R*). It had previously appeared in [A. Wright, ed.,] *Parnassus Biceps* (London, 1656), pp. 154–6, (*PB*), and it appears in BL Harley MS 4955, fo. 216, (*H*) one of the most important manuscript collections of Jonson's poems, BL Sloane 1446 fols. 56r–57r (*Sl*); and Bodleian MSS Ashmole 38, p. 71; 47 fols. 108v–110r; and 71 fol. 108v.

4. THOMAS CAREW'S REPLY TO JONSON'S 'ODE TO HIMSELF'

To Ben Jonson upon Occasion
of his Ode to Himself

'Tis true, dear Ben, thy just chastising hand
Hath fixed upon the sotted age a brand
To their swoln pride and empty scribbling due:
It can nor judge nor write. And yet 'tis true
Thy comic muse from the exalted line 5
Touched by thy *Alchemist* doth since decline
From that her zenith, and foretells a red
And blushing evening when she goes to bed;

50. gather] *R;* gain her *PB.* 51. humour] *R;* humerous *PB.* 57. your] *R;* the *PB.* 58. puts] *R;* put *PB;* pull *Sl.* 59. you . . . draw] *R;* you may applause to wonder drawe *H, Sl.*
2. brand] *A;* band *Fo2.* 6. thy] *A;* the *H.*

60. *Phoebus*] or Apollo was god of music, especially the lyre.

0.1 *Carew*] the poet Thomas Carew (1595?–1639?), one of the leading 'sons of Ben'; see *H.& S.*, I, 112.

6. Alchemist] *The Alchemist* was regularly revived during the Jacobean and Caroline periods.

Yet such as shall outshine the glimmering light
With which all stars shall gild the following night.   10
Nor think it much, since all thy eaglets may
Endure the sunny trial, if we say
This hath the stronger wing, and that doth shine
Tricked up in fairer plumes, since all are thine.
Who hath his flock of cackling geese compared   15
To thy tuned choir of swans, or who hath dared
To call thy births deformed? But if thou bind
By city custom or by gavelkind
In equal shares thy love to all thy race,
We may distinguish of their sex and place.   20
Though one hand shape them, and though one brain strike
Souls into all, they are not all alike.
Why should the follies, then, of this dull age
Draw from thy pen such an immodest rage
As seems to blast thy else immortal bays   25
When thine own tongue proclaims thy itch of praise?
Such thirst will argue drought: no, let be hurled
Upon thy works by the detracting world
What malice can suggest; let the rout say,
The running sands that, ere thou make a play,   30
Count the slow minutes, might a Goodwin frame

11. thy] *A;* yᵉ *Fo2.*   12. we] *A;* we doe *Fo2.*   18. custom] *Fo2, H, P;*
customs *A.*   19. to] *A;* on *P.*   21. shape] *A;* form *P.*   28. by] *A;* what
Fo2.

---

11. *eaglets*] 'Gesner, *Historiae Animalium Liber III*, 1585, p. 171 says that
eagles test their young by forcing them to gaze steadfastly at the sun' (*The
Poems of Thomas Carew*, ed. Dunlap, (Oxford, 1949), p. 246).

18. *city custom*] 'Giles Jacob, *A New Law-Dictionary*, 1729, s.v. "Custom of
London": By the *Custom of London*, when a citizen and Freeman dies, his
Goods and Chattels shall be divided into three parts; the Wife to have one
Part; the Executors another, to discharge Legacies, &c, and the Children
unprovided for the other third Part' (Dunlap).

gavelkind] 'The name of a land-tenure existing chiefly in Kent ... by
which a tenant's land at his death was divided equally among his sons'
(*O.E.D.*).

25. *bays*] The laurel, from which the poet's crown was made, was supposed
to be immune from lightning (see Pliny, *Nat. Hist.*, II.56).

30–1.] The charge that Jonson brooded overlong on his comedies is also
alluded to in Jasper Mayne's poem in *Jonsonus Virbius*, ll. 49ff. (*H.& S.*, XI,
453). Jonson did not write for the stage between 1616 and 1626.

31. *Goodwin*] The Goodwin sandbanks lie seven miles off Ramsgate in
Kent.

To swallow when th' hast done thy shipwrecked name,
Let them the dear expense of oil upbraid,
Sucked by thy watchful lamp, which hath betrayed
To theft the blood of martyred authors, split   35
Into thy ink, whilst thou growst pale with guilt.
Repine not at thy taper's thrifty waste,
That sleeks thy terser poems; nor is haste
Praise, but excuse; and if thou overcome
A knotty writer, bring the booty home;   40
Nor think it theft if the rich spoils so torn
From conquered authors be as trophies worn.
Let others glut on the extorted praise
Of vulgar breath, trust thou to after days.
Thy laboured works shall live when Time devours   45
Th'abortive offspring of their hasty hours.
Thou art not of their make: the quarrel lies
Within thine own verge. Then let this suffice:
The wiser world doth greater thee confess
Than all men else, than thyself only less.   50

From the autograph in the Domestic State Papers, Charles I clv., no. 79, 1629
(*A*). Printed in Carew's *Poems* (London, 1640), pp. 108–10 (*P*). It also appears
in BL MSS Harley 4955, fol. 214 (*H*), Add. 11,811 fol. 12; Sloane 1446 fols.
55v–56r; Folger V.a.170, pp. 190–2 (*Fo2*); Bodleian MS Rawl. Poet 209, fol.
12; *Don.b.9, fol. 26; Firth d.7, fol. 135.

5. R. GOODWIN ON JONSON'S SPLENETIC OUTBURST

Vindiciae Jonsonianae

Since, what past ages only had begun

40. the booty] *A;* thy trophies *Fo2*.   47. their make] *A;* their rank *P;* the
ranke *Fo2*.

---

38. *terser*] more refined, smoother; cf. *Poet.*, III.i.35: 'I am enamour'd of
this street . . . 'tis so polite and terse'.
40 *knotty*] rugged (*O.E.D.*, 4).
45–6. *Time . . . offspring*] Time was identified with Saturn or Chronos who
devoured his own children; see Panofsky, *Studies in Iconology*, pp. 73ff.
48. *verge*] 'An area subject to the jurisdiction of the Lord High Steward,
defined as extending to a distance of twelve miles round the King's court'
(*O.E.D.*).
0.1 R. Goodwin] *H.& S.*, I, 210n. indicates that Jonson had received a

And ventured at, thou hast exactly done,
And that the ancients more precede not thee
In time than thou dost them in poesy,
Stain not that well gained honour with the crude 5
Or the rash censure of a multitude
Of silken fools, who cannot understand
(For they were born not to have wit but land)
Thy sublimed soul, but daily do prefer
Those who almost as diligently err 10
As thou dost write, more comic rules mistake
Than thou observedst of old, or new dost make;
Revenge those wrongs with pity, for we see
'Tis ignorance in them, no crime in thee,
That moulds their judgments. Who e'er chanced to see 15
That vast prodigious Louvre gallery,
But at his entrance, judging by his eyes,
Would think the roof inclined, the floor did rise,
And at the end each equidistant side
Met in one point – though there they be as wide 20
As where he stood – so they who nowadays
Come to behold, not understand, thy plays
With weak-eyed judgment, easily may depress
Thy lofty muse, extol the lowliness
Of trampled poets, with sinister wit 25
Contract thy dextrous vein to answer it,
And be deceived like him. Or as those eyes
Which, through gross vapours and thick air that flies
Close to the earth, the rising sun can view,
And with deluded sense do judge it true 30
That then he's twice as great as when he hath ran
And is enthroned in their meridian –
Though at that time he was more distant far

---

poem from Goodwin (which may be this one) by 4 February 1631/2. Nothing else is known of him.

9. *sublimed*] refined by chemical process, exalted.
25. *trampled*] downtrodden.
sinister] malicious (*O.E.D.* 1b).
26. *dextrous*] from Lat. *dexter* = right, echoing, 'sinister' (Lat. *sinister* = left) above.
answer it] correspond with their wit (*O.E.D.*, 28).
27. *him*] the visitor to the Louvre – see ll. 15ff. above.

Than the whole earth's semidiameter –
Even so these gallants, when they chance to hear   35
A new wit peeping in their hemisphere
Which they can apprehend, their clouded brains
Will straight admire, and magnify his strains
Far above thine – though all that he hath done
Is but a taper to thy brighter sun –   40
Wound them with scorn! Who grieves at such fools' tongues,
Doth not revenge but gratify their wrongs.
Who's doomed to err, unto himself must be
An heretic, if he judge right of thee;
Icteric eyes all different colours think   45
The same; what feverish palates drink
Tastes ill, though n'er so good; we find by sense
E'en contraries may have coincidence;
For, to a smiling statue let a hand
Add some few tears, though all the lines else stand,   50
And lineaments untouched, it will appear
Like sorrow's figure, and the lively cheer
Drowned into sadness: so when these bold men,
Blindly misled, shall temerate thy pen,
Adding their censures, thou mayst seem to be   55
As different from thyself as they from thee.
Were't not the sense I had of sacred writ,
I should have called it blasphemy 'gainst wit
And sacrilege 'gainst art; but when I see
They little know themselves and far less thee,   60
Their dislike is thine honour. He that's moved
With such men's censures, granteth it half proved
That he is guilty. Innocence no laws,
Virtue fears no detraction. 'Tis no cause,
Yet argument of worth, in that 'tis true   65
Your wit cannot suit them nor their brains you.
Could such poor intellectuals as theirs

---

34. *semidiameter*] N. Carpenter, *Geography Delineated forth in Two Books*,
1625, I.v, p. 117 (1635 ed.): 'Astronomers measure the magnitude of the
Starres by Diameters and Semidiameters of the Earth' (cited *O.E.D.*).
36. *peeping*] sounding small (*O.E.D.*, vb.1.2).
45. *Icteric*] affected with jaundice.
54. *temerate*] profane (first use recorded in *O.E.D.* is 1635).
64. *detraction*] disparagement.
67. *intellectuals*] intellects, wits.

But reach thy pitch, the mind that now admires
Would then contemn thee. He's esteemed by none,
That can be understood by everyone.   70
Fearst then thy fame that wars 'gainst time, thy pen
That triumphs, can be foiled by outside men?
Such aromatic trees – is't such a grace
T' have precious barks when as the timber's base?
Had they been half so versed in wit, so bred   75
In learned authors as they're deeply read
In subtle shop-books, I confess their doom
That gives thee a laurel now had given thee a tomb.
But scorn to stand, fear not to fall, by votes
Of such embroidered-glittering-silver coats!   80
The Capitol was saved, I do confess,
By watchful geese; but when Rome's thankfulness
A silver goose erected which there stood,
Did that discover foes or do Rome good?
Nor can these gilt-men thee. Thy daring pen   85
That may contend with fate, can that fear men?
When Rome, that quelled the world, to thee had been
A debtor for her safety (had she seen,
Or been so blessed as to have heard one line
Which thy pen wrote of bloody Catiline)   90
More than to that vain consul's glorying style,
Whose every period seems a German mile;
Whose fluent tongue more lively, at that time,
Expressed his own vainglory than their crime;
For words and actions might be easily known,   95
The thoughts were only Cataline's and thine own,
And thou didst write what he durst think or dare,
Could we now question Catiline and compare
Him with thy writings, we should swear, almost,

76–7. *read . . . shop-books*] Goodwin asserts that Jonson's detractors are base
tradesmen.

81–2. *Capitol . . . geese*] When the Gauls occupied Rome in 390 B.C. the
Romans under Marcus Manlius Capitolinus were awakened by the cackling
of geese and were able to repel their attackers from the Capitol; see Livy,
V.xlvii.

91. *vain consul*] Cicero, consul from 64/3 BC had prosecuted Catiline – see
his *In Catalinam*.

96. *thoughts . . . own*] Goodwin contrasts the Senecan directness of Jonson's
style in *Catiline* with Cicero's elaborate periods.

Thy muse had been confessor to his ghost   100
And his soul's characters in his front had read,
Which threatened death when he himself was dead.
Had she read thy Sejanus' life and fate,
World's second head, that tympany of state,
She had a wonder seen far greater, then,   105
Than was himself. Him, equalled by thy pen!
Nay, more a miracle: for on thy stage
Caesar's outdone in craft, Rome in her rage.
The other works, raised by thy skilful hand,
Pitying the world's old wonders, they shall stand   110
As monuments of thee, more firm amids
All envy's blasts than Egypt's pyramids,
Those burdens of the earth, 'gainst labouring storms.
Thus then secured above the reach of harms
Low souls can meditate, use not that pen   115
That could affright the world 'gainst such poor men.
He is more fool than tyrant that would kill
His enemy at once: too great an ill
It is to them. They cannot hurt thee: be
Then wise to them as they are fools to thee.   120
For if those men that built th'Ephesian pile
Did feed the toiled out asses all the while
On public charge, whose younger strength did bring
Materials to that structure as a thing
As great in charity for them to yield   125
Food to those beasts, as piety to build
Their goddess such a temple – shall't be thought
That the ridiculous asses, which once brought
Thee such materials as have made thy stage
To be the greatest wonder of our age,   130
Should not at last, tired out in follies, get
Licence to banquet their decrepit wit

---

102. *threatened . . . dead*] According to Sallust, *De Coniuratione Catilinae*,
lxi, the dead countenance of Catiline was as fierce as it had been while he was
alive.

104. *tympany*] a morbid swelling or tumour.

121. *Ephesian pile*] the temple of Diana; the reference to the asses may
derive from the account in Vitruvius, *De Arch.*, X, Pref., of how, during the
construction of buildings at Ephesus, the property was assigned to a
magistrate in order that the architect's estimates might not be exceeded.

On offal poets, on the common store
And scraps of wit? Nay, grieve there are no more
To please their tastes. For when fools plenty be,   135
Wise men are miracles. When Rome did see
At Caesar's triumph all the figures there
Of rich materials, gold, and silver were,
And in the triumph next to his not one
But carved in wood, in ivory, or stone,   140
They did conceive the last which they had seen
Served as a case to keep great Caesar's in:
So, after thy rare pieces, when we hear
Such blockish poems, do they not appear
Like dark foils, closely set, which cannot shine,   145
Yet give, what in themselves they want, to thine
Lustre and life? As they were only shown
To lock thy memory up in, not their own,
And that so safely too that fate from thee
Cannot take life – it may mortality.   150
Other oblivion, then, thou ne'er shalt find
Than that which, with thee, must put out mankind.

Printed from BL Harley MS 4955, fols. 186–7.

6. AN ANONYMOUS CRITICISM OF 'THE NEW INN'

The Country's Censure on Ben Jonson's
'New Inn'

Listen, decaying Ben, and counsel hear,
Wits have their date and strength of brains may wear,
Age steeped in sack hath quenched thy enthean fire,
We pity now whom once we did admire.
Surrender, then, thy right to th' stage; forbear   5
To dare to write what others loath to hear –
And justly, since thy crazy muse doth now

133–4. *common . . . wit*] See Jonson's Ode, ll. 25–30.
137. *Caesar's triumph*] the series of four triumphs after the defeat of Scipio; they are described in Appian, *Civil Wars*, II.ci ff., and Dio Cassius, *Roman History*, XLIII.xixff.
3. *enthean*] inspired by an indwelling god (*O.E.D.*).
7. *crazy*] broken down, decrepit.

To quit her Spartan province faintly know.
Swear not by God 'tis good, for if you do,
The world will tax your zeal and judgment too.   10
For in a poet, if that's last regarded,
New Inn's discretion hath thee quite discarded
From Aganippe's pale, and placed thee among
Not the giddy-headed but the unbrowed throng.
Rail not at the actors, do not them abuse,   15
Action to dullness cannot life infuse;
For Velvet, Scarlet, Plush do tell you true,
'Twas not their clothes but they did blush for you
To see. And was not that just cause of rage?
Weakness and impudence possessed the stage,   20
Injured the strength of wit now cloyed and dry:
Goodstock, Pru, Frampul, Huffle, Burst, Tip, Fly,
And their comrades, whose language but to hear
Might strike a surfeit into a gentle ear.
But let me tell you this, Ben, by the way,   25
Thy argument's as tedious as thy play.
Thou sayst no palsy doth thy brain-pan vex:
I pray thee tell me what? An apoplex?
Thy Pegasus can stir, yet thy best care
Makes her but shuffle; like the parson's mare   30
Who from his own side wit says thus by me,
He hath bequeathed his belly unto thee
To hold that little learning, which is fled
Into thy guts from out thy empty head.
Yet thou art confident, and darst still swear   35
The fault's not in thy brain but in their ear.
What dismal fate is this thus on thee seizeth?

---

8. *Spartan province*] the stage now held by Jonson's rival dramatist, Richard Brome – *spartum* is Latin for broom; Jonson had used the jest himself, see II.vi.45n.

12. *discretion*] judgment on (*O.E.D.*, 2).
discarded] forced away (*O.E.D.*, 2b).

13. *Aganippe*] a spring sacred to the Muses, below the Hippocrene on Mount Helicon.

14. *unbrowed*] a nounce word = faceless (see *O.E.D.*, 'brow' 5b).

16. *infuse*] dissolve (*O.E.D.*, 3b).

24. *gentle*] well-born.

29. *Pegasus*] the winged horse of the Muses which produced the Hippocrene spring with a stamp of its hoof. Jonson refers to it at III.ii.269.

30. *shuffle . . . mare*] echoes III.i.142–5.

Thy worth doth fail, thy arrogance increaseth,
Pride and presumption hath dethroned thy wit,
And set up philauty in place of it,   40
Thy inn-bred darling, whose strong self-conceit
Forestalling praise, did thy just praise defeat.
Worth being self-praised doth fall: he is the best poet
Can justly merit praise and yet scarce know it.
But 'tis *New Inn*'s disaster not to know   45
What or thyself or others can allow.
We wrong thee not, for take thy enraged appeal,
'Twill rather fester thy mad wound than heal.
For know what knowledge justly doth despise
Doth prove a greater scandal to our eyes;   50
And sure that censure must impartial be,
Where readers and spectators both agree.
Yet if pure need enforce thee to this shame,
We proner are to advise thee than to blame.
Since wits do fail, thou wert best, poor crack-brained elf,   55
To turn mine host, and keep *New Inn* thyself:
But change thy sign if thou'lt be ruled by me,
No more 'Light Heart' but 'Light Brain' let it be.
        Thy hostler Peck abusèd thus the jade
        Of this fat-bellied parson who this made.   60

From Bodleian MS Ashmole, 38, pp. 79–80. The references to Pru (l. 22) and
to the Argument (l. 26) indicate that the poem was written after the play was
published in 1632.

7. JOHN POLWHELE ON 'THE NEW INN'

To the admired Ben Jonson to encourage him to write,
after his farewell to the stage, 1631;
alluding to Horace, Ode xxvi, Lib.I:
'Musis amicus', etc.

Ben, thou art the muses' friend;
Grief and fears cast to the wind;

---

40. *philauty*] self-love; the name of a character and the main theme in *C.R.*
60. *fat-bellied parson*] echoes III.i.142–5.
0.1 *John Polwhele*] otherwise unknown.

Who wins th'emperor is swayed,
Soul secure, you nothing dread.
Inhabitant near Hippocrene,   5
Pluck sweet roses by that stream.
Put thy laurel crownet on:
What is fame, if thou hast none?
See Apollo with the nine
Sings; the chorus must be thine.   10
                    Jo. Polw.

From the manuscript *Poems of John Polwhele*, c. 1660, in Bodleian MS Eng.
Poet. f.16, fol. 10; *H.& S.* omit the third line.

8. A POSSIBLE REFERENCE TO THE PLAY BY 'C.G.' IN 1640

I do not wonder that great Jonson's play
Was scorned so by the ignorant that day
It did appear in its most glorious shine,
And comely action graced each learned line.
There was some reason for it: 'twas above   5
Their reach, their envy, their applause or love,
Whereas the wiser few did it admire,
And warmed their fancies at his genuine fire.
    But I commend the wisdom of thy fate
To sell thy labours at a better rate   10
Than the contempt of the most squeamish age
Or the exactest Roscii of the stage,
Which might provoke our laureate to repine,
That thine should rival his brave *Albovine*.
Thy muse in this birth doth unhappy prove   15
In that it is abortive. Let thy love
Appear to us in getting such another,
That she may boast herself a happy mother.

    Prefixed to Nabbe's *Unfortunate Mother*, 1640.

3. is swayed] *conj. this ed.;* or sweade *ms.*

---

5. *Hippocrene*] the spring sacred to the Muses.
10. *nine*] the Muses.
0.1. *C.G.*] This unknown author also wrote a verse for Brome's *The Antipodes* (1640).
8. *genuine*] native.
12. *Roscii*] emulators of the great Roman comic actor Roscius (d. 62 BC).
14. *Albovine*] Davenant's tragedy *Albovine, King of the Lombards*, (1628).

APPENDIX II

The New Inn and Love's Pilgrimage

In the first scene of *Love's Pilgrimage*, a play that appeared posthumously in the Beaumont and Fletcher Folio of 1647, there appear two passages of 38 and 81 lines that bear a very close resemblance to II.v.48–73 and III. i.57–93, 130–68 of *The New Inn*. The play's most recent editor, L. A. Beaurline, dates the play about 1615 or 1616.[1] On 16 September 1635 the licence for the play was renewed and 'one pound was paid Herbert's assistant, the usual price charged for a revised play'.[2] The two passages in question could therefore have been incorporated into *Love's Pilgrimage* during its revision and could well derive from Jonson's original. (The play was acted by the King's Men before the King and Queen at Hampton Court on 16 December 1636, presumably in its revised form.) It is also conceivable that Jonson adapted the lines from a passage that Cyrus Hoy judges to be by Beaumont.[3] However, there is nothing similar in texture elsewhere in *Love's Pilgrimage* and the passages are quite in harmony with *The New Inn*'s other scenes of 'wild life'. Jonson's version is manifestly superior, and although, as Beaurline points out, 'artistic superiority is no test for a source' and 'it is possible that *Love's Pilgrimage* originally contained the speeches that

---

1 *The Dramatic Works of Beaumont and Fletcher*, II (Cambridge, 1970), 569.

2 *Ibid.*, p. 570.

3 *S.B.*, II (1958), 85–106; Baldwin Maxwell, *Studies in Beaumont, Fletcher, and Maxwell* (North Carolina, 1939), argues the case that Jonson borrowed from lines he takes to be by Fletcher. His case rests on the assertion that the phrase *in cuerpo* is in keeping with the Spanish source for *Love's Pilgrimage*. But the phrase had passed into Elizabethan usage. It is found in the text of what may be Massinger's revision of Beaumont and Fletcher's *Love's Cure* (possibly as early as 1606), II.i.2, and in Massinger and Field's *The Fatal Dowry* (1619), II.ii.101. (This is six years earlier than the first recorded use in *O.E.D.*) His argument is therefore weakened and there is no confirmatory evidence to support his speculation that 'Jonson began a revision of *Love's Pilgrimage* and, having abandoned his plan, later put parts of his revision to use in *The New Inn*'.

were later used by Jonson in a more skilful way', it is to be presumed that in fact Jonson provided the original lines which were adapted just before his death by an unknown reviser for his familiar company, the King's Men. The relevant lines are printed in Beaurline, ed., *Love's Pilgrimage*, I.i.20–64 and 330–411.

APPENDIX III

Table of Press Corrections

The following table should be conflated with that given by *H.& S.*, VI, 386–7. It shows the pattern of press-corrections in the additional copies I have collated: uncorrected readings in the left column, corrected readings on the right. Abbreviations are identified in the Introduction, p.14.

Sig. B1r	Fo, G, H1, H2, T, W. Y.	
Sig. B1v	Fo, H2, T, Y.	G, H1, W.
Sig. B2r	Fo, H2, T, Y.	G, H1, W.
Sig. B3v	Fo, H2, T, Y.	G, H1, W.
Sig. B4r	Fo, H2, T, Y.	G, H1, W.
Sig. B5v	Fo, H2, T, Y.	G, H1, W.
Sig. B6r	Fo, H2, T, Y.	G, H1, W.
Sig. B7v	Fo, H2, T, Y.	G, H1, W.
Sig. B8r	Fo, H2, T, Y.	G, H1, W.
Sig. C1v	Fo, G, H1, H2, T, W, Y.	
Sig. C2r	Fo, G, H1, H2, T, W, Y.	
Sig. C3v	Fo, G, H1, H2, T, W, Y.	
Sig. C4r	Fo, G, H1, H2, T, W, Y.	
Sig. C5v	Fo, G, H1, H2, T, W, Y.	
Sig. C6r	Fo, G, H1, H2, T, W, Y.	
Sig. C7v	Fo, G, H1, H2, T, W, Y.	
Sig. C8r	Fo, G, H1, H2, T, W, Y.	
Sig. D8v	Y.	Fo, G, H1, H2, T, W.
Sig. E4v	H2, T.	Fo, G, H1, W, Y.
Sig. E6v	H2, T.	Fo, G, H1, W, Y.
Sig. E8v	H2, T.	Fo, G, H1, W, Y.

Glossarial Index to the Commentary

An asterisk before a word indicates that the annotation contains information regarding meaning, usage, or date which supplements that given in the *O.E.D.*

Arg. = Argument; C.C. = 'The Country's Censure'; C.G. = C.G.'s 'I do not wonder'; Carew = Thomas Carew's Reply; Ded. = Dedication; Ep. = Epilogue; Fel. = Owen Felltham's 'Answer'; Good. = R. Goodwin's *Vindiciae Jonsoniae*. I.C. = I.C's Reply; Ode = The Ode ('Come leave the loathèd stage'); Pers. = The Persons of the Play; Pol. = John Polwhele's Ode; Pr. = Prologue; Rand. = Thomas Randolph's 'Answer'; T.P. = Title Page.

231